Comparative
Criminal Procedure

Carolina Academic Press
Comparative Law Series

Michael Louis Corrado
Series Editor

Comparative Constitutional Review
Cases and Materials
Michael Louis Corrado

Comparative Law: An Introduction
Vivian Grosswald Curran

Comparative Consumer Bankruptcy
Jason Kilborn

Comparative Law of Contracts
Alain Levasseur

Comparative Criminal Procedure, Second Edition
Stephen C. Thaman

Comparative Human Rights Law, Vol. 1:
Expression, Association, Religion
Arthur Mark Weisburd

Comparative Human Rights Law, Vol. 2:
Detention, Prosecution, Capital Punishment
Arthur Mark Weisburd

Comparative Criminal Procedure

A Casebook Approach

Second Edition

Stephen C. Thaman
SAINT LOUIS UNIVERSITY
SCHOOL OF LAW

CAROLINA ACADEMIC PRESS
Durham, North Carolina

Library of Congress Cataloging-in-Publication Data

Thaman, Stephen, 1946-
  Comparative criminal procedure : a casebook approach / by Stephen C.
Thaman. -- 2nd ed.
      p. cm. -- (Comparative law series)
  Includes bibliographical references and index.
  ISBN-13: 978-1-59460-500-0 (alk. paper)
  ISBN-10: 1-59460-500-9 (alk. paper)
1. Criminal procedure--Europe--Cases. 2. Criminal procedure--European
Union countries--Cases. I. Title. II. Series.

  KJC9405.T52 2008
  345'.05--dc22

                                                            2007044851

Carolina Academic Press
700 Kent Street
Durham, North Carolina 27701
Telephone (919) 489-7486
Fax (919) 493-5668
www.cap-press.com

Printed in the United States of America

To the memory of two beloved fatherly friends on whose premises I wrote parts of this book:

Robert Jacques de Trey
(London, April 26, 1912–
Bodega Bay, California, August 7, 2000)

German Mikhaylovich Makarov
(Poselok Togul, Altay, December 31, 1927–
Magnitogorsk, Russia, May 31, 2000)

Contents

Chapter One   Criminal Law and Its Procedures   3

I. Introduction   3

  A. The Flagrant Crime   4

    Assises de la cour des Bourgeois (Ch. CCLIX)   4

    § 16 Constitutio Criminalis Carolina (German Empire, 1532)   5

    Questions   6

  B. The Circumstantial Evidence or "Who-Done-It?" Case   7

    Regulations Regarding Exculpation of William I

      (England, Late 11th Century)   7

    Law II of Edmund (England, 10th Century)   9

    §§ 23, 25–27 Constitutio Criminalis Carolina

      (German Empire, 1532)   10

    Questions   11

  C. The Secret Victimless Crime   12

    Livre de Justice et des Plets I, 3, § 7

      (France, 12th Century)   12

    Entick v. Carrington

      (English Court of Common Pleas, 1765)   14

    Questions   15

  D. A Brief History of European Criminal Procedure   16

  E. Outline of the Book   20

    Selected Readings (History & Theory)   21

    Selected Readings (Comparative, Country-Related)   21

Chapter Two   The Criminal Investigation: Procedures and Participants   23

I. The Continuing Role of the Victim in Prosecuting Criminal Cases   23

  A. The Institution of Private Prosecution   23

    Decision of December 8, 1906 (Placet) (French Supreme Court)   23

    § 100 LECr (Spain)   25

    § 105 LECr (Spain)   25

Questions   27
Selected Readings   27
B. The Institution of Popular Prosecution   28
Art. 125 Const. (Spain)   28
§ 101 LECr (Spain)   28
§ 270(1) LECr (Spain)   28
Decision No. 241 of December 21, 1992
    (Spanish Constitutional Court)   28
Questions   30
II. The Role of the Police Before
    Initiation of Formal Criminal Proceedings: The Police Inquest   30
§ 282 (para. 1) LECr (Spain)   30
§ 286 LECr (Spain)   31
III. The Formal Criminal Investigation   32
A. The Search for Truth and the Compilation
    of the Investigative Dossier   32
§ 80 CPP (France)   32
§§ 81 (paras. 1–2,4) CPP (France)   32
Questions   36
Selected Readings   36
B. Confrontation and Adversarial Rights during
    the Preliminary Investigation   36
1. The Right to Be Present with Counsel   36
§ 118 LECr (Spain)   36
2. The Right to Make Evidentiary Motions   37
§ 82-1(paras. 1–2) CPP (France)   37
3. Proceedings to Preserve or "Anticipate" Evidence   38
§ 392(1) CPP (Italy)   38
§ 394 CPP (Italy)   39
§ 401 (1–3,5) CPP (Italy)   39
§ 403(1) CPP (Italy)   39
4. Identification Procedures   40
5. The Adversarialization of the Preliminary Investigation   40
§ 25 LOTJ (Spain)   41
§ 27(1) LOTJ (Spain)   41
Questions   42
Relevant U.S. Case Law   42
IV. Avoiding the Preliminary Investigation   43
§ 449 (1–5) CPP (Italy)   43
Questions   44

Chapter Three   Search and Seizure: Search for Truth and Protection of
Privacy   45
I. Police Powers of Investigation, Search and Seizure
   during the Police Inquest   45
   A. Temporary Investigative Detentions   45
      Decision of July 12, 1995 (Spanish Supreme Court)   45
      §§ 1.4, 2.2, 2.3 PACE, Code of Practice A (England)   46
      Questions   47
      Relevant U.S. Case Law   47
   B. Police Power to Arrest in Flagrant Cases   48
      § 380(1) CPP (Italy)   48
      § 381 (1,4) CPP (Italy)   48
      Questions   49
      Relevant U.S. Case Law   49
   C. Definition of a Flagrant Crime   49
      Decision of March 29, 1990 (Spanish Supreme Court)   49
   D. Police Powers to Search in Situations of Flagrancy and
      Incident to Arrest   51
      § 352(1) CPP (Italy)   51
      Decision No. 303 of October 25, 1993
         (Spanish Constitutional Court)   52
      Questions   53
      Relevant U.S. Case Law   53
   E. Consent Searches   54
      § 5 PACE Code of Practice B (England)   54
      Decision of July 8, 1994 (Spanish Supreme Court)   55
      Questions   55
      Relevant U.S. Case Law   56
II. The Requirement of Judicial Authorization for Invasions of Privacy   56
   A. The Special Protection of Dwellings   56
      1. The Requirement of a Warrant   56
      Art. 13(1,2) Const. (Germany)   56
      § 98 StPO (Germany)   56
      2. The Requirement of Probable Cause   57
      Decision of June 28, 1994 (Spanish Supreme Court)   57
      Questions   59
      Relevant U.S. Case Law   59
      3. Procedural Safeguards Required during the Search   59
      Decision of October 30, 1992 (Spanish Supreme Court)   59

Decision of November 14, 1992
    (Spanish Supreme Court)   60
Questions   61
Selected Readings   61
B. The Protection of Confidential Communications   61
1. Intercepting Private Conversations   61
Decision No. 49 of March 26, 1996
    (Spanish Constitutional Court)   61
§ 266 CPP (Italy)   64
§ 267(1–3) CPP (Italy)   64
§ 268 (4,6) CPP (Italy)   65
Decision of June 25, 1993 (Spanish Supreme Court)   66
Questions   68
Relevant U.S. Case Law   69
Selected Readings   69
2. Right to Privacy in the Identity of One's
    Conversation Partners   69
Decision No. 81 of March 11, 1993
    (Italian Constitutional Court)   69
Questions   71
Relevant U.S. Case Law   71
3. Informant-Citizen Taping and Interception
    of Communications   72
Decision of June 14, 1960 (German Supreme Court)   72
Decision of July 5, 1988 (Italian Supreme Court)   73
Decision of October 8, 1993 (German Supreme Court)   76
Questions   77
Relevant U.S. Case Law   78
C. The Limits on Police Undercover Activity in the
    Proactive Investigation of Crime   78
Teixeira de Castro v. Portugal
    (European Court of Human Rights) (June 9, 1998)   78
Questions   80
Relevant U.S. Case Law   80
Selected Readings   80
D. Seizure and Reading of Private Writings   81
Entick v. Carrington
    (English Court of Common Pleas 1765)   81

Decision of February 21, 1964
   (German Supreme Court)   82
Questions   83
Relevant U.S. Case Law   83

Chapter Four   The Defendant as a Source of Evidence:
                The Privilege against Self-Incrimination   85
I. Police Interrogations Before the Initiation of Criminal Proceedings   85
  A. Privilege against Self-Incrimination and
      Right to Counsel during Police Interrogation   85
    1. The Requirement of Admonitions ("Miranda Rights")   85
    Decision of October 29, 1992 (German Supreme Court)   85
    Decision of May 21, 1996 (German Supreme Court)   87
    § 64(3)(a,b)(3-bis) CPP (Italy)   88
    § 350 CPP (Italy)   88
    §§ 10.1, 10.5 Code of Practice C. PACE (England)   90
    Questions   90
    Relevant U.S. Case Law   91
    2. When Must Police Give a Suspect the
       Miranda-Type Admonitions?   91
    Decision of February 27, 1992 (German Supreme Court)   91
    Decision of May 31, 1990 (German Supreme Court)   92
    § 63 CPP (Italy)   93
    Questions   94
    Relevant U.S. Case Law   94
    3. The Problem of Undercover Interrogation   94
    Regina v. Bryce (English Court of Appeals) (1992)   94
II. The Prevention of Involuntary Confessions   96
    § 136a StPO (Germany)   96
    Decision of February 16, 1954 (German Supreme Court)   97
    Decision of April 28, 1987 (German Supreme Court)   98
    Decision of November 25, 1997
      (Court of Appeal of Frankfurt/Main, Germany)   99
    Regina v. Fulling (English Court of Appeal) (1987)   101
    Questions   102
    Relevant U.S. Case Law   102
III. The Formal Interrogation of the Accused during
  the Preliminary Investigation   103
    § 65 CPP (Italy)   103

Questions   104
Selected Readings   104

Chapter Five   Determining the Admissibility of Evidence at Trial   105
I. Exclusion of Illegally Gathered Evidence   105
    A. From Nullities to Non-Usability   105
        § 170 CPP (France)   105
        § 171 CPP (France)   105
        § 174 (para. 3) CPP (France)   106
        Decision of July 9, 1993 (Spanish Supreme Court)   106
        § 191 CPP (Italy)   109
    B. The Proportionality Test of Exclusion   110
        Decision of February 27, 1992 (German Supreme Court)   110
        Decision of February 21, 1964 (German Supreme Court)   112
    C. Case-by-Case Fairness Test: The English Approach   114
        Regina v. Samuel (English Court of Appeal) (1987)   114
    D. Presumption of Innocence and Equality of Arms:
        The Spanish Approach   115
        Decision No. 49 of March 26, 1996
            (Spanish Constitutional Court)   115
        Art. 24(2) Canadian Charter of Rights and Freedoms   117
        Questions   118
        Relevant U.S. Case Law   118
    E. Fruits of the Poisonous Tree   118
        Decision of June 5, 1995 (Spanish Supreme Court)   118
        Decision of February 22, 1978 (German Supreme Court)   119
        Regina v. McGovern (English Court of Appeal) (1990)   121
        Decision of March 27, 1996 (Italian Supreme Court)   122
        Questions   124
        Relevant U.S. Case Law   124
II. Admissibility of Evidence and the Right to Confrontation   125
    A. The Transformation of the Inquisitorial
        "Written" Trial   125
        Decision of July 18, 1884 (French Supreme Court)   125
        Kostovski v. The Netherlands (European Court of
            Human Rights) (November 20, 1989)   126
        Delta v. France (European Court of Human Rights)
            (December 19, 1990)   129
    B. Admissibility of Statements of Unavailable Witnesses   131

Decision of March 5, 1993 (Spanish Supreme Court)   131
Regina v. Cole (English Court of Appeal) (1989)   132
Questions   135
Relevant U.S. Case Law   135
C. Admissibility of Prior Statements to Impeach or
   Contradict a Testifying Witness   135
   Decision No. 52 of February 23, 1995
      (Spanish Constitutional Court)   135
   Decision of November 3, 1982 (German Supreme Court)   136
   Questions   137
D. Anonymous Witness Testimony   137
   Kostovski v. The Netherlands (European Court of
      Human Rights) (November 20, 1989)   137
   Doorson v. The Netherlands European Court of
      Human Rights (March 26, 1996)   140
   Questions   142
   Relevant U.S. Case Law   142
E. The Admissibility of Hearsay as Corroborative Evidence   143
   Decision of March 31, 1989 (German Supreme Court)   143

Chapter Six   Procedural Economy:
              Avoiding the Trial with All Its Guarantees   147
I. Different Procedures for Different Substantive Crimes:
   Avoiding Trials with Lay Participation   147
   Regina v. Canterbury et al. (English Divisional Court) (1982)   148
   Questions   150
II. Procedural Encouragement of Confessions to Avoid or
    Simplify the Trial   151
    Decision of August 28, 1997 (German Supreme Court)   151
    Decision of June 10, 1998 (German Supreme Court)   156
III. Accepting the Prosecution's Pleadings: A Way around
     the Guilty Plea for Lesser Crimes   158
     Decision No. 313 of July 3, 1990 (Italian Constitutional Court) 159
     Decision of February 19, 1990 (Italian Supreme Court)   162
     § 655 LECr (Spain)   164
IV. Submitting the Case on the Investigative Dossier:
    Return of the Written Inquisitorial Trial?   165
    Decision of November 21, 1991 (Italian Supreme Court)   166
V. Significance of Alternative Procedures   168

Questions   168
Suggested Readings   169

Chapter Seven   The Trial   171
  I. Presumption of Innocence and
    Burden of Proof   171
    A. Presumption of Innocence and Right to Remain Silent   171
      1. The Use of a Defendant's Silence as Evidence of Guilt   171
      Murray v. United Kingdom (European Court of
        Human Rights) (February 8, 1996)   171
      Decision of October 26, 1965 (German Supreme Court)   177
      Questions   178
      Relevant U.S. Case Law   179
    B. Role of the Trial Judge: Investigator of the Truth,
      Impartial Evaluator of the Evidence, or Impartial
      Guarantor of a Fair Adversarial Trial?   179
      1. The Judge's Power to Question Witnesses and
        Introduce Evidence   179
      Decision of October 10, 1991 (Italian Supreme Court)   179
      Decision of March 26, 1993 (Italian Supreme Court)   180
      Regina v. Foxford
        (Northern Ireland Court of Appeals) (1974)   182
      Regina v. Roncoli (English Court of Appeal) (1997)   183
      § 683 LECr (Spain)   184
      § 310 CPP (France)   184
      2. The Judge as Investigator and Evaluator of the Evidence   185
      Decision No. 145 of July 12, 1988
        (Spanish Constitutional Court)   185
      Decision No. 455 of December 30, 1994
        (Italian Constitutional Court)   186
      Decision of April 20, 1999 (Russian Constitutional Court)   187
      Questions   190
      Relevant U.S. Case Law   191
  II. The Evaluation of the Evidence and Rendering of Judgment   191
    A. Who Evaluates the Evidence?   191
      Regina v. Consett Justices, Ex Parte Postal Bingo Ltd.
        (Queen's Bench, England) (1966)   191
    B. Evaluating the Evidence in a Flagrant Case:
      Circumstantial Evidence of Mental State   193

Decision of February 9, 1957 (German Supreme Court)   193
Case of Otegi (Guipuzcoa Regional Court, Spain)
    (Verdict of March 6, 1997)   195
Otegi Case: Decision of March 11, 1998
    (Spanish Supreme Court)   199
§ 339 (1–5) UPK (Russia)   201
Case of Kraskina (Ivanovo Regional Court, Russia)
    (Verdict of March 10, 1995)   203
Decision of June 7, 1995 (Kraskina Case)
    (Russian Supreme Court)   204
§ 353 CPP (France)   205
§ 63(1)(d) LOTJ (Spain)   206
C. Evaluating the Non-Flagrant Case Based on
   Circumstantial Evidence   206
Regina v. Turnbull (English Court of Appeal) (1976)   206
Case of Monika Weimar. Decision of November 6, 1998
    (German Supreme Court)   209
Decision of November 17, 1983 (German Supreme Court)   214
D. Was There a Crime Committed?
   The Evaluation of the Credibility of Witnesses   216
Decision of January 1, 1988 (German Supreme Court)   217
Decision of December 17, 1997 (German Supreme Court)   219
E. Concluding Remarks   220
   Questions   220
   Relevant U.S. Case Law   221
   Selected Readings   222

Case Register   223

Statutes and Other Texts   229

Appendix   233

Glossary   265

Index   275

Comparative
Criminal Procedure

Chapter One

Criminal Law and Its Procedures

I. Introduction

Criminal procedure is society's organized response to crime. The type of crime and the mode of its commission have always conditioned the choice of procedures used to investigate alleged criminal conduct and, if necessary, to prove it in court. Three prototypes of crimes have been selected as leitmotifs throughout this short casebook on comparative criminal procedure: these are the flagrant crime, the circumstantial evidence (who-done-it?) crime, normally the subject of reactive criminal investigations, and the secretly committed, often victimless crime, which is usually the subject of proactive criminal investigations.

The focus of this book will be on European law, which gave birth to the two classic models of criminal procedure, the adversarial and inquisitorial, which made their way to most other countries through European colonization or independent reform processes. It is from these two classic models that most of the universally recognized principles of criminal procedure, which are today found in modern constitutions, criminal procedure codes and international human rights conventions, have been derived.

This book was originally designed to teach comparative criminal procedure to American law students, and thus presumes knowledge of American jurisprudence in the area, which has been extremely influential in this area in the last half century. It thus contains no American cases or statutes, though reference will be made to American jurisprudence in the text and in the notes to each separate section, where appropriate.

The focus is on Europe, as well, because, since the end of World War II, it has undergone a marked and progressive democratization which has been reflected, in some countries, in interesting innovations in the old criminal procedure paradigms. It is also an area where the author is fluent enough in the major languages to be able to read the statutory and case law in the original and translate the materials into English using homogeneous terms for similar procedural realities so as to reduce, to the greatest extent possible, confusion among the English readers.[1]

The study of comparative criminal procedure enables one to trace the development of procedural forms from their customary law origins to their present day realities, and to use the knowledge gained to try to reform one's own criminal justice system to better achieve what are perceived as being its three main goals: (1) to determine, if possible, whether a crime has been committed, who is guilty thereof, and what sanctions, if any, should be imposed (the search for material truth); (2) to use procedures in the search for truth that are humane, fair, and consistent with principles of democracy and a state under the rule of law (principle of due process); and (3) to achieve the first two goals in an efficient way, without excessive waste of government time and resources (principle of procedural economy).

Just as continental European countries have borrowed from Anglo-American adversary procedure to modernize their inquisitorial systems, students from America and other common law countries can learn from the constitutions, statutes and case law presented in this book and gain new insights into the functioning and possible reform of, our own system.

A. The Flagrant Crime

Assises de la cour des Bourgeois (Ch. CCLIX)[2]

If peradventure it happens that one man assault another and kill him, or a woman, and two vassals pass the spot and see him commit the offense and arrest him, as all vassals should hold and arrest (for) all the rights of their lord and all the wrongs done to him, and if they deliver him over to the court and they say faithfully in the court, before the sheriff and the *échevins* on the faith and homage which they owe to the king, that they saw him commit this murder, reason judges and commands that it be adjudged that such person is attainted without battle and that it avail him not to say "no, as God wills, he did not do it," but he should be immediately hanged. For to this extent should

---

1. For a glossary of terms, matching the original concepts in English, French, German, Italian, Russian and Spanish, *see* Glossary, at the end of the book.

2. Reprinted in ADHEMAR ESMEIN, A HISTORY OF CONTINENTAL CRIMINAL PROCEDURE WITH SPECIAL REFERENCE TO FRANCE 61 (1913).

the testimony of two vassals be equal to two sworn men or *échevins* in such a matter."[3]

Here is the ancient societal response to a flagrant crime, where the culprit is caught in the act either, in relation to crimes against property, with the stolen object in his hand ("hand-having") or, in relation to crimes against the person, "red-handed," with the blood of the victim on him and his clothing. Such was the procedure triggered by flagrant crimes in times of old. The proof was obvious, no further investigation (and there were no criminal investigators in those days!), no further witnesses, no admission of guilt was necessary. The procedure closely approximates simple revenge. Criminal procedure is society's attempt to eliminate blood revenge, perhaps the most primitive social response to crime. Note also that the court was composed of an official, the sheriff, and the *échevins*, lay judges from the community. It was the people from the local community affected by the crime who judged whether the person was guilty and whether she should be executed or otherwise removed from the community. When a person was caught red-handed there appeared to have been a non-rebuttable presumption of guilt—no real trial was needed.

Note how the old procedure was modified in a famous 16th Century inquisitorial code, the *Carolina*, which was considered to be a great advance over the primitive attempts to prove guilt and impose punishment in earlier arrangements:

§ 16 Constitutio Criminalis Carolina (German Empire, 1532)[4]

It is especially to be noted by judges and judgment-givers, where a crime is or has been openly and undoubtedly committed without lawful and urgent occasion (apart from legally sufficient cause which

---

3. For a similar procedure, *see* FREDERICK POLLOCK & FREDERIC WILLIAM MAITLAND, THE HISTORY OF ENGLISH LAW BEFORE THE TIME OF EDWARD I, Vol. II 579 (2nd ed. 1952): "Now if a man is overtaken by hue and cry while he has still about him the signs of the crime, he will have short shrift. Should he make any resistance, he will be cut down. But even if he submits to capture, his fate is already decided. He will be bound, and if we suppose him a thief, the stolen goods will be bound to his back. He will be brought before some court (like enough it is a court hurriedly summoned for the purpose), and without being allowed to say one word in self-defense, he will be promptly hanged, beheaded or precipitated from a cliff, and the owner of the stolen goods will perhaps act as an amateur executioner."

4. English translation from JOHN H. LANGBEIN, PROSECUTING CRIME IN THE RENAISSANCE 271 (1974).

properly exculpates from criminal penalty) — for example (...) when someone has actually been caught in the act of committing a crime; or when such a person knowingly has the robbed or stolen property with him and cannot on any ground explain it away or legally justify it or deny it, in the manner hereafter to be found with regard to the said crimes when there is exculpation: In these and similar obvious and undoubted crimes, when the culprit brazenly denies the obvious and undoubted crime, the judge shall examine him under severe torture to induce him to confess the truth, in order that the ultimate judgment and penalty as regards such obvious and undoubted crimes be proceeded to and executed at the least possible cost.

Note how the *Carolina* requires the inducement of a confession of guilt despite the arrest *in flagrante*. There is also concern for the cost of the administration of justice, to arrive at a judgment "at the least possible cost." Chapter Six will address how countries have strived for procedural economy through arrangements aimed at inducing defendants to admit, or at least not contest their guilt.

Legal systems have always provided for special procedures to respond to flagrant crimes. Police may make arrests, conduct searches and seize property without judicial authorization in the case of flagrant crimes, or, as Americans say, under "exigent circumstances." Several European countries provide, as well, for expedited or abbreviated trial procedures in flagrant cases. Expedited procedures in cases of flagrancy, however, may not lead to execution of the culprit, as in the good old days, for the death penalty is considered to be a violation of human rights and has been effectively abolished in Europe.[5]

Questions

1. Is it fair to expedite the criminal trial when a suspect is caught in the act?

2. Can we even call the summary justice meted out in the old French and English procedures a "trial?"

3. Is there any need to induce a confession from a suspect who is actually caught in the act?

---

5. Protocol No. 6, European Convention for the Protection of Human Rights and Fundamental Freedoms, ETS 114 (April 28, 1983). *See* in general, ROGER HOOD, THE DEATH PENALTY. A WORLDWIDE PERSPECTIVE 11–23 (2nd ed. 1996).

4. Can we always be sure that a person arrested *in flagrante* is actually guilty of the alleged crime? If a suspect is caught "red-handed" after killing someone, can we be sure whether he has committed a crime? What crime?

B. The Circumstantial Evidence or "Who-Done-It?" Case

Regulations Regarding Exculpation of William I (England, Late 11th Century)[6]

1. If an Englishman summons a Frenchman to trial by combat for theft or homicide or for anything for which it is fitting that there should be trial by combat or judicial suit between two men, he shall have full permission to do so.

§ 1.If the Englishman declines trial by combat, the Frenchman, who is accused by the Englishman, shall clear himself against him with an oath supported by those who are qualified by Norman law to be his compurgators.

2. Further, if a Frenchman challenges an Englishman to trial by combat for the same things, the Englishman shall have full permission to defend himself by combat or by the ordeal of iron, if he prefers it.

§ 1. And if he is infirm and will not or cannot undertake trial by combat, he shall procure a lawful substitute.

§ 2. And if the Frenchman is defeated, he shall give the king £ 3.

§ 3. And if the Englishman will not defend himself by combat or by compurgation, he shall clear himself by the ordeal of iron.

No one was caught red-handed. Two eyewitnesses are not to be found. We see here the origins of what we now call accusatory procedure: one side accuses the other of a crime and has the burden of proving guilt. The accuser was always the victim or the victim's family or tribe. The methods of proof in non-flagrant cases were often quite primitive.

For instance, the accused could summon compurgators or oath-helpers, upstanding citizens, often twelve in number, to swear unanimously that the accused was an honorable man and should be believed. The result was ac-

---

6. The Laws of the Kings of England from Edmund to Henry I 233 (A.J. Robertson ed. 1925).

quittal even though those swearing the oath likely knew nothing about the facts of the alleged crime. In this procedure lurks most likely the origin of the Anglo-American tradition of requiring unanimous verdicts of 12 jurors (the word jury comes from the French verb *jurer* ("to swear"). Sometimes the accuser or victim could also summon 12 compurgators on his side as well.

The accuser could summon the accused to a duel, or trial by combat, where it was often possible to hire "champions" to fight for you, especially if one of the parties was a woman, or old and infirm. In duels and the exchange of oaths between compurgators for the prosecution and the defense we have the precursors of what we now call adversarial procedure and the notion that when two sides present their best arguments (either by force of arms or persuasion) the truth will out.

The right to a public trial and the right to confront the state's witnesses have their roots in these early procedures which were usually conducted in public places, often under sacred oak trees. If twelve good men vouch for the defendant, perhaps he is not a dangerous person (even if he did commit the crime) and a majority of the community would permit him to continue to live within its confines.

If the accused were a drifter or vagabond, i.e., not a member of the community, an outsider or enemy, then he could not cleanse himself by oath or oath-helpers and would most likely have to rely on God to prove his innocence. He would have to go through an ordeal—be thrown into a river with weighs on him, or hold a hot iron in his hand. If did not come to the surface, or was not burned or his wound healed without infection, then he was considered innocent and could go free. Such a supposed sign from God, though a chimera, was believed by the people and provided a way out, a solution for a crime for which there were no witnesses, no real proof. For even in the early Middle Ages, disputes had to be resolved, they could not just remain pending. The social peace had to be restored to prevent blood revenge and feuds.[7]

---

7. On the history of ordeals in Europe, *see* ROBERT BARTLETT, TRIAL BY FIRE AND WATER (1986); on the interplay of ordeals, duels and use of compurgators in early Gaul, *see* Ian Wood, *Disputes in Late Fifth and Sixth Century Gaul: Some Problems,* in THE SETTLEMENT OF DISPUTES IN EARLY MEDIEVAL EUROPE 7–22 (1986). Not limited to Europe, ordeals were used to solve non-flagrant cases among early peoples throughout the world. A.S. DIAMOND, PRIMITIVE LAW, PAST AND PRESENT 228 (1971).

Law II of Edmund (England, 10th Century)[8]

§ 1. Now, it has seemed to us first of all especially needful that we steadfastly maintain peace and concord among ourselves throughout all my dominion. I myself and all of us are greatly distressed by the manifold illegal deeds of violence which are in our midst. We have therefore decreed:

> 1. Henceforth, if anyone slay a man, he shall himself [alone] bear the vendetta, unless with the help of his friends he pay composition for it, within twelve months, to the full amount of the slain man's wergeld, according to his inherited rank.

A consensual resolution of the controversy, short of trial, was also possible. Often the victim or the victim's family or clan would agree to a monetary payment or "composition" in a fixed amount depending on the status of the victim ("wergeld"). Then there would be no trial and blood revenge, and ensuing feud or war would be avoided. Criminal procedure was a private adversary affair which could, following a payment, lead to conciliation of the parties. These procedures existed not only in Europe, but throughout the world, and sometimes involved the use of mediators, usually in the form of wise men or elders who had the trust of the community.[9] These procedural forms still survive today in modern codes in the form of victim-offender conciliation, usually reserved for less serious crimes.[10]

With the growing complexity of society and the increased centralization of governmental power, crime also became more complex. It was no longer restricted to crimes of passion or theft. Highwaymen roamed the land and people were afraid. Princes and kings tried to gain legitimacy by "keeping the peace." The State moved in and took upon itself the prosecution of criminals, declaring that crimes against its citizens were simultaneously crimes against the State. Look at the early inquisitorial approach to the circumstantial evidence case:

---

8. The Laws of the Kings of England, *supra* note 6, at 9.

9. On so-called "bloodwealth" payments in customary law, *see* Diamond, *supra* note 7, at 260–67. In Africa, payment was often in cattle, *id.*, at 268–70. *See also*, P.P. Howell, A Manual of Nuer Law 40–43 (1954) on cattle payments and the role of the "leopard-skin chief" as mediator.

10. *See* Stephen C. Thaman, *Plea-Bargaining, Negotiating Confessions and Consensual Resolution of Criminal Cases* in General Reports of the XVIIth Congress of the International Academy of Comparative Law 951, 966–968 (2007).

§§ 23, 25–27 Constitutio Criminalis Carolina (German Empire, 1532)[11]

§ 23. Every sufficient indication upon which it is sought to examine under torture shall be proven with two good witnesses, as described below in several articles concerning sufficient proof. When, however, the essential element of the crime is proven with one good witness, then this, as a half proof, serves as sufficient indication, as set out below. (...)

§ 25. To begin with: concerning matters which raise suspicion, with explanation following, how and when these suffice as legally sufficient indication.

[And as a second purpose of this article:] When the indication does not appear among those described in numerous following articles and regulating sufficiency for examination under torture, investigation shall correspond to the following and to similar circumstances of suspicion, because not all can be set forth.

First: When the accused is an insolent and wanton person of bad repute and regard, so that the crime could be credibly ascribed to him, or when the same person shall have dared to perform a similar crime previously or shall have been accused of having done so. However, this bad repute shall not be adduced from enemies or wanton people, rather from impartial and upright people.

Second: When the suspected person has been caught or found at a place suspicious in the context of the deed.

Third: When a culprit has been seen in the deed or while on the way to or from it; in the case when he has not been recognized, attention shall be paid to whether the suspect has such a figure, such clothes, weapon, horse, or whatnot corresponding to what the above-mentioned culprit was seen to have.

Fourth: When the suspected person lives with or associates with such people who commit similar crimes.

Fifth: In cases of damage to property or person, attention shall be paid to whether the suspected person could have been motivated to the present crime out of envy, enmity, former threat, or in the expectation of some advantage.

Sixth: When a victim injured in person or property himself accuses someone of the crime on various grounds, and thereafter dies or affirms it with his oath.

---

11. Langbein, Prosecuting crime, *supra* note 4, at 273–75.

Seventh: When someone flees on account of a crime.

Eighth: § 26. When someone is in litigation with another concerning substantial property, which thereby constitutes the larger part of his support, goods, and possessions, he will be regarded as a grudge-holder and great enemy of his opponent; should the opponent be secretly murdered, a presumption arises against the other party that he committed this murder; and when this person is otherwise inherently suspect of having done the murder, he may be gaoled and examined under torture, when he has in the matter no legally sufficient excuse.

In circumstantial evidence crimes, there is usually no doubt that a crime has been committed, for property has been stolen or a person killed, but the identity of the perpetrator is not obvious as in flagrant crimes. To prove such crimes, inquisitorial procedure required the testimony of two eyewitnesses, or in the absence thereof, a confession corroborated by independent facts. "Legally sufficient indication," as required in the *Carolina*, was something akin to what we call "probable cause" or "reasonable suspicion," which is required to conduct an arrest or temporary detention, to search for and seize property, or to file a criminal charge.

Circumstantial evidence, of course, is also necessary to prove the intent of someone who may have been apprehended *in flagrante* after killing someone. Did he kill in self-defense, heat of passion, or with cool, calculated intent? Despite the official prohibition of torture, criminal investigators still try to induce defendants to confess, either by using illegal force, threats, deception or promises, or through legal persuasion. Prosecutors try to get defendants in non-flagrant cases to admit by offering to dismiss or reduce charges, so as not to have to present the many pieces of circumstantial evidence needed to prove identity or guilty *mens rea*. Even judges will try to get them to admit by promising them a mitigated sentence so as to avoid a full trial, or one in which members of the community participate as jurors or lay assessors.[12]

Questions

1. Which method of proving guilt in circumstantial evidence cases seems to you to be the best in attempting to ascertain the truth: the old

---

12. We will address the issue of confessions induced by the police in Chapter Four and that of confessions induced through guilty pleas or similar procedures in Chapter Six, *supra*.

customary forms (compurgators, ordeals, trial by battle, "wergeld") or the inquisitorial extraction of a confession upon the finding of "legally sufficient indication?"

2. Which method is more apt to restore the peace in the community which has been disturbed by the crime?

C. The Secret Victimless Crime

Livre de Jostice et des Plets I, 3, § 7
(France, 12th Century)[13]

The king by advice of his barons makes the following "établissement" or law; when a man shall be suspected of heresy, the ordinary judges should request the king or his court to make the "aprise" in regard to the case. He should be apprehended and imprisoned. Afterwards the bishop and the prelates of the place, that is, the Church officials, should hold an inquisition upon his case and inquire of him concerning his faith. And if he is condemned by their judgment and holy Church takes what belongs to it, the king afterwards takes possession of the prisoner and causes his execution, and all his goods belong to the king, except his wife's dowry and his heritage.

Centralized monarchies, in order to protect and consolidate their powers over local potentates and communities and enforce ideological and spiritual hegemony, invented crimes such as seditious libel, heresy, blasphemy, etc. These were crimes that could not be seen and could not be proved or disproved by eyewitnesses. They were political crimes without victims in the traditional sense. To prove them, a new type of procedure was needed.

The old procedural forms with participation of the victim, accused and community were not adequate for this new subject matter and the politicized character of the administration of justice. Crimes like homicide or theft violated private interests, such as the right to life, personal integrity or dignity and the right to property. This new kind of crime had no private victim and was designed to protect state interests, originally intimately related to its own political hegemony. It required a new kind of criminal procedure: the secret inquisition aimed at ascertaining the so-called "truth" of these political crimes.[14]

---

13. ESMEIN, *supra* note 2, at 99.

14. *Id.*, at 10–11. *See also* LUIGI FERRAJOLI, DIRITTO E RAGIONE 577, 656–57 (5th ed. 1998).

No longer were lay decision makers adequate to the new task. Royal judges replaced them to administer this centralized and politicized from of criminal law. Judges performed their duties in secular and ecclesiastical courts and were called upon to replace the God that had spoken through the ordeals, a God that was found to be too unsure a diviner of the truth of criminal charges. These judges were vetted as scientists, who, in applying the "science" of the law, would determine the truth of the charge. They were bound by strict formal rules of evidence which allotted to certain types of witnesses and testimony predetermined weight.[15]

This inquisitorial procedure, which was first used in the prosecution of political and ecclesiastical crimes, was gradually applied in the prosecution of normal criminal acts as the state took over the "keeping of the peace." It was a secret procedure, based on a pedantic assembling and analysis of written documents gathered in an investigative dossier which reflect the interrogations, searches and seizures, questioning of witnesses and other investigative measures conducted by an investigating magistrate. The "trial" in such systems amounted to no more than a perfunctory judicial review of the contents of the investigative dossier to ensure that the evidence was properly collected and analyzed by the investigating magistrate. There was no role for victims, much less the accused, who is a mere object of the proceedings with no procedural rights. He is like an insect being prepared for dissection.

In these early inquisitorial procedures are the roots of the official state monopoly on prosecution which exists in many countries. With the state moving into criminal prosecution, the victim is pushed into the background in most continental European countries and completely out of the picture in the U.S. The inquisitorial system is also the source of the so-called "principle of legality," which makes it incumbent on police, prosecutors and judges to pursue all violations of the law (to guarantee the equal protection of the law) and the "principle of material truth," which obligates investigating and adjudicating officials *sua sponte* to ascertain the truth of the charges.

In the Anglo-Saxon world the self-informing grand jury also carried out secret investigations in an inquisitorial manner and turned over information as to crimes committed in their communities to itinerant royal judges who would visit at regular intervals from London. But only with the development

---

15. Such as the requirement of two eyewitness to convict, or certain types of evidence to authorize torture in the *Carolina, supra* at 10–11.

of the inquisitorial system on the European continent can we really speak of a criminal investigation in the modern sense.

Entick v. Carrington
(English Court of Common Pleas, 1765)[16]

In trespass; the plaintiff declares that the defendants on the 11th day of November in the year of our Lord 1762, at Westminster in Middlesex, with force and arms broke and entered the dwelling-house of the plaintiff in the parish of St. Dunstan, Stepney, and continued there four hours without his consent and against his will, and that all that time disturbed him in the peaceable possession thereof, and broke open the doors to the rooms, the locks, iron bars &c. thereto affixed, and broke open the boxes, chests, drawers, &c of the plaintiff in his house and broke the locks thereto affixed, and searched and examined all the rooms, &c, in his dwelling-house, and all the boxes, &c, of the plaintiff there found, whereby the secret affairs, &c, of the plaintiff became wrongfully discovered and made public; and took and carried away 100 printed charts, 100 printed pamphlets, &c of the plaintiff there found, and other 100 charts, &c took and carried away, to the damage of the plaintiff (...)

This power assumed by the secretary of state [to conduct a general search] is an execution upon all the party's papers, in the first instance. His house is rifled; his most valuable secrets are taken out of his possession, before the paper for which he is charged is found to be criminal by any competent jurisdiction, and before he is convicted either of writing, publishing, or being concerned in the paper (...)

Lastly, it is urged as an argument of utility, that such a search is a means of detecting offenders by discovering evidence (...)

In the criminal law such a proceeding was never heard of; and yet there are some crimes, such for instance as murder, rape, robbery and house-breaking, to say nothing of forgery and perjury, that are more atrocious than libeling. But our law has provided no paper-search in these cases to help forward the conviction.

Whether this proceedeth from the gentleness of the law towards criminals, or from a consideration that such a power would be more pernicious to the innocent than useful to the public, I will not say.

It is very certain, that the law obligeth no man to accuse himself; because the necessary means of compelling self-accusation, falling upon

16. 19 Howell's State Trials, 1029, 1030, 1064, 1073 (1765)

the innocent as well as the guilty, would be both cruel and unjust; and it should seem, that search for evidence is disallowed upon the same principle. There too the innocent would be confounded with the guilty.

Observe the wisdom as well as mercy of the law. The strongest evidence before a trial, being only *ex parte*, is but suspicion; it is not proof. Weak evidence is a ground of suspicion, though in a lower degree; and if suspicion at large should be ground of search, especially in the case of libels, whose house would be safe?

The secretly committed crime (often without a typical victim) must be investigated in ways which invade our private spaces through searches, or our private thoughts or knowledge through eavesdropping, seizure of writings or compelled testimony. Searches of dwellings, wiretapping, electronic eavesdropping, undercover agents and other means to invade the citizen's private sphere are now widespread. Modern criminal procedure laws seek to determine to what extent the use of such practices can be tolerated in a democratic society and when the goal of ascertaining the truth must yield to the citizen's right to privacy and to remain silent and not divulge his or her secrets.

Today, the criminalization of the use of narcotics and marijuana and the rise of organized crime in the commerce in such controlled substances and pornography are often the context in which law enforcement agencies use these investigative techniques to penetrate into constitutionally protected spheres. When secret criminal organizations commit crimes against life and property to further their business interests, or have this as their political goal, as is the case with organized terrorist groups, then secret inquisitorial methods of investigation are clearly not limited to traditionally victimless crimes.

Questions

1. What limits should be placed on the criminalization of our thoughts, ideas or beliefs?

2. Should we ever be compelled in a criminal investigation or prosecution to reveal them?

3. What limits should the criminal law place on what we can do in the privacy of our own homes as long as it does not harm others?

4. When should the law allow an invasion of the privacy of one's home or communications?

D. A Brief History of European Criminal Procedure

Customary lay courts existed in most continental European lands, and especially in northern Europe, until the 14–16th Centuries, when they were gradually eliminated with the turn to inquisitorial procedure. In the inquisitorial system, legally educated judges, which we will refer to as "investigating magistrates," presided over the elaborate pretrial gathering and analysis of evidence, which we will call the "preliminary investigation" which was collected in written form in what we will call the "investigative dossier" which formed the legal foundation for the final judgment. It was a two-stage, secret procedure in which the first, investigative stage was decisive. The trial, a perfunctory review of the paperwork in the investigative file did not require the presence of members of the community, the victim or the defendant to disturb the "scientific" work of the Bench. The existence of several layers of appeal permitted higher courts to review the work of the courts of first instance.

Only in the British Isles and parts of Scandinavia were the lay courts maintained. In England the trial remained an oral affair before a court made up of twelve laypersons presided by a professional judge. Although there was no investigative dossier like on the European continent, elaborate rules of evidence (including the hearsay rule) gradually developed to make sure that only the most direct and reliable evidence was presented orally to the jury. The judge decided which evidence could be heard by the jury and which criminal laws should be applied by them in their deliberations. The jury alone decided the guilt or innocence of the defendant. We will call this bifurcated court, in which the judge decides questions of law and the jury questions of fact and guilt, a "jury court." The jury's verdict was final, with but few exceptions. The English judiciary tried, most notably during the prosecution of dissidents for seditious libel in the 17th and early 18th Centuries, to wrest some of the power over the guilt decision from the jury. But this attempt failed and the jury remained sovereign within the parameters of its competence. The tradition of this independent, sovereign jury was transplanted to the United States and took root in 1787 with the enactment of the U.S. Constitution.

Towards the end of the 18th Century in Europe, Enlightenment thinkers such as Beccaria in Italy and Voltaire and Montesequieu in France subjected the inquisitorial system to stinging criticism and with the French Revolution of 1789 an open revolt against it began. France adopted trial by jury and open, public trials and grafted them on to the inquisitorial mode of criminal investigation in what many have called a "mixed system" of criminal procedure. Although jury verdicts were final as in England, French juries were asked to answer a list of specific questions related to the elements of the charged crime(s) and the guilt of the defendant(s) contained in a special verdict. Sometimes the list contained dozens if not hundreds of questions. The inquisitorial written tradition on the European continent preferred reasoned judgments and a particularized special verdict would make the jury's reasoning process clear, enable the Bench to formulate judgment reasons, and facilitate appellate review. The professional judiciary and the appellate courts at various times interpreted the special verdicts or question lists so as to restrict the jury to answering only factual questions, while preserving for the professional Bench the application of the law to the facts found to have been proved and thus the ultimate determination of guilt. The French jury model, in which a jury of twelve was presided by three professional judges and a simple majority verdict sufficed for a guilt-finding, was adopted in nearly all European countries in the 19th Century, the only major exception being The Netherlands. In Germany, however, another form of lay court was gradually introduced in the 19th Century for the trial of less serious crimes. It usually consisted in a unified panel of one professional and two lay judges which collegially decided all questions of fact, law, guilt and sentence and was named after an old German customary tribunal, the *Schöffengericht*. We will call this court a "mixed court" and the lay members thereof, "lay assessors."

Jury courts were always controversial on the European continent and many jurists sought to abolish them or convert them into mixed courts. This was finally accomplished in many countries by the totalitarian regimes of the first half of the 20th Century (1917 in Russia, 1931 in Italy, 1939 in Spain and 1941 in Vichy France). The only exception was Germany, which transformed its jury court into a mixed court by decree in 1924 before Hitler's rise to power.

After the defeat of Nazism and Fascism in World War II, Italy, France and Germany did not return to the jury court but stayed with the mixed court, thus avoiding the complicated and often Byzantine 19th Century discussions as to which questions should be left to the jury and which to the professional judge. With the mixed court, the professional judge could exert his or her influence over the lay assessors in the secrecy of the deliberation room in deciding the question of guilt and could then issue judgment reasons which reflected this decision. The mixed court clearly enabled European judges to maintain their dominant, inquisitorial roles during the trial and was more consistent with the legality principle and the necessity of issuing reasoned judgments in all criminal cases. The chances of a runaway, nullifying mixed court are virtually nil.

With the democratization of Germany, Italy and France after 1945 and Spain after General Franco's death in 1975, these countries began to systematically eliminate many of the vestiges of the old inquisitorial systems which had survived the French Revolution. The investigating magistrate was eliminated in Germany in 1974 and in Italy in 1988. The preliminary investigation was opened up, allowing more participation of the accused, the victim, and their counsel. The high courts interpreted constitutional rights to give more protection to the citizenry against practices which infringed on constitutionally protected rights, such as oppressive interrogation practices, warrantless searches and seizures, etc. The jurisprudence of the European Commission and Court of Human Rights, which were set up after World War II to handle petitions alleging violations of the European Convention of Human Rights (ECHR) has also had great influence.[17] Signed in 1950 by the major Western European democracies, the ECHR has now been ratified by all of the formerly Communist countries in Eastern and Southeastern Europe as well as all of the former Soviet republics of Europe with the exception of Belarus. The jurisprudence of the European Court of Human Rights (Eur. Ct. HR), in interpreting the provisions of the ECHR, has given a vital push towards the reform of many inquisitorial practices which remained in Western Europe, as well as to some of the sloppier practices in Common Law England. It has also led to the elimination of the death penalty and the institution of more judicial control over invasions of privacy, and oppressive use of pretrial detention and torture in the former socialist bloc. In general, trials have become speedier and more open and adversarial with stricter rules limiting the admissibility of documents from the investigative dossier. Exclusionary rules have been developed to limit admissibility of illegally obtained evidence. The role of the victim during the preliminary investigation and trial has been enhanced.

Another notable development, triggered by rising crime rates and the cumbersome nature of the preliminary investigation, has been the introduction of consensual, abbreviated and simplified trial procedures. A type of sentence bargaining has even reared its head in Germany, the bastion of the legality principle, according to which all cases, whether big or small, whether with overwhelming evidence of guilt or not, must be tried.

---

17. ETS 5, November 4, 1950.

Finally, the new democratic constitutions in Spain (1978) and Russia (1993) provided for the classic jury court after the end of Franco's dictatorship and the collapse of the Soviet Union. It was seen as a catalyst for the introduction and strengthening of adversarial procedure in both countries. This surprising turn of events raises another crucial question which must be addressed by modern reformers: to what extent does the proper functioning of many of the universally accepted principles of criminal procedure, such as the presumption of innocence, the privilege against self-incrimination, the right to a public and oral trial and the right to confront and cross-examine the witnesses, ultimately depend on the form of trial court from which they were originally derived: the Anglo-American jury court. For only there is the court separated into a neutral Bench, which decides questions of law unburdened by inquisitorial duties of determining the truth of the charges, and where a jury decides facts and guilt, unprejudiced by prior knowledge of the facts of the case or institutional closeness to prosecutorial organs.

This textbook will present a thematic comparative view of criminal procedure, concentrating on some of the most controversial and problematic areas, i.e., those in which the principles of European criminal procedure often conflicted with those in the common law Anglo-American realm, and which have been the focus of major reforms. There will be no systematic description of how any one system of criminal procedure works, but the bulk of the statutes and court decisions presented will be from the most influential European countries in the area of criminal law and procedure, England, France, Germany, Italy and Spain, and from the jurisprudence of the European Court of Human Rights.

In studying English law we will see how a system with similar roots as the U.S. system has developed in the overall European context, influenced by the jurisprudence of the European Court of Human Rights. England was also the inspiration for the great reforms in France after the revolution in 1789, which in turn became the model for criminal procedure systems throughout Europe in the 19th Century. Germany has preserved many classic inquisitorial principles, such as the legality principle and the principle of material truth but has also substantially reformed its preliminary investigation and is now tacitly accepting a kind of plea bargaining. Italy, on the other hand, has made the most consequential attempt to move from the mixed French system to a purely adversarial system when it enacted a new code of criminal procedure in 1988 which abolished the investigating magistrate and introduced a panoply of new forms of consensual, abbreviated and simplified procedures. Unlike Italy, however, Spain introduced the jury court in 1995, viewing it as being the crucial foundation for turning to adversarial procedure. Like Italy,

Spain also banished the investigative dossier from the trial court in jury cases in an effort to reinforce the immediacy of the evidence-taking at trial and reduce the importance of the preliminary investigation which is still conducted by an investigating magistrate. Brief mention will be made of Russia, a country in transition from Communist dictatorship and an inquisitorial system of criminal justice, to democracy and adversary procedure.

E. Outline of the Book

Chapter Two will deal with the preliminary investigation in general and the roles of police, public prosecutor, investigating magistrate and victim in investigating crimes and deciding if criminal charges will be brought. It will also describe the participatory rights of the victim, defendant, defense counsel and prosecutor during the pretrial stages.

Chapter Three will discuss the limits placed on criminal investigators in carrying out investigative acts which impinge on the privacy rights of citizens, whether it be through searches and seizures, wiretaps, other forms of eavesdropping or use of secret informants, or seizure of private writings.

Chapter Four will discuss the limits placed on criminal investigators in interrogating suspects.

Chapter Five will discuss the admissibility at trial of evidence gathered during the preliminary investigation.

Chapter Six will address procedures which are aimed at avoiding the full trial with all of its guarantees and especially those which involve the inducement of admissions of guilt.

Chapter Seven will discuss how the presumption of innocence is protected during the full-blown trial with emphasis on the passive or active role of the judge, procedural pressures placed upon the defendant to testify, the interplay between professional and lay judges in deciding guilt and the control over the guilt decision as exercised through judicial instructions and reasoned verdicts and judgments.

Each chapter will be followed by references to seminal U.S. cases in the area being discussed and to other suggested reading. An Appendix will contain translations of selected statutory material mentioned in the text arranged according to country. A glossary will correlate the generalized English terms I use in the text with the actual terms used in our primary non-English-speaking countries: France, Germany, Italy, Russia and Spain.

Selected Readings (History & Theory)

MIRJAN R. DAMASKA, THE FACES OF JUSTICE AND STATE AUTHORITY (1986).

Mirjan R. Damaska, *Models of Criminal Procedure*, 51 ZBORNIK PFZ 477 (2001) (Collected Papers of Zagreb Law School).

JOHN PHILIP DAWSON, A HISTORY OF LAW JUDGES (1960).

ADHEMAR ESMEIN, A HISTORY OF CONTINENTAL CRIMINAL PROCEDURE WITH SPECIAL REFERENCE TO FRANCE (1913).

THOMAS ANDREW GREEN, VERDICT ACCORDING TO CONSCIENCE (1985).

JOHN H. LANGBEIN, PROSECUTING CRIME IN THE RENAISSANCE (1974).

JOHN H. LANGBEIN, TORTURE AND THE LAW OF PROOF (1977).

Erik G. Luna, *The Models of Criminal Procedure*, 2 BUFF. CRIM. L. REV. 389 (1999).

FREDERICK POLLOCK & FREDERIC WILLIAM MAITLAND, THE HISTORY OF ENGLISH LAW BEFORE THE TIME OF EDWARD I, Vol. II (2nd ed. 1952).

RICHARD VOGLER, A WORLD VIEW OF CRIMINAL JUSTICE (2005).

Selected Readings (Comparative, Country-Related)

Ennio Amodio, *The Accusatorial System Lost and Regained: Reforming Criminal Procedure in Italy*, 52 AM. J. COMP. L. 489 (2004).

Ennio Amodio & Eugenio Selvaggi, *An Accusatorial System in a Civil Law Country: the 1988 Italian Code of Criminal Procedure*, 62 TEMPLE L. REV. 1211 (1989).

CRIMINAL PROCEDURE, A WORLDWIDE STUDY (2nd ed. Craig M. Bradley, ed. 2007).

CRIMINAL PROCEDURE SYSTEMS IN THE EUROPEAN COMMUNITY (Christine Van Den Wyngaert ed. 1993).

Joseph J. Darby, *Lessons of Comparative Criminal Procedure: France and the United States*, 19 SAN DIEGO L. REV. 277 (1982).

MIREILLE DELMAS-MARTY, THE CRIMINAL PROCESS AND HUMAN RIGHTS. TOWARDS A EUROPEAN CONSCIOUSNESS (1995).

FLOYD F. FEENEY & JOACHIM HERRMANN, ONE CASE — TWO SYSTEMS: A COMPARATIVE VIEW OF AMERICAN AND GERMAN CRIMINAL JUSTICE SYSTEMS (2005).

Phil Fennell et al, The Criminal Process and Human Rights. Toward a European Consciousness (1995).

Richard S. Frase, *Comparative Criminal Justice as a Guide to American Law Reform: How Do the French Do It, How Can We Find Out, and Why Should We Care?*, 78 Cal. L. Rev. 539 (1990).

Richard S. Frase & Thomas Weigend, *German Criminal Justice As a Guide to American Law Reform: Similar Problems, Better Solutions?*, 18 B.C. Int'l & Comp. L. Rev. 317 (1995).

Stephen P. Freccero, *An Introduction to the New Italian Criminal Procedure*, 21 Am. J. Crim. L. 345 (1994).

Elisabetta Grande, *Italian Criminal Justice: Borrowing and Resistance*, 48 Am. J. Comp. L. 227 (2000).

John Hatchard et al, Comparative Criminal Procedure (1996).

Jacqueline Hodgson, French Criminal Justice: A Comparative Account of the Investigation and Prosecution of Crime in France (2007).

Giulio Illuminati, *The Frustrated Turn to Adversarial Procedure in Italy*, 4 Wash. U. Global Studies L. Rev. 567 (2005).

John H. Langbein & Lloyd L. Weinreb, *Continental Criminal Procedure: 'Myth' and Reality*, 87 Yale L. J. 1549 (1978).

John H. Langbein, Comparative Criminal Procedure: Germany (1977).

William T. Pizzi & Luca Marafioti, *The New Italian Code of Criminal Procedure: The Difficulties of Building an Adversarial Trial System on a Civil Law Foundation*, 17 Yale J. Int'l L. 1 (1992).

William T. Pizzi & Mariangela Montagna, *The Battle to Establish an Adversarial Trial System in Italy*, 25 Mich. J. Int'l L. 429 (2004).

Stephen Seabrooke & John Sprack, Criminal Evidence and Procedure: The Essential Framework (2nd ed. 1999).

John Sprack, Emmins on Criminal Procedure (11th ed. 2006).

Stefan Trechsel, Human Rights and Criminal Procedure (2005).

Chapter Two

The Criminal Investigation: Procedures and Participants

I. The Continuing Role of the Victim in Prosecuting Criminal Cases

A. The Institution of Private Prosecution

Decision of December 8, 1906 (*Placet*)
(French Supreme Court)[18]

Whereas a complaint against various persons, with a count of fraud and complicity in such felony, was filed by Mr. Placet in the hands of one of the investigating magistrates at the Court of the Seine on February 24, 1906; that, after having received the declarations of the complainant, who was constituted as civil party, and having referred the documents to the public prosecutor, the latter concluded: "that it was unnecessary to issue an order to investigate," whereupon the investigating magistrate declared in an order dated March 2: "unnecessary to prosecute;" (...)

Whereas the public prosecutor, the petitioner in this appeal in cassation, maintains that the complaint of the civil party (...) does not trigger the public prosecution; that, consequently, the investigating magistrate had necessarily to conform to the order not to investigate, which prohibited him in an absolute manner from making any other decision. (...)

But, whereas this interpretation of the texts cannot be accepted in this manner; that (...) "any person who claims to be injured by a felony

---

18. LES GRAND ARRÊTS DU DROIT CRIMINEL,Vol. 2, 38–40 (Jean Pradel & André Varinaud eds. 1995). Unless otherwise noted all French, German, Italian, Russian and Spanish texts (cases and statutes) have been translated into English by the author.

or misdemeanor can file a complaint and be constituted as a civil party before the investigating magistrate, either at the place of the felony or misdemeanor, at the place of residence of the accused, or at the place where he can be found;" It follows, furthermore (...), that penal jurisdictions can only rule on a civil action when the public prosecution has been simultaneously brought to them and that, thus, in investing the aggrieved party with the right to bring a civil action before the investigating magistrate, the legislator has necessarily intended that the filing itself of the complaint in the hands of this magistrate, with constitution as civil party, would similarly initiate the public prosecution; (...) that the right of the civil party to initiate, at her risk and peril, the public prosecution before the investigating magistrate (...), establishes for this party a parallel right to that of the public prosecutor; (...)

Whereas a prosecution initiated by the civil party before the investigating magistrate, just like that begun by direct summons, necessarily assumes, of course, the same characteristics as if it had been requested by the public prosecutor; it is necessary, therefore, as a consequence, to apply (...) the absolute rule according to which the investigative jurisdiction has, like any other, the right and duty to exercise it in complete independence from the orders of the public prosecutor;

Whereas it follows from the preceding, that whatever orders are issued by the public prosecutor (...), once a complaint with a proper constitution of the civil party has been submitted to the investigating magistrate (...), he has (...) the duty to investigate the complaint to the extent deemed appropriate; that this obligation does not cease until the investigating magistrate decides, in fact, either that from the outset the accusation has been sufficiently established (...) or, due to reasons affecting the public prosecution itself, the facts cannot legally justify a prosecution or that, supposing they have been disproved, they could not admit of any penal qualification.

With the rise of inquisitorial procedure an investigating magistrate trained in the law becomes the first professional criminal investigator. An executive official, the public prosecutor, becomes the prosecuting party in most cases, with the aggrieved party playing a subsidiary role in all but minor cases in most post-inquisitorial systems on the European continent.[19]

---

19. The victim will hereafter be referred to as the "aggrieved party," a broader term which includes family members who, particularly in homicide cases, represent the actual victims in bringing the civil action and the private prosecution.

In the old *Placet* case, the public prosecutor did not want to pursue the charges proffered by the complainant. French prosecutors have discretion, as in the United States, not to bring criminal charges even if they could be theoretically proved in court. In Europe this is called the "opportunity principle."

§ 100 LECr (Spain)[20]

From every felony and misdemeanor[21] arises a criminal action to punish the guilty person, and may also arise a civil action for restitution of the thing, reparation of the harm, or indemnification for the damages caused by the criminal act.

§ 105 LECr (Spain)

Officials in the public prosecutor's office have the obligation to bring, in accordance with the provisions of the law, all criminal actions which they consider to be legitimate, whether or not there is a private prosecutor in the case, with the exception of those which the Penal Code reserves exclusively for private complaint.[22]

Note the mandatory obligation placed on the public prosecutor to charge crimes which violate public interests or important private interests, such as is the case with the crimes of homicide, rape, burglary, serious thefts, etc. In

---

20. *See Ley de Enjuiciamiento Criminal*, Gaceta, No. 260, Sept. 16, 1882, Gaceta, No. 283, Oct. 10, 1882, hereafter LECr (Spain) (Spanish Code of Criminal Procedure) all cites from Ley de enjuiciamiento criminal y otras normas procesales 37–207 (10th ed. Julio Muerza Esparza ed. 2005).

21. There is no consistency across the board in how various levels of crime are defined in national penal codes. In general I will use the term "infraction" for crimes where only a fine may be imposed, the term "misdemeanor" for less-serious crimes where shorter terms of deprivation of liberty may be imposed, and "felony" for the most serious crimes subject to long prison terms or life imprisonment. Some countries, however, like Spain, only have two global distinctions, others, like France and the U.S., have three, etc.

22. Cf. § 152(2) *Strafprozessordnung*, Feb. 1, 1877, RGBL, p. 253, New version of April 7, 1987, BGBl I, p. 274, 1319, hereafter StPO (Germany) (German Code of Criminal Procedure), all cites from Strafprozessordnung (42nd ed. DTV 2007). § 50 *Codice di Procedura Penale*, Decree of the President of the Republic, Sept. 22, 1988, No. 447, hereafter CCP (Italy) (Italian Code of Criminal Procedure), all cites from Mario Chiavario et al, Codici e leggi per l'udienza penale 167–449 (2005–2006); §§ 1,2 *Code de Procédure Pénale*, (Appendix, 245–46), L. no. 47-1426, Dec. 31, 1957, hereafter CPP (France), all cites from Code de procédure pénale (48th ed. Dalloz 2007).

Europe this is called the "legality principle," in contrast to the aforementioned "opportunity principle," which reigns in common law countries as well as in France. In France, as well as in Spain, the person whose private interests have been violated by a crime may file a private "complaint" in order to initiate a criminal prosecution and may also attach a "civil action" for damages arising out of the criminal act. The consolidation of civil and criminal actions is allowed in most continental European countries. The aggrieved party may play the role of both "private prosecutor" and/or "civil party" (plaintiff). The division of roles between public and private prosecutor depends in general on two factors: (1) the type of interest violated by the criminal act; and (2) whether or not the public prosecutor has discretion not to charge in relation to the type of crime involved.

When a less-serious crime affects the private interests of a citizen, the codes of some many countries require the aggrieved party to file a complaint and constitute herself as private prosecutor. Thus, in Germany, misdemeanors such as disturbing the peace, libel, battery, minor threats, destruction of property, etc., may only be prosecuted by private complaint.[23] Although the public prosecutor may enter the case if she deems it is in the public interest, she is not obliged to do so, which means one could have a criminal prosecution brought by a private person against another private person with no state participation,[24] thus perpetuating in a sense the ancient mode of initiating criminal prosecutions before the advent of the public prosecutor. Although aggrieved parties in Germany may always act as a civil party by joining a civil action to a pending criminal action, they may act as "private prosecutors" only in cases requiring a private complaint or in those involving certain serious felonies such as murder, assault, kidnapping or sexual assault.[25] If a German aggrieved party reports a crime that is not charged by the public prosecutor, however, she may appeal to a court for a writ of mandamus to order the prosecutor to bring charges.[26]

There are obvious advantages for an aggrieved party in being able to combine a civil action with a criminal prosecution and, in addition, to be able to

---

23. §374 StPO (Germany) (Appendix, 250).

24. §377 StPO (Germany) (Appendix, 251).

25. §395 StPO (Germany). The Germans call this "auxiliary prosecution" (*Nebenklage*). 67% of the cases in which an aggrieved party has chosen to exercise this right in serious felony cases have been in sexual assault cases. William Pizzi & Walter Perron, *Crime Victims in German Courtrooms*, 32 STAN. J. INT'L L. 7, 55 (1996).

26. §172 StPO (Germany) provides for this "procedure to compel prosecution." (*Klageerzwingungsverfahren*).

prosecute in her name and request a particular legal qualification of the criminal act and the amount of punishment that she feels should be imposed. But there are also risks much like those which confront a civil plaintiff. The private prosecutor must usually post bond upon filing the complaint[27] and may, in the event of an acquittal or dismissal of the charge, be subject to a civil fine,[28] the payment of damages to the defendant,[29] the payment of the defendant's costs[30] or even to criminal punishment.[31]

Questions

1. Do you see any advantages for an aggrieved party in acting as a private prosecutor alongside the public prosecutor in bringing the alleged culprit to justice?

2. Would consolidating the civil with the criminal trial have produced better results for the victims' families in the O.J. Simpson case?

Selected Readings

M.E.I. Brienen & E.H. Hoegen, Victims of Crime in 22 European Criminal Justice Systems (2000).

George P. Fletcher, With Justice for Some. Protecting Victim's Rights in Criminal Trials (1996).

Jacqueline Hodgson, *Suspects, Defendants and Victims in the French Criminal Process: The Context of Recent Reform*, 51 Int'l & Comp. L. Q. 781 (2002).

William Pizzi & Walter Perron, *Crime Victims in German Courtrooms: A Comparative Perspective on American Problems*, 32 Stan. J. Int'l L. 7 (1996).

---

27. § 88 CPP (France); § 379 StPO (Germany); § 280 LECr (Spain).
28. § 91(1) CPP (France).
29. § 472 CPP (France).
30. § 379(1) StPO (Germany); § 427 CPP (Italy).
31. § 226-10 Code Pénale (French Penal Code), a charge of calumnious denunciation. Cf. Jean Pradel, Procédure Pénale 478 (9th ed. 1997). Under the *Carolina* the private prosecutor could be imprisoned until he provided surety and also had to pay compensation if the defendant was acquitted. § 12 *Constitutio Criminalis Carolina, supra* note 4, at 270. In ancient times the aggrieved party who brought a false charge would be subject to the same punishment the accused would have received if guilty!

B. The Institution of Popular Prosecution

Art. 125 Const. (Spain)

Citizens may initiate a popular prosecution and participate in the administration of justice through the institution of the jury, in the form and with respect to those criminal proceedings determined by law (...)

§ 101 LECr (Spain)

The criminal action is public. All Spanish citizens may exercise it in accordance with the prescriptions of the Law.

§ 270(1) LECr (Spain)

All Spanish citizens can, whether or not they were victimized by the crime, file a criminal complaint, exercising the right of popular prosecution established in Article 101 of this Law.

Known to the Romans as *quivis ex populo*, popular prosecution also existed in old Germanic legal systems in the right of the victim's tribe or clan to seek redress for the crime.[32] Spain is the only country in Europe where any citizen properly constituted as a "popular prosecutor" has procedural equality or "equality of arms" with the public prosecutor.[33]

Decision No. 241 of December 21, 1992 (Spanish Constitutional Court)[34]

By written motion presented to the Municipal Court on February 28, 1990, (...) the "Association of Mothers of the National Police of Guipúzcoa," files a constitutional appeal against the Order of (...) the Court of Appeal of the Autonomous Community of the Basque Country of February 6, 1990 (...), in preliminary investigation no. 23/1987 involving apologizing for terrorism. (...)

The reasons why, in the opinion of the Court of Appeal, the appellant Association may not initiate a popular prosecution are, on the one hand, that such action is constitutionally reserved for "citizens"—and

---

32. Claus Roxin, Strafverfahrensrecht 71 (24th ed. 1995).
33. Vicente Gimeno Sendra et al, Derecho procesal penal 289 (1996).
34. 141 BJC 134, 135,139.

it should be understood thereunder only natural persons—and, on the other hand, that among the statutory aims of the Association-petitioner none is included which legitimates its initiation of public prosecution. For its part, both the appellant and the public prosecutor maintain that, in relation to the former, the expression "citizens" in Art. 125 of the Const. must be understood to include all persons, natural or juridical (...). Moreover, (...) the petitioner and the public prosecutor understand that, to the extent that what is intended by the exercise of popular prosecution is to give satisfaction to the common interest in the defense of the legal order, it is not necessary in order to exercise it that any particular or direct interest exist independent from the fact that, of course, it is not difficult in this case to also identify an obvious specific interest on the part of the Association in the criminal prosecution of those who apologize for activities primarily directed against the spouses, family members and members of the Association like that of the appellant, the "Mothers of the National Police of Guipúzcoa."

[As to the term] "citizens," this Court has been maintaining for a long time that with it one refers both to natural as well as juridical persons (...), but, above all, also because "if all persons have the right of access to the courts and to a fair trial and if one legitimately recognizes the personifications which, in order to achieve a common goal together have been given the name of juridical persons, one can affirm that Art. 24.1 [Const.] includes in the reference to 'all persons,' both natural and juridical." (...) [I]t is obvious that the person to which Art. 24.1 [Const.] refers as the holder of the right which includes (...) the right to access to justice through popular prosecution, is both the natural or physical person as well as the juridical or collective and, therefore, only by a restrictive interpretation of the expression "citizens" in Art. 125 Const. (...) can one justify the judicial decision now under discussion. (...) On the contrary, the full constitutional recognition of the associative phenomenon and of the articulation of collective entities equipped with personality, necessitates the assumption of a broad interpretation of the expressions with which, in each case, one designates the holder of rights which are constitutionally recognized and legislatively developed.

Note how non-victim citizens and even interest groups defending social or collective interests[35] can launch and participate in a criminal prosecution in

---

35. Interest groups may also bring popular prosecutions in Italy, *see* §§ 91, 92(1) CPP (Italy) (Appendix, 252–53). In France, §§ 2-2 through 2-14 CPP (France) provide for a right of civil action to non-profit organizations which for at least five years have had a record of, for instance, defending the rights of workers, consumers, chil-

some European countries. In Spain popular prosecution is guaranteed in the same constitutional provision as that providing for the right of the public to participate in deciding criminal cases as jurors.

With the institutions of private and popular prosecution and procedural consolidation of civil and criminal actions arising from the commission of unlawful acts, we can see that the criminal prosecution on the European continent includes a broader array of participants than does the bipolar battle between prosecution and defense in the United States.

Questions

1. Is it fair that a number of prosecutors, public, private and popular, square off against a single defendant in a criminal case? Does this violate the principle of equality of arms?

2. Does the consolidation of the civil suit with the criminal prosecution turn the focus of the trial from that of personal guilt to one of maximization of monetary damages?

3. Does the procedural empowerment of the victim constitute a return to earlier procedural paradigms which focused on personal revenge and prevent the future re-socialization of the convicted defendant?[36]

II. The Role of the Police Before Initiation of Formal Criminal Proceedings: The Police Inquest

§ 282 (para. 1) LECr (Spain)

The judicial police have as their objective, and it shall be the duty of all members of which it is composed, to ascertain the public offenses which are committed in their territory or district; to conduct, de-

---

dren, the environment, women, racial minorities, the disabled, animals, the family and the French language. Other groups who have been granted the right to join in criminal prosecutions as a civil party are those who fight against sexual violence, drugs, alcohol, tobacco, drunk driving, crimes against humanity, abortion, etc. PRADEL, *supra* note 31, at 254–67.

36. ROXIN, *supra* note 32, at 454.

pending on their particularities, the investigative acts necessary to prove them and to discover the offenders and collect all the fruits, instruments or evidence of the crime which are in danger of disappearing, and to place them at the disposition of the judicial authorities (...).

§ 286 LECr (Spain)

When the investigating or municipal magistrate commence to initiate the preliminary investigation, the investigative acts of prevention being conducted by any police agent or authority shall cease; they are obligated to deliver the records thereof to said magistrate as well as the fruits relating to the crime which they have collected, and place the arrestees at his disposition, if there are any.[37]

Continental European criminal justice systems make a clear distinction between the powers of the police before initiation of criminal proceedings, which we will call the "police inquest," and those afterwards. As we shall later see, the police continue investigating after the initiation of criminal proceedings, but only when the authority to do so has been delegated by the investigating official, whether investigating magistrate or public prosecutor.

The authority of the police to act on their own initiative stops as soon as the charging process is initiated. This usually short period before the initiation of formal criminal proceedings,[38] has always been a very productive investigative period for law enforcement organs and a very critical one from the point of view of the person under investigation, whom we shall call the

---

37. For similar provisions, *see* § 14 CPP (France); § 163(1) StPO (Germany); § 354 CPP (Italy).

38. Following a warrantless arrest police normally only have a short window of time to conduct investigative measures *ex officio*. In Europe, as in the United States, the arrested person must be brought before a judge within a short time, usually from 24 to 48 hours, after which the police's independent powers of investigation usually cease or the prerequisites therefor are radically altered. *See* § 63 CPP (France), allowing for 24 hours of pre-charge detention (*garde à vue*) with a further 24 hour extension; § 128 StPO (Germany) (no later than the next day); § 390(1) CPP (Italy) (48 hours); § 496 LECr (Spain) (24 hours), with up to 72 hours in terrorism cases (§ 520bis LECr (Spain). Although the U.N. Human Rights Commission recently required that arrested persons be brought before a judge within 48 hours, Sarah Joseph et al, The International Covenant on Civil and Political Rights. Cases, Materials and Commentary 324–25 (2d. ed. 2004), the European Court of Human Rights has, of yet, not found a violation unless the delay exceeded four days. Stefan Trechsel, Human Rights and Criminal Procedure 512–16 (2005).

"suspect," because of the difficulty to protect one's right to silence and privacy in police custody.[39]

III. The Formal Criminal Investigation

A. The Search for Truth and the Compilation of the Investigative Dossier

§ 80 CPP (France)

The investigating magistrate may only investigate pursuant to a petition of the public prosecutor (...).

§§ 81 (paras. 1–2,4) CPP (France)

The investigating magistrate conducts, in conformance with the law, all investigative acts that he deems useful to ascertain the truth. He investigates inculpatory and exculpatory evidence.

A copy of such acts as well as all procedural documents shall be prepared; each copy shall be certified to be in compliance by the clerk of the court or the judicial police mentioned in paragraph 4. All the documents of the investigative dossier shall be marked by the clerk of the court in the order of their compilation or receipt by the investigating magistrate. (...)

If it is impossible for the investigating magistrate to carry out all the investigative acts himself, he may issue a rogatory commission to officers of the judicial police that they may conduct all the necessary investigative acts (...).

The formal preliminary investigation, the centerpiece of inquisitorial criminal procedure, is still conducted in secrecy.[40] Formal preliminary inves-

---

39. After formal proceedings are initiated by a document we shall call the "complaint," the person under investigation will be referred to as the "accused." The decision to bring the accused to trial (often by a judge or magistrate) will be called the "committal order." The prosecutor's charging document in the trial court will be referred to as the "accusatory pleading." The person on trial will be referred to as the "defendant."

40. See § 11(1) CPP (France); § 329(1) CPP (Italy) (Appendix, 253); § 301(1) LECr (Spain).

tigations are often lengthy affairs and the suspect-accused is often subject to long periods of pretrial detention.[41] Nowadays the formal preliminary investigation is reserved for the most serious crimes.[42] As can be seen above, the reports of all investigative acts carried out are placed in the investigative dossier which then forms the basis for judgment at trial. In inquisitorial times the "trial" consisted in a judicial reading of the dossier to make sure it was compiled in accordance with the statutory rules evidence gathering.[43] Note also the interaction between public prosecutor and investigating magistrate during the preliminary investigation in France. The initiation of criminal proceedings in most systems is strictly in the hands of the public prosecutor.[44] In Spain, on the contrary, the investigating magistrate may initiate criminal proceedings *ex officio*.[45]

As can be seen, the investigating magistrate may delegate performance of investigative acts to the "judicial police" through what are called "rogatory commissions." As in the United States, police in Europe conduct most of the investigative work pursuant to rogatory commission or pursuant to legislation which has given them more authority to investigate less serious crimes *sua sponte*. The investigating magistrate's role has gradually been reduced to: (1) authorizing invasions into protected interests of the accused, such as searches, seizures, wiretapping, other secret investigative measures, and

---

41. Pretrial detention is at least theoretically questionable in relation to the presumption of innocence and the principle that no one should be punished until found guilty by a court of law. Nonetheless the European Court of Human Rights has held that pretrial detention of from 27.5 to 41 months does not violate the ECHR, TRECHSEL, *supra* note 37, at 530–31, and Spanish legislation from 2004 permits pretrial detention of four years in serious cases. § 504(2) LECr (Spain).

42. In France a preliminary investigation is mandatory for felonies and discretionary for misdemeanors. § 79 CPP (France).

43. The preparation of the investigative dossier follows the same general rules in non-jury cases in Spain, §§ 299 et seq LECr (Spain) and in Italy, where the public prosecutor is the investigative official. § 373 (1,5) CPP (Italy) (Appendix, 254).

44. The same is true in the Netherlands, but once the investigating magistrate has begun an investigation, the public prosecutor loses all control over its further course. Ingrid van Reyt, *Niederlande*, in DIE BEWEISAUFNAHME IM STRAFVERFAHRENSRECHT DES AUSLANDS 294–95 (Walter Perron ed. 1995).

45. *See* § 303 (para. 1) LECr (Spain). As was noted *supra*, Chapter 2, I, A. and B, the private and popular prosecutors may directly trigger an investigation by the investigating magistrate by filing a complaint without prior approval of the public prosecutor. On the preliminary investigation which is exclusively in the hands of the public prosecutor, *see* §§ 326, 327 CPP (Italy) (Appendix, 253); § 260 StPO (Germany).

pretrial detention; (2) conducting interrogations of the accused; (3) preserving evidence which cannot be repeated at trial by presiding over depositions, line-ups or other investigative acts while guaranteeing the rights of the defense to be present and cross-examine witnesses, etc;[46] and (4) deciding the admissibility at trial of the evidence gathered during the preliminary investigation.

In 1974 Germany formalized this trend by abolishing the office of investigating magistrate and turning the supervision of the preliminary investigation over to the public prosecutor and creating a new impartial judicial figure to preside over the four aforementioned tasks involving violations of protected rights of the accused and issues relating to the admissibility of evidence. Italy took a similar step in 1988. We will call this new pretrial judge the "judge of the investigation."[47] The theoretical rationale for separating the judicial from the investigative function is that an investigator, who is pursuing a particular theory of a case, can no longer be impartial in making decisions which impact on the suspect's constitutional rights. Politically, therefore, the modern trend is to allocate investigation and prosecution of criminal cases to the executive branch of government, and decisions which affect constitutionally protected rights to privacy, human dignity and freedom, including the judgment in criminal cases, to the judicial branch.

Despite a relative rise in serious crime in Europe over the last several decades, formal preliminary investigations have become less frequent. In France in the 1830s about 41% of criminal investigations were conducted by the investigating magistrate, but by 1988 the percentage had fallen to around 8%.[48] In the Netherlands, only about 3% of cases are investigated by the investigating magistrate.[49]

---

46. We will use the Spanish term for the evidence thus preserved: "anticipated evidence." On the difference between "anticipated" and "preconstituted" evidence in Spain, see RAQUEL LÓPEZ JIMÉNEZ, LA PRUEBA EN EL JUICIO POR JURADOS 151–96 (2002).

47. A French penal reform commission coined this name (*juge de l'instruction*) to differentiate the new role from that of the traditional *juge d'instruction*. COMMISSION JUSTICE PÉNALE ET DROITS DE L'HOMME, LA MISE EN ÉTAT DES AFFAIRES PÉNALES. RAPPORTS 31 (1991). The name used in Germany is *Ermittlungsrichter* (investigation-judge) and in Italy, *giudice per le indagine preliminari* (judge of the preliminary investigation).

48. In 1969 still about 20% of cases were in the hands of investigating magistrates. Richard Vogler, *Criminal Procedure in France*, in JOHN HATCHARD ET AL., COMPARATIVE CRIMINAL PROCEDURE 69 (1996).

49. Stewart Field et al, *Prosecutors, Examining Judges and Control of Police Investigations*, in PHIL FENNELL ET AL, CRIMINAL JUSTICE IN EUROPE. A COMPARATIVE STUDY 240–41 (1995).

In the United States, the United Kingdom and some Scandinavian countries, criminal investigation is almost exclusively in the hands of the police, with the public prosecutor's role restricted almost exclusively to prosecuting cases in the courts. England did not even have a public prosecutor's office until quite recently.[50] What actually is the difference between having a prosecutor or a judge in charge of the investigation? Italy has switched from investigating magistrate to public prosecutor—but both officials are legally educated, members of the magistracy, and often switch positions during their careers. The same is true of prosecutors, investigating magistrates and judges in France who all attend the National Judicial College and where traditionally prosecutors are called "standing magistrates" and judges "sitting magistrates."[51] If the officers of the judicial police had a legal education, would it make any difference if they were entrusted with the formal education of criminal cases?[52]

Regardless of under whose tutelage, the continental European preliminary investigation requires a more or less secret investigation by a legally trained official who is duty-bound to ascertain the truth and to officially and impartially collect evidence which will be admissible in court and be sufficient to justify a criminal charge. The search for truth, if taken seriously, cannot be partisan and must include an investigation of potentially exculpatory evidence as well. Lawyers on the European continent do not usually conduct parallel investigations as would an American lawyer, but must rely on the objectivity and impartiality of the investigating official to investigate exculpatory as well as incriminating evidence. There is a modern trend, however, to permit defense investigations with Italy leading the way.[53]

---

50. The Crown Prosecution Service was only established in 1985. John Hatchard, *Criminal Procedure in England and Wales*, in HATCHARD ET AL, *supra* note 48, at 182. Before this time, private barristers were employed to prosecute criminal cases.

51. Vogler, *supra* note 48, at 62.

52. The French investigating magistrate was originally tightly associated with the judicial police and was called an "officer of the judicial police." Only in 1958 was the investigating magistrate assigned to the judicial branch. MIS EN ÉTAT, *supra* note 47, at 127–28. The legally trained Russian investigator is still integrated into the Ministry of Internal Affairs alongside the police.

53. The CCP (Italy) of 1988 allowed for defense investigations but, in the early years, defense lawyers claimed they did not have the funds to conduct them. Hans-Heinrich Jescheck, *Grundgedanken der neuen italienischen Strafprozeßordnung in rechtsvergleichender Sicht*, in FESTSCHRIFT FÜR ARTHUR KAUFMANN ZUM 70. GEBURTSTAG 661 (1993); Susanne Hein, *Italien*, in BEWEISAUFNAHME, *supra* note 44, at 159. In 2000, however, the code was amended to add a new chapter, §§ 391bis–391decies CCP (Italy), which statutorily regulates the possibilities of defense interviewing of

Questions

1. Does it really matter who investigates a criminal case as long as humane methods are used and the investigator honestly seeks the truth?

2. Should criminal investigators be trained in the law? Should they have higher degrees in criminology or other forensic sciences?

3. Should a judge independent of the investigation decide the propriety of investigative acts which impact on protected constitutional rights of the suspect-accused?

Selected Readings

Stanley Z. Fisher, *The Prosecutor's Ethical Duty to Seek Exculpatory Evidence in Police Hands: Lessons from England*, 68 FORDHAM L. REV. 1379 (2000).

JULIA FONDA, PUBLIC PROSECUTORS AND DISCRETION. A COMPARATIVE STUDY (1995).

Abraham Goldstein & Martin Marcus, *The Myth of Judicial Supervision in Three "Inquisitorial" Systems: France, Italy, and Germany*, 87 YALE L. J. 240 (1977).

Joachim Herrmann, *The Rule of Compulsory Prosecution and the Scope of Prosecutorial Discretion in Germany*, 41 U. CHI. L. REV. 468 (1974).

John H. Langbein, *Controlling Prosecutorial Discretion in Germany*, 41 U. CHI. L. REV. 439 (1974).

B. Confrontation and Adversarial Rights during the Preliminary Investigation

1. The Right to Be Present with Counsel
§ 118 LECr (Spain)

Every person imputed to be responsible for a punishable act can exercise the right of defense, acting in proceedings of whatever type, from the moment she is notified of the existence of the imputation, has

---

witnesses, use of private investigators, creation of a "defense file" and the integration of the defense file with the prosecutor's investigative file. *See* Nicola Triggiani, *La L. 7 diciembre 2000 No. 397 ("Disposizione in materia di indagine difensivi"): Prime riflessioni*, CASS. PENALE #1120, 2272–91 (2001).

been the object of an arrest or of any other preventive measure, or as to whom the prosecution has been initiated, and shall be informed of this right in furtherance thereof.

The receipt of a crime report or complaint and any procedural act from which results the imputation of a crime against a determinate person or persons, shall be immediately made known to the presumptive accuseds.

To exercise the right conceded by the first paragraph, the interested persons should be represented by a solicitor and defended by counsel, and if they have requested them and not named them themselves, they should be officially appointed. (...)

The right to counsel is guaranteed in most European countries from the moment of arrest or charge, whichever comes first.[54] Continental European law also often permits the defendant, defense counsel and sometimes even the aggrieved party to be present when investigative measures are carried out.[55] For instance, the defendant often has the right to have defense counsel present when he is interrogated or subjected to a confrontation with another witness,[56] or even when investigative officials conduct searches and seizures[57] or examinations of prosecution witnesses.[58]

2. The Right to Make Evidentiary Motions
§ 82-1(paras. 1–2) CPP (France)

During the course of the preliminary investigation, the parties may submit a reasoned written motion to the investigating magistrate that he conduct their examination or interrogation, the examination of a witness, a confrontation, a visit to the scene of the crime, order production by any of them of evidence useful to the investigation, or that all other acts be conducted which appear necessary to them for the ascertainment of the truth. (...)

---

54. Cf. § 104 CPP (Italy); §§ 46(4)(3), 47(4)(9) *Ugolovno-protsessual'nyy kodeks Rossiyskoy Federatsii*, enacted by Russian State Duma, November 22, 2001 (Code of Criminal Procedure of the Russian Federation, hereafter UPK (Russia), all cites from UGOLOVNO-PROTSESSUAL'NYY KODEKS ROSSIYSKOY FEDERATSII (Os' 89 2006) (with amendments through January 9, 2006).

55. *See* § 302 LECr (Spain) (Appendix, 258).

56. *See* § 364 (1–4,7) CPP (Italy) (Appendix, 254).

57. *See* § 365 CPP (Italy) (Appendix, 254).

58. *See* § 168c(2–3) StPO (Germany).

The investigating magistrate should, if he does not intend to grant [the motion], issue a reasoned order within a month calculated from the receipt of the motion (...).[59]

As can be seen, the "parties," including both defendant and the aggrieved party, have the right to make evidentiary motions during the preliminary investigation, i.e., to ask the investigating magistrate or public prosecutor to pursue a certain line of inquiry, to interview witnesses, seek expert opinions, perform tests, etc. The parties are also given nearly complete discovery of the results of the preceding police and official investigations unless revelation would jeopardize the success of the investigation.[60]

3. Proceedings to Preserve or "Anticipate" Evidence
§ 392(1) CPP (Italy)

(1) During the course of the preliminary investigation the public prosecutor and the accused can request the judge to preserve ("anticipate") evidence:

(a) by taking testimony from a person when there is reasonable cause to believe that she will not be able to be examined at trial due to illness or another grave impediment;

(b) by taking testimony when, due to concrete and specific facts there is reasonable cause to believe that the person is exposed to violence, threats, offers or promises of money or other benefits so that she will not testify or will testify falsely;

(c) by examining the accused as to facts concerning the responsibility of others;

(d) by examining persons indicated in § 210 [those charged in separate related cases];

(e) by arranging a confrontation between persons who have made contradictory declarations in other acts to preserve evidence;

---

59. Cf. § 166(1) StPO (Germany); §§ 311 (para. 1), 384(2) LECr (Spain) (Appendix, 259).

60. Cf. § 147 StPO (Germany). On the Netherlands, see Van de Reyt, supra note 44, at 296. On the other hand, in France full discovery for the defense is only allowed after the committal order, PRADEL, supra note 31, at 486. The liberal approach to discovery in Europe should be compared with the extremely restrictive approach taken in the United States, especially in the federal courts. See Fed. R. Crim. P. 16.

(f) by taking expert testimony or conducting a judicial experiment if the evidence regards a person, thing or place, the status of which is subject to unavoidable modification;

(g) by conducting an identification proceeding, if certain exigent circumstances do not permit postponing the act to the trial.

§ 394 CPP (Italy)

(1) The aggrieved party may request the public prosecutor to move for the preservation (anticipation) of evidence.

(2) If he does not grant the request, the public prosecutor shall issue a reasoned order and notify the aggrieved party.

§ 401 (1–3,5) CPP (Italy)

(1) The hearing takes place *in camera* with the obligatory participation of the public prosecutor and the accused's defense counsel. The aggrieved party's counsel also has a right to participate.

(2) If the defense counsel of the accused fails to appear, the judge appoints another defense counsel pursuant to § 97(4).

(3) The accused and the aggrieved party have the right to be present at the preservation of evidence when a witness or other person must be examined. (...)

(5) Evidence is taken according to the rules established for trial. The aggrieved party's counsel may ask the judge to pose questions to the person subject to examination.

§ 403(1) CPP (Italy)

(1) The evidence taken as anticipated evidence is usable at trial only in relation to the defendants whose defense counsel have participated when it was taken.

The procedures outlined in the above sections are required in order to preserve or "anticipate" evidence so that it will be admissible at trial. Admissibility is ensured by requiring that witnesses be examined in the presence of all the parties so that each will have a right to test the evidence in adversarial fashion much as is the case with pretrial depositions provided for in many American jurisdictions. The right to confrontation has thus been guaranteed in case the witness is not available for trial.

4. *Identification Procedures*

Observe how the right to counsel is guaranteed at identifications pursuant to § 392(1)(g) CCP (Italy), *supra*. Counsel must be present during line-ups in nearly all European jurisdictions.[61] In England, which does not have a two-stage investigation procedure, police are allowed to conduct pre-charge identification procedures, such as lineups, called "identification parades," video identifications and group identifications. English law regulates in detail the procedures for identification and gives suspects "a reasonable opportunity to have a solicitor or friend present" during the identification procedure.[62]

Mistaken identifications by eyewitnesses are one of the main sources of the conviction of the innocent in the United States. Nonetheless, there is no right to counsel when the great majority of lineups and show-ups are conducted, i.e., before the initiation of criminal proceedings.[63]

5. *The Adversarialization of the Preliminary Investigation*

Observe what has become of the old inquisitorial preliminary investigation. It is no longer the secret, *incommunicado*, coercive institution of the past. Now the defendant, defense counsel, the aggrieved party and her lawyer actively participate in the investigative acts and the role of the judge, whether investigating magistrate or judge of the investigation, has become more like that of a trial judge: an impartial arbiter responding to motions of the parties.

When Spain reintroduced trial by jury in 1995,[64] the jury law included changes in the role of the investigating magistrate in cases subject to the jurisdiction of the jury court. Note what happens when the investigating magistrate decides that a case is subject to the jurisdiction of the jury court:

---

61. *See* § 520(2)(c) LECr (Spain) (Appendix, 259–60).

62. §§ 1–3, 8–9, 11–13, 16 , Annex B, Code of Practice D, Police and Criminal Evidence Act 1984 (Appendix, 240–41), hereafter PACE (England), all citations from MICHAEL ZANDER, THE POLICE AND CRIMINAL EVIDENCE ACT 1984 (5th ed. 2005).

63. United States v. Wade, 388 U.S. 218 (1967); Kirby v. Illinois, 406 U.S. 682 (1972).

64. Ley Orgánica 5/1995, del Tribunal del Jurado, BOE no. 122, of May 23, 1995, modified by LO 8/1995 of November 16, 1995 and LO 10/1995, of November 23, 1995 (Organic Law on the Jury Court, hereafter LOTJ (Spain)). All citations from LEY DE ENJUICIAMENTO CRIMINAL Y OTRAS NORMAS PROCESALES, *supra* note 20, at 208–41.

§25 LOTJ (Spain)

(1) Once a proceeding has been initiated for a crime the adjudication of which is within the jurisdiction of the jury court, the investigating magistrate immediately gives notice to the accuseds. For the purpose of concretizing the charges, they are summoned to appear within five days along with the public prosecutor and the other parties. At the time of the summons, the accuseds are notified of the crime report or complaint admitted for consideration if notice had not already been effectuated. The accused must be assisted by counsel of his choice, or if not designated, by officially appointed counsel.

(2) If the persons aggrieved or damaged by the crime are known and are not present, they shall be summoned to be heard during the appearance provided in the above section and at the time of the summons they shall be informed in writing of their rights (...) if they had not been so informed earlier. They shall be especially notified of their right to formulate allegations and solicit what they deem necessary if they appear according to law during this act and to solicit (...) the right to free legal assistance.

(3) At the aforementioned appearance the investigating magistrate shall first hear the public prosecutor and successively the other prosecuting parties, who will concretize their pleadings. He then will hear counsel for the accused, who will express what he deems necessary for the defense, and can move for a dismissal if there is a reason therefor (...). In their interventions the parties can solicit investigative acts they deem necessary.

§27(1) LOTJ (Spain)

(1) If the investigating magistrate agrees to a continuation of the proceedings, he shall decide the relevance of the acts solicited by the parties, ordering the conduct of, or himself conducting only those he considers indispensable for deciding the legitimacy of a committal order for trial (...).

Observe that the scope of the preliminary investigation is no longer that of determining the entire truth of the charge and all personal characteristics of the accused relevant to the assessment of punishment.[65] It is strictly limited to deciding whether to commit the accused for trial. As in the CCP (Italy) of

---

65. As is required in a preliminary investigation not subject to the jurisdiction of the jury court. *See* §299 LECr (Spain).

1988, evidence should be normally introduced for the first time at trial unless it is in danger of disappearing and must be anticipated to preserve the confrontation rights of the defendant. This modern version of the preliminary investigation appears like an adversarial mini-trial much broader in scope than the adversary preliminary hearing in American jurisdictions and a far cry from the eminently inquisitorial procedure before the American grand jury.

Questions

1. Which method of investigating a criminal case and preparing it for trial is preferable if the goal is the ascertainment of the truth? Which is most fair to the accused?

2. Can we rely on investigating magistrates or public prosecutors to fairly investigate exculpatory evidence?

3. Does defense investigation in American cases constitute an appropriate substitute for the supposedly independent investigative official in Europe?

4. Do you believe that opening the preliminary investigation to defense (and aggrieved party) participation compromises the ability of the prosecution to gather evidence and prepare the case for trial?

5. Do you believe that the openness of the preliminary investigation and the defense's full knowledge of the evidence against him will prejudice the ascertainment of the truth at the trial?

Relevant U.S. Case Law

United States v. Wade, 388 U.S. 218 (1967)

Kirby v. Illinois, 406 U.S. 682 (1972)

United States v. Williams, 504 U.S. 36 (1992)

IV. Avoiding the Preliminary Investigation

§ 449 (1–5) CPP (Italy)[66]

(1) When a person is arrested *in flagrante* for a crime, the public prosecutor, if he deems he must prosecute, may present the accused directly while under arrest before the trial judge to validate the arrest and for arraignment within 48 hours of the arrest (…).

(2) If the arrest is not validated, the judge remands the file to the public prosecutor. The judge proceeds nevertheless to the expedited trial if the accused and the public prosecutor consent.

(3) If the arrest is validated, one proceeds immediately to trial.

(4) The public prosecutor may, in other cases, proceed to the expedited trial if the arrest *in flagrante* has already been validated. In such case the accused is brought to the hearing within 15 days of arrest.

(5) The public prosecutor may, in addition, proceed to the expedited trial in relation to persons who during the course of the interrogation (…) have given confessions. The accused who is not in custody is summoned to appear at a hearing no later than 15 days from the inscription of the crime into the register. The accused in pretrial detention for the crime which is the subject of the procedure is brought to the hearing within the same time.

As can be seen from the above provisions, when a person has been arrested *in flagrante*, and this fact has been verified by a judge, the preliminary investigation is eliminated and the trial date is set within a few days. Recall how arrest *in flagrante* in ancient procedures could mean immediate execution or torture without further ado. In modern times the presumption of innocence still reigns and requires a trial before the imposition of punishment, but the presumed simplicity of flagrant cases has led in many countries to simplified, expedited procedures. In Italy the preliminary investigation may also be leapfrogged and the case immediately set for trial if the evidence in non-flagrant cases otherwise appears to be clear.[67]

---

66. Cf. § 395 CPP (France); § 795 LECr (Spain).

67. *See* § 453(1) CPP (Italy) (Appendix, 256) for the regulation of the "immediate trial." The new Spanish procedure for "speedy trials" applies to flagrant crimes, some other simple offenses such as the infliction of injuries, drunk driving, robbery, some drug crimes, but also to crimes the investigation of which appears "simple." § 795(1–2) LECr (Spain). The German "expedited trial," §§ 417–420 StPO (Germany), is limited to cases punishable by no more than one year, but has traditionally

Questions

1. Is it fair to bring someone to trial in a very short time just because they were arrested in the act?

2. If no death penalty existed and penalties for crimes were reasonable, would there be any reason why a flagrantly arrested person would not want an expedited trial?

3. Can we be sure that the person arrested *in flagrante* is always guilty?

4. How could a flagrantly arrested person benefit by spending more time in pretrial detention?

---

been mainly used in cases involving foreigners. Barbara Huber, *Criminal Procedure in Germany*, in HATCHARD, *supra* note 48, at 157.

Chapter Three

Search and Seizure: Search for Truth and Protection of Privacy

I. Police Powers of Investigation, Search and Seizure during the Police Inquest

A. Temporary Investigative Detentions

Decision of July 12, 1995 (Spanish Supreme Court)[68]

It is the settled doctrine of this Chamber in its consistent case law (...), that the right to liberty and, on the contrary, not to be deprived of it except in those cases and in the manner established by law, are not affected by police acts of stop-and-frisk and identification. Even though these inevitably constitute a nuisance, their realization and the resulting immobilization of the citizen during the time indispensable for conducting them, constitute for the affected person a legitimate submission, from the constitutional perspective, to the police measures.

In the present case, the detention of the accused was not the result of an arbitrary police action, but justified by rational grounds to believe in the existence of an act with criminal characteristics and the participation therein of the detained person, such as the circumstances of the existence of a confidential tip indicating that the accused could be dedicating himself to the small-scale trafficking of narcotic substances, that he frequented areas where this traffic was habitually conducted, that the subjects were persons related to the world of narcotics, along with the suspicious activity of the accused, who, when the agents approached him to identify him, put something in his

---

68. RJ 1995, No. 5775, 7737.

mouth which made them suspect that it was a narcotic substance
(...).

These are sufficient reasons for the inadmissibility of the alleged
ground of a violation of Art. 17.1 Const. (...).[69]

What are the police usually trying to accomplish when conducting what
Americans call a "temporary detention" or a "stop-and-frisk?" In the context
of a narcotics investigation they are usually trying to determine if a secret
victimless crime is being committed. If a frisk turns up drugs, then the rules
relating to flagrant crimes are applicable and the police may arrest. European
law often requires citizens to identify themselves and even permit detentions
for several hours to identify suspects.[70]

§§ 1.4, 2.2, 2.3 PACE, Code of Practice A (England)

1.4 The primary purpose of stop and search powers is to enable officers to allay or confirm suspicions about individuals without exercising their power of arrest. (...)

2.2 Reasonable grounds for suspicion depend on the circumstances in
each case. There must be an objective basis for that suspicion based
on facts, information, and/or intelligence which are relevant to the
likelihood of finding an article of a certain kind (...). Reasonable
suspicion can never be supported on the basis of personal factors
alone without reliable supporting intelligence or information or some
specific behaviour by the person concerned. For example, a person's
race, age, appearance, or the fact that the person is known to have a
previous conviction, cannot be used alone or in combination with
each other as the reason for searching that person. Reasonable suspicion cannot be based on generalisations or stereotypical images of certain groups or categories of people as more likely to be involved in
criminal activity. A person's religion cannot be considered as reasonable grounds for suspicion and should never be considered as a reason
to stop or stop and search an individual.

---

69. Art. 17.1 Const. (Spain) guarantees the right to personal liberty and security.
70. See § 78-1 (para. 2), 78-2 (para. 1), 78-3 (paras. 1,3) CPP (France) (Appendix, 246–47). Pursuant to § 163b StPO (Germany), police may detain suspects and
non-suspects for identification as long the detention is "proportional to the seriousness of the case" and not "against the will of the person concerned." The law allows
up to twelve hours for this purpose. § 163b StPO (Germany). In the U.S. a suspect
who fails to identify herself may be arrested and criminally prosecuted. Hiibel v.
Sixth Judicial District, Court of Nevada, 542 U.S. 177 (2004).

2.3 Reasonable suspicion can sometimes exist without specific information or intelligence and on the basis of some level of generalisation stemming from the behaviour of a person. For example, if an officer encounters someone on the street at night who is obviously trying to hide something, the officer may (depending on the other surrounding circumstances) base such suspicion on the fact that this kind of behaviour is often linked to stolen or prohibited articles being carried. (...)

Note how English law attempts to categorize the situations which give rise to suspicion of criminal activity, such as to justify a stop and search. We saw earlier how a similar list of suspicious facts were used to justify torture in the *Carolina*.[71]

Questions

1. Do the Spanish and British approaches give more or less protection to citizens in their confrontations with police than an American citizen would enjoy where probable cause to arrest is not yet articulable?

2. Which standard gives the citizen more protection from arbitrary police action?

3. Which standard is best suited to deal with street crime such as drug trafficking?

4. Could one fashion codified rules for temporary detentions based on the case law of the U.S. Supreme Court that would look similar to the English rules?

5. Is there any articulable difference between the English "reasonable suspicion" to search and American "probable cause" when applied to the search of persons for fruits, evidence or instrumentalities of crime?

Relevant U.S. Case Law

Terry v. Ohio, 392 U.S. 1 (1968)

United States v. Sokolow, 490 U.S. 1 (1989)

Alabama v. White, 496 U.S. 325 (1990)

Minnesota v. Dickerson, 508 U.S. 366 (1993)

---

71. *See* §§ 23, 25–27 *Carolina, supra* at 10.

Illinois v. Wardlow, 528 U.S. 119 (2000)

Florida v. J.L., 529 U.S. 266 (2000).

United States v. Arvizu, 534 U.S. 266 (2002).

Hiibel vs. Sixth Judicial District Court of Nevada, 542 U.S. 177 (2004).

B. Police Power to Arrest in Flagrant Cases

§ 380(1) CPP (Italy)

The officials and agents of the judicial police shall arrest anyone caught *in flagrante* after a non-negligent completed or attempted crime, for which the law sets a punishment of life imprisonment or imprisonment for no less than a minimum of five years and a maximum of 20 years.

§ 381 (1,4) CPP (Italy)

(1) The officials and agents of the judicial police may arrest anyone caught *in flagrante* after a non-negligent completed or attempted crime for which the law sets a punishment of imprisonment for a maximum of three years or for a negligent crime for which the law sets a punishment of imprisonment for a maximum of five years.

(4) Pursuant to the circumstances provided in this article, an arrest *in flagrante* should only be made if the measure is justified by the gravity of the act or the dangerousness of the subject deduced from his personality or the circumstances of the act.[72]

Custodial arrest for flagrant crimes in Italy or England is only possible for serious felonies and is subject to a requirement of proportionality. The principle of proportionality is of crucial importance in European law in relation to decisions involving law enforcement infringement of the privacy or liberty interests of citizens. Thus, the same type of "exigent circumstances" which warrant a judicial order of pretrial detention must be present to arrest in

---

72. Cf. § 492 LECr (Spain), which permits the police to arrest for serious felonies committed *in flagrante*, if a correctional prison sentence could be imposed, or if the person has a record of not appearing in court and the person cannot post adequate bail. In Germany, arrests *in flagrante* may be made if a person is in danger of fleeing, her identity cannot be readily determined, or if the prerequisites for an order of pretrial detention exist in relation to the person. § 127(1,2) StPO (Germany) (Appendix, 249).

cases involving less-serious crimes. American police, on the other hand, may arrest anyone suspected of committing a felony, whether or not it was committed *in flagrante*, if the arrest is made in public,[73] and may in some states arrest for any flagrant misdemeanor even if it is only punishable by a minor fine and the police only make the arrest as a pretext to investigate someone for a more serious crime, for which adequate suspicion is lacking.[74]

Questions

1. Why do all countries allow for arrests of persons caught in the act of committing a serious crime, or shortly thereafter?

2. Should the invasion of liberty we call an arrest be limited to serious crimes?

3. Should arrests for non-serious crimes be allowed solely as a pretext for conducting investigations or searches which otherwise lack probable cause or reasonable suspicion?

Relevant U.S. Case Law

Warden v. Hayden, 387 U.S. 294 (1967)

United States v. Watson, 423 U.S. 411 (1976)

Whren v. United States, 517 U.S. 806 (1996)

Atwater v. City of Lago Vista, 532 U.S. 318 (2001)

C. Definition of a Flagrant Crime

Decision of March 29, 1990 (Spanish Supreme Court)[75]

The facts occurred, in short, in the following manner: on June 15, 1983, some police officials who had been conducting surveillance of him, detained Julián R.S. when he exited apartment 3B at No. 22 Cruz Verde Street in Madrid, which he occupied as a tenant, and during the frisk he was subjected to, a bindle of heroin was found which

---

73. United States v. Watson, 423 U.S. 411 (1976).

74. Atwater v. City of Lago Vista, 532 U.S. 318 (2001); Whren v. United States, 517 U.S. 806 (1996).

75. RJ 1990, No. 2647, 3534, 3535–37.

weighed one gram. Immediately after this detention and without a judicial warrant or the consent of the owner of the aforementioned apartment, and in the company of the concierge of the building, the four police officers who had intervened in the act, entered it, made a search and found, among other objects, 170 grams of heroin which was hidden in six envelopes in a maroon purse which was hidden in a suitcase (...).

Art. 18.2 Const.[76] appears, as formulated, to allow entry into the dwelling of another without the consent of the owner and without a judicial warrant, authorizing such entry, only in cases of flagrant crime, a situation which constitutes an exception to the content of a fundamental right. Thus the application of this exception and the very concept of flagrant crime have to be given a restrictive interpretation in the interest of giving the maximum possible respect to a fundamental right.

[There follows a discussion of the definition of "flagrant crime" contained in the now repealed §779 LECr, which defined cases subject to a now repealed abbreviated procedure.]

(...) [I]t may be said that the concept of a flagrant crime, in the context of Art. 18.2 Const. (Spain) and the correlative §553 LECr, remains delimited by the following three requirements:

1. Temporal immediacy, that is, that one is committing the crime or had been committing it moments before:

2. Personal immediacy, consisting in the fact that the offender is found at this moment in a situation in relation to the object or the instruments of the crime such as to offer evidence of his participation in the act;

3. Urgent necessity, of the sort that the police, due to the circumstances present in the concrete case, consider themselves impelled to immediately intervene with the double goal of putting an end to the existing situation, impeding in all possible ways the propagation of the evil which the penal violation gave rise to, and to achieve the arrest of the perpetrator of the acts, a necessity which will not exist when the nature of the facts allows one to appear before a judicial authority to obtain an appropriate warrant.

In the present case, of the three requirements indicated, only the first was present. The other two are thus missing in relation to the facts that were the object of the charges and which served as the foundation for the conviction being appealed.

---

76. *See* Art. 18(2) Const. (Spain) (Appendix, 264).

The first existed because, as the public prosecutor said, we are here confronted with a permanent crime.

The second is missing because the convicted person now appealing was not in the apartment searched where the 170 grams of heroin were found.

The third is also missing, because there were no reasons of special urgency which would not have permitted the police to appear before a judicial authority to obtain an appropriate warrant, while simply leaving surveillance at the scene of the crime to prevent, in the meantime, the frustration of the police operation.

Most European jurisdictions define when a crime is committed *in flagrante*[77] for it is the manner in which a concrete crime is committed or detected which conditions the powers the police have in pursuing investigative measures *sua sponte*, or when they require judicial authorization.

D. Police Powers to Search in Situations of Flagrancy and Incident to Arrest

§ 352(1) CPP (Italy)

In the case of a flagrant offense or flight, officials of the judicial police shall conduct searches of the person or places when they have reasonable cause to believe that things or indicia relevant to the offense are being hidden on the person which could be destroyed or removed or that such things or indicia can be found in a particular place or that the suspect can be found there.

English law allows police, incident to a lawful arrest of a person, "to enter and search any premises in which he was when arrested or immediately before he was arrested for evidence relating to the offence for which he has been arrested."[78] These searches without judicial authorization, whether conducted *in flagrante* or incident to arrest, still require "reasonable cause" and must be related to actual exigent circumstances articulated in the case. While the original American doctrine of search incident to arrest was based on a similar rationale,[79] the United States Supreme Court now allows searches in-

---

77. Cf. § 53 CCP (France) (Appendix, 246)

78. § 32(2)(b) PACE (England) (See Appendix, 235–36), for the complete section on searches incident to arrest.)

79. Chimel v. California, 395 U.S. 752 (1969).

cident to arrest even when there are no exigent circumstances and no evidence related to the offense which can be destroyed.[80] On the other hand, English law permits a full search of a dwelling incident to arrest, rather than the more limited "wingspan" search permitted by American case law.

If the police in making a flagrant or non-flagrant arrest have probable cause to believe that an automobile contains evidence of a crime, European law usually does not require the police to secure a search warrant.

Decision No. 303 of October 25, 1993 (Spanish Constitutional Court)[81]

[W]ith respect to the act which produced the discovery of ten balls of hashish in the interior of the searched vehicle "two days before" by officers of the Corps of the Guardia Civil, we are obliged to affirm that, in contrast to the first search effectuated with negative results that day, here there is no note of urgency which affects the character of this investigative act of seizing the integral fruits and tools of the *corpus delicti*. The delay, on the other hand, in the realization of this investigative act could permit the occupants of the vehicle (at the time detained at the police station) to be present, duly assisted by their lawyers (...). Thus, once the expressed reasons of urgency are gone, the lack of judicial intervention and the absence of confrontation in the execution of the search of the vehicle of the accuseds, deprived it of evidentiary value (...).

Note that the "automobile exception" to the requirement of judicial authorization in Spain applies only upon a showing of exigent circumstances and cannot justify a later search at the police station at a time when the suspect's rights to counsel and to confrontation could be guaranteed.[82] In the United States, the police may search an automobile with probable cause that it contains evidence of crime without requiring flagrancy or "exigent circum-

---

80. United States v. Robinson, 414 U.S. 218 (1973); Gustafson v. Florida, 414 U.S. 260 (1973); New York v. Belton, 453 U.S. 454 (1981).

81. STC 303/1993, 151 BJC 108, cited in Eduardo de Urbano Castrillo & Miguel Ángel Torres Morato, La prueba illícita penal. Estudio jurisprudencial 195–96 (1997).

82. In France, old case law has been repealed which had allowed automobile searches without probable cause and there is also now a requirement of exigent circumstances. In addition, the police may not search vehicles when investigating vehicle code violations. Pradel, *supra* note 31, at 333–34.

stances" and need not give the defense an opportunity to be present.[83] Unlike dwellings which have constitutional protection, an automobile in Spanish jurisprudence is "a simple object of investigation, as to which there is no reason to apply the protective guarantees which must be considered when there is a question of defending personal and familial intimacy."[84]

Questions

1. Why should the police be able to search a person in the act of, or immediately after committing a crime?

2. Why should police be able to search a house or an automobile without judicial authorization when a person is arrested therein?

3. If an automobile has been secured so as to prevent entry of persons to remove evidence, why should the police be able to search it without judicial authorization?

4. Should a search for evidence or weapons be allowed incident to arrest for an offense if the arresting officer is not in fear for his safety and there is no reasonable suspicion that evidence related to the offense will be found?

Relevant U.S. Case Law

Carroll v. United States, 267 U.S. 132 (1925)

Chimel v. California, 395 U.S. 752 (1969)

Vale v. Louisiana, 399 U.S. 30 (1970)

United States v. Robinson, 414 U.S. 218 (1973)

Chambers v. Maroney, 399 U.S. 42 (1975)

New York v. Belton, 453 U.S. 454 (1981)

California v. Carney, 471 U.S. 386 (1985)

---

83. Chambers v. Maroney, 399 U.S. 42 (1975); California v. Carney, 471 U.S. 386 (1985).

84. Decision of April 21, 1995 (Spanish Supreme Court), RJ 1995, No. 2871, 3828, 3829. Pursuant to § 1 (2–5) PACE (England), police may search vehicles upon "reasonable grounds" without securing a warrant unless the automobile is located "in a garden or yard or other place occupied with and used for the purposes of a dwelling or on other land so occupied and used" and the automobile belongs to someone residing at those premises.

Knowles v. Iowa, 525 U.S. 113 (1998)

Thornton v. United States, 541 U.S. 615 (2004)

E. Consent Searches

§ 5 PACE Code of Practice B (England)

5.1 Subject to paragraph 5.4 below, if it is proposed to search premises with the consent of a person entitled to grant entry to the premises the consent must, if practicable, be given in writing on the Notice of Powers and Rights before the search. The officer must make enquiries to be satisfied the person is in a position to give such consent. (...)

5.2 Before seeking consent the officer in charge of the search shall state the purpose of the proposed search and its extent. This information must be as specific as possible, particularly regarding the articles or persons being sought and the parts of the premises to be searched. The person concerned must be clearly informed they are not obliged to consent and anything seized may be produced in evidence. If at the time the person is not suspected of an offence, the officer shall say this when stating the purpose of the search.

5.3 An officer cannot enter and search or continue to search premises under paragraph 5.1 if consent is given under duress or withdrawn before the search is completed.

5.4 It is unnecessary to seek consent under paragraphs 5.1 and 5.2 if this would cause disproportionate inconvenience to the person concerned.

Note how the English police advise suspects or concerned parties of the right to refuse to consent to a search and that express waiver forms to that affect are used.[85] Consider the following Spanish case:

---

85. For a similar provision, *see* § 76 CPP (France). French police use a form that reads: "Knowing that I can oppose the visit to my home, I consent expressly that you conduct searches and seizures which you judge to be useful in their course." In France, most people do consent despite the admonitions. PRADEL, *supra* note 31, at 411. The U.S. Fourth Amendment, however, does not require police to admonish suspects of the right to refuse consent to search. Scheckloth v. Bustamonte, 412 U.S. 218 (1973).

Decision of July 8, 1994 (Spanish Supreme Court)[86]

[162 capsules of ecstasy were found in a car. After his arrest, defendant David de O. consented to the search of his house in which another 32 capsules were found.]

These questions relative to the search [dealing with absence of the court clerk] of the appellant's dwelling definitely lack importance because there is a defect of constitutional relevance which results in the radical nullity of said search.

As is related in the statement of proved facts, the obligatory assistance of counsel for the arrestee was lacking.

In effect, when the police arrested David de O. they transported him to the corresponding police station and there obtained in writing his consent for the search of the dwelling where he lived without previously having informed him of his right to be assisted by counsel, an assistance which was especially important to him as an arrestee, in view of the importance said search could have for his later defense.

If the assistance of counsel is necessary for the arrestee before he makes a statement (§ 520.2 LECr), it appears logical that it should be even more necessary upon arrest to be advised before giving one's consent to a police search of one's dwelling. It seems inadmissible that the police must wait for the appointment of counsel before the act of taking a statement yet can obtain the aforementioned consent before counsel could have intervened.[87]

Questions

1. Do you think informing suspects of their right to refuse to consent to a police search will hamper law enforcement?

2. Should people be presumed to know their constitutional rights?

3. Should law enforcement rely on the people's ignorance of their rights in the investigation of criminal cases?

---

86. RJ 1994, No. 6261, at 7983, 7983–84.

87. In the United States the prevailing view is that a person in custody need not be advised of her right to remain silent or right to counsel before being asked to consent to a search. If the person has been charged, however, it is likely that presence of counsel would be required. WAYNE R. LA FAVE ET AL, CRIMINAL PROCEDURE 253 (4th ed. 2004).

4. Should police rely on consent searches rather than searches based on probable cause and judicial authorization?

5. Should jailed suspects have the right to consult with counsel before making any decisions which could undermine their defense?

Relevant U.S. Case Law

Schneckloth v. Bustamonte, 412 U.S. 218 (1973)

Gentile v. United States, 419 U.S. 979 (1974)

II. The Requirement of Judicial Authorization for Invasions of Privacy

A. The Special Protection of Dwellings

1. The Requirement of a Warrant

Art. 13(1,2) Const. (Germany)

(1) The dwelling is inviolable.

(2) Searches may only be ordered by a judge or under exigent circumstances by other organs authorized by law and may only be executed in the legally prescribed manner.[88]

§ 98 StPO (Germany)

1. Seizures may only be ordered by the judge, or in exigent circumstances, by the public prosecutor or her auxiliary officials (...)

2. The official who seizes an object without a judicial warrant, shall request judicial confirmation within three days, if neither the person affected nor an adult relative was present or if the person affected, or in his absence, an adult relative, expressly objected to the seizure. The person affected can at any time request a judicial decision (...)

Art. 13(1,2) Const. (Germany) and several other European constitutions have a separate section dealing with the protection of dwellings, unlike the

---

88. Cf. Art. 14 Const. (Italy); Art. 18(2) Const. (Spain) (Appendix, 264). The German term for what Americans call "exigent circumstances" is *Gefahr im Verzug*, which means "danger in delay."

U.S. Fourth Amendment which lumps together the protection of "houses, persons, papers and effects." It is also typical that judicial authorization for a search or seizure is not required when exigent circumstances exist, but most European law requires the officials who conduct the search or seizure to get confirmation from a judge within a few days.[89]

2. The Requirement of Probable Cause
Decision of June 28, 1994 (Spanish Supreme Court)[90]

In the instant case, the police, when requesting the judicial warrant, told the investigating magistrate that they had become aware of the presence in Córdoba in the company of two other individuals of the accused, María Rosa M.C., whom they associated with the traffic of drugs and who had reserved a room in the Hotel "El Cisne," suspecting, that the reason for the journey could be the introduction of a certain quantity of drugs. (...) Similarly, in the first section of the police report, a report indicated that "by means of established controls in hotel establishments for the prevention of terrorist acts and drug trafficking, the presence of María Rosa M.C., a resident of Erandio (Vizcaya), was detected, who had rented two rooms, paying in advance and who had remained in them for some two hours and then left without baggage to continue her travels." The report added that "due to this strange conduct, an investigation has been initiated because of her known record in relation to drug trafficking, but excluding any relationship to terrorism."

Such are the facts despite, from a formal point of view, the paucity of a factual record included in the controverted judicial warrant which authorized the entry and search of the hotel room occupied by the appellant—which without doubt could have been more explicit—it is beyond doubt that an examination of the record in the police application reflected in the warrant makes it clear that in the instant

---

89. See also § 105(1) StPO (Germany) (Appendix, 248), which allows prosecutors to order searches without judicial authorization when there is "danger in delay." Up until recently, the German authorities conducted around 90% of house searches without judicial authorization, with their claims of "danger in delay" routinely accepted by the courts. Thomas Weigend, *Germany*, in CRIMINAL PROCEDURE. A WORLDWIDE STUDY (Craig M. Bradley ed. 1999). The German Constitutional Court, however, recently ruled that such a situation was intolerable in a state under the rule of law, that duty judges had to be available during all hours of the night to issue warrants, and that the courts would review claims of exigent circumstances with higher scrutiny. BVerfGE 103, 142 (2001).

90. RJ 1994, No. 5157, at 6797, 6797–98.

case one cannot speak of mere suspicions lacking an objective foundation and that, taking into account the peculiarities of drug trafficking and its grave social importance, the questioned judicial authorization should be deemed sufficiently justified and proportionate to the gravity of the act under investigation, and, as a result, it is correct to conclude that the appellate issue examined lacks foundation and must be rejected.

Notice the similarity with U.S. "probable cause" analysis, though that phrase is not explicitly used. A mere suspicion is insufficient to justify search of a dwelling. It also appears as if a deficiency in the police application for a warrant, called the "affidavit" in the U.S., can be corrected by facts in the police file. Many U.S. jurisdictions do not allow looking beyond the affidavit or the warrant to rectify deficiencies in probable cause.[91]

Both in England and Italy, police may search dwellings with judicial authorization upon a showing of "reasonable grounds" that evidence of crime or criminal suspects may be found in a given location.[92] In Italy, the judge issuing a search warrant must include written reasons in the warrant supporting its issuance.[93] Many European countries require that reasons be given for important judicial decisions in order to prevent arbitrary application of the law.[94] The giving of reasons in the context of search warrants makes it easier for appellate courts to evaluate the strength of the suspicion which gave rise to the invasion of important constitutional rights. Spain, on the other hand, requires only that "there are indicia that the defendant or fruits or instruments of the crime, or books, papers and other objects which could serve for the discovery or proof of the crime may be found there."[95] German statutes require only a mere suspicion.[96]

---

91. One may not augment a deficient police affidavit in support of a search warrant by referring to information possessed by the police which was not conveyed to the magistrate who issued the warrant. Whiteley v. Warden, 401 U.S. 560 (1971). In addition, where the search warrant itself is defective by not properly describing the things to be seized, one may not cure such a defect by referring to the police affidavit. Groh v. Ramirez, 540 U.S. 551 (2004).

92. §8 PACE (England) (Appendix, 233–34); §247 CPP (Italy) (Appendix, 253).

93. §247(2) CPP (Italy) (Appendix, 253); Cf. §558 LECr (Spain) (Appendix, 260).

94. The requirement of reasons has achieved constitutional status, at least in relation to judgments of conviction, in some European countries. Cf. Art. 111 Const. (Italy) and Art. 120(3) Const. (Spain).

95. §546 LECr (Spain).

96. §102 StPO (Germany) (Appendix, 248). A warrant for a seizure requires only that the object "be of significance to the preliminary investigation." §94 (1,2) StPO

Questions

1. Does the American standard of "probable cause" give more protection to dwellings than the standards used in Spain or other European countries?

2. What protects the privacy of the home to a greater extent, the amount of suspicion required to search or the procedure of having a judge review the evidence of such suspicion before the search is undertaken?

3. Do you think more searches for criminal evidence are carried out with judicial authorization or under claims of exigent circumstances or consent? Why do you think people consent to police searches which uncover evidence of serious crime?

Relevant U.S. Case Law

Whiteley v. Warden, 401 U.S. 560 (1971)

Illinois v. Gates, 462 U.S. 213 (1983)

Groh v. Ramirez, 540 U.S. 551 (2004)

3. Procedural Safeguards Required during the Search
Decision of October 30, 1992 (Spanish Supreme Court)[97]

[The defendant was arrested, police got a warrant and searched certain houses in her absence without notifying her of the right to be present with counsel.]

Without doubt the acts which occupy us were not clothed with the necessary and required guarantees as the public prosecutor proclaims in his appeal. The absence of the interested party due to being detained at the police station, implies an unacceptable violation of the guarantee which her presence constitutes in such cases, which is of such pronounced significance, obligatorily required by § 569 LECr, which only allows conduct of a search without the effective presence of the interested party when he "cannot be found" or "wants to neither be present nor name a representative,"[98] none of which require-

---

(Germany) (Appendix, 247). On the almost non-existent requirement of probable cause in Germany, see Weigend, *supra* note 89, at 193.

97. RJ 1992, No. 8553, 11247.

98. See § 569 (1–4) LECr (Spain) (Appendix, 260). Cf. § 106(1) StPO (Germany) (Appendix, 249). In Italy the defendant also has a right to have defense counsel present during the search. § 365(1) CPP (Italy) (Appendix, 254).

ments are present which would permit a substitution for the procedure provided in the law. Apart from the mentioned requirements it is impermissible to conduct an entry and search without the affected person being present in the dwelling or closed area being inspected. An exception, of course, is provided by the consent of the interested party (...). It should also be emphasized that the situation of detention in which the accused found herself should have required that she be informed of the possibility of being assisted by counsel during the execution of the search (...).

The following case indicates one reason why the suspect or owner of the house has a right to be present, sometimes along with counsel, or to designate a friend or relative in his stead:

Decision of November 14, 1992
(Spanish Supreme Court)[99]

The absence of the interested party during the aforementioned act [i.e., the search], as well as, in this case, of his defense counsel due to lack of notification and summons, deprives—due to the inability of repeating it subsequently—of the character of preconstituted evidence, because the interested party was unable to exercise therein his right of "confrontation" (...) and results in a violation of the right to due process[100] (...).

Spanish law also requires the presence of the clerk of the investigating magistrate during judicially authorized searches.[101] Note how the right of the defendant to be present during investigative acts is closely linked with the right of privacy. The police may not go off on their own and search private spaces without the interested party and/or neutral civilian witnesses present to verify if and where the alleged evidence, contraband or instrumentalities were found.[102]

---

99. RJ 1992, No. 9661, 12662, at 12664.

100. The American phrase "due process" is used for the Spanish *indefensión* which literally means "defenselessness."

101. §569(4) LECr (Spain) (Appendix, 260). German law requires the public prosecutor or the judge of the investigation to be present and, where this is not possible, a "community official or two members of the community in whose district the search takes place." §105(2) StPO (Germany) (Appendix, 248). These witnesses of the search may not be police employees.

102. In the U.S. there is no requirement that the suspect be present when a search warrant is served. Indeed, federal law explicitly allows covert-entry search warrants in which notification of the interested party may be delayed indefinitely. §13 U.S. PATRIOT Act, 18 U.S.C. §3103(a) (2001).

Questions

1. Would it be a good idea for civilian witnesses or impartial judicial officials to be present during searches of dwellings or other private buildings in the U.S.?

2. Should the defendant be present during such searches, where it is practicable?

3. Why do you think European law requires the presence of a judicially trained official or civilian witnesses during the execution of such searches?

4. Can we trust the police to honestly testify to how a search was conducted, what was found and where if no neutral persons are present to observe the investigative act?

Selected Readings

RICHARD STONE, THE LAW OF ENTRY, SEARCH AND SEIZURE (4th ed. 2005).

MICHAEL ZANDER, THE POLICE AND CRIMINAL EVIDENCE ACT, 1984 (5th ed. 2005).

B. The Protection of Confidential Communications

1. Intercepting Private Conversations

Decision No. 49 of March 26, 1996
(Spanish Constitutional Court)[103]

Art. 18(3) Const. establishes: "Secrecy of communications, especially postal, telegraphic and telephonic, is guaranteed, unless there is a judicial decision." For its part, Art. 8 of the ECHR of November 4, 1950, provides a detailed regulation of the rights to private and family life, home and correspondence destined to safeguard and eliminate any interference in the ambit of these fundamental rights:

"1. Every person has the right to respect for his private and family life, his home and his correspondence.

2. There shall be no interference by a public authority with the exercise of this right except such as is in accordance with the law and is necessary in a democratic society in the interests of national security, public safety or the economic well-being of the country, for the pre-

---

103. 180 BJC 133, 138–39.

vention of disorder or crime, for the protection of health or morals, or the protection of the rights and freedoms of others."

The Eur. Ct. HR has had occasion to apply the aforementioned rule in numerous judgments. Among the most significant, the judgment of September 6, 1978 (*Klass* Case), in which it held that "telephonic communications are included within the notions of private life and correspondence;" the judgment of August 2, 1984 (*Malone* Case) also declared that "the interception of a telephonic conversation in the case referred to implied an interference by a public authority in the exercise of a right which Art. 8 [ECHR] guaranteed to the petitioner; the judgments of April 24, 1980 (*Huvig* and *Kruslin* Cases) dealt with the theme of wiretaps carried out by order of an investigating magistrate, declaring that "the wiretaps and other procedures for intercepting telephonic conversations are a grave attack on privacy and correspondence," which should be based on a "law of singular precision. It is indispensable that the norms which regulate it be clear and detailed;" the aforementioned judgment of August 2, 1984, requires, for an interference to be considered legitimate, that, beyond being provided by law, "it pursue one or more legitimate objectives in light of paragraph 2 of Art. 8 [ECHR] and, moreover, that it be "necessary in a democratic society" to achieve them.

In harmony with this doctrine of the Eur. Ct. HR and in line with our own case law, we recently affirmed (...) that "the right to secrecy of communications can only be limited by a decision which is based on sufficient reasons. The existence of a judicial warrant authorizing the intervention, along with strict observance of the principle of proportionality in the execution of the investigative act constitute non-excusable constitutional requirements which affect the essential nucleus of the right to secrecy of communications to such an extent that the absence of judicial authorization or the lack of reasons determine inevitably the violation of the constitutional right and, as well, the prohibition of the use of any evidence which could be deduced from the content of the intercepted conversations, not only of the results of the intervention itself, but also of any other evidence derived from the telephonic surveillance, given always that there exists a causal connection between both evidentiary results." (...)

To summarize:

(A) Strict observance, thus, of proportionality. The principle of proportionality "refers not only to the gravity of the punishable offense to justify the type of measure, but also to the required guarantee of a specific and reasoned judicial authorization, comparing its execution with other types of control of communication." (...)

(B) The reasons are necessary because only through them can the right to due process be preserved and the necessary decision on proportionality be made, between the sacrifice of the fundamental right and the reasons which require it. (...)

(C) The legitimacy of the measure of telephonic intervention is determined, finally, by the consideration by the authorizing judge of its necessity for the investigation of determinate facts within a specific penal classification; the decision should expressly mention the factual and legal reasons which support the necessity of the intervention, that is, should elucidate the evidence which exists in relation to the presumed commission of a grave criminal act by a specific person and, in relation to this evidence, to classify it under one of the criminal categories which justify the application of the measure. It is indispensable that the judicial decision specify the object of the intervention: the telephone number or numbers and persons whose conversations are to be intercepted, who, in principle, should be the persons implicated by the aforementioned evidence, the time and duration of the intervention, who must carry it out and how, and the period after which one must report to the magistrate to control its execution.

Effective judicial control in the development and termination of the measure is indispensable for keeping the intervention in the fundamental right within constitutional limits. The magistrate who authorizes it should, in the first place, be notified of the results obtained by the intervention and, in cases where there is a divergence between the crime which is purportedly the object of the investigation and that which is in fact being investigated, should adopt the decision which is appropriate, given that otherwise (...) the intervention constitutes an interference by public authority in the affected person's right to respect for his correspondence and privacy (...).[104]

As can be seen, the Eur. Ct. HR has played a pivotal role in this important area of law which has such grave impact on the right to privacy. The continental European countries we are highlighting have enacted fairly elaborate statutes which regulate wiretapping, bugging and the interception of electronic communications.

---

104. Despite the Spanish Constitutional Court's attempt to interpret the Spanish wiretapping law in a progressive, very protective manner, the Eur. Ct. HR found that the law violated Art. 8 ECHR because these protections had not themselves been enacted into the criminal procedure statute. Valenzuela Contreras v. Spain, 28 E.H.R.R. 43 (1998).

§ 266 CPP (Italy)

1. The interception of conversations or telephonic communications and of other forms of telecommunications is permissible relative to the following offenses:

(a) non-negligent crimes punishable by life imprisonment or imprisonment fir five years or more (...);

(b) crimes against public administration punishable by at least five years imprisonment (...);

(c) crimes relating to narcotic or psychotropic substances;

(d) weapons and explosives crimes;

(e) crimes involving smuggling;

(f) offenses of insults, threats, usury, abusive financial activity, molestation or harassment using the telephone;

(f-bis) crimes listed in § 600(3) of the Penal Code.

2. In the same types of cases it is permissible to intercept communications of people amongst themselves [i.e. not involving telecommunications] (...)

§ 267(1–3) CPP (Italy)

1. The public prosecutor shall request the judge of the investigation for authorization to put in motion the operations provided for in § 266. The authorization is given in a reasoned order when there are grave indicia of an offense and the interception is absolutely indispensable to the goals of carrying out the investigation.

1bis. (excluded).

2. In cases of urgency, when there is reasonable cause for believing that delay will cause grave prejudice to the investigation, the public prosecutor shall set in motion the interception with a reasoned order, which shall then immediately, and in any case no later than twenty-four hours, be brought to the attention of the judge indicated in paragraph 1. The judge, within forty-eight hours of the measure, decides whether to ratify it with a reasoned order. If the order of the public prosecutor is not ratified within the established period, the interception may not be continued and the results thereof may not be used.

3. The order of the public prosecutor which sets in motion the interception shall indicate the procedure for the operation and its duration. The duration may not exceed fifteen days, but may be extended

by the judge with a reasoned order for successive periods of fifteen days as long as the presuppositions noted in paragraph 1 persist.[105]

§ 268 (4,6) CPP (Italy)

4. The reports and recordings shall be immediately turned over to the public prosecutor. Within five days of the conclusion of the operations they shall be deposited with the clerk of the court along with the orders which set in motion, authorized, ratified or extended the interception and shall remain there for the time fixed by the public prosecutor unless the judge deems that an extension is necessary (...).

6. The defenders of the parties shall be immediately given notice that, within the period fixed by the provisions of paragraphs 4 and 5, they have the power to examine the documents and listen to the recordings or take note of the flow of electronic or telecommunications (...).

Note the heightened standard of probable cause, that of "grave indicia of an offense" and the "indispensability" of the measures, which are more rigorous than the requirements in other European countries.[106] Note that wiretaps in Italy are available only for the investigation of serious crimes, either those

---

105. Some recent decisions rendered by Italian judges of the investigation have held that §§ 266, 267 CPP (Italy) apply only to "intercepted" communications and not to the seizure of stored electronic communications. Order of December 16, 1998 (Judge of the Investigation of the Court of Rome), CASS. PENALE 1623 (1999); Order of January 5, 1999 (Judge of the Investigation of the Court of Rome), CASS. PENALE 1627 (1999). For a discussion of similar distinctions in U.S. law, see Steve Jackson Games, Inc. v. U.S. Secret Service, 36 F.3d 457 (5th Cir. 1994).

106. House searches in Italy require only "reasonable cause," § 247 CPP (Italy) (Appendix, 253). Wiretap warrants are allowed in France, "when the necessities of the investigation require it." § 100 (para. 1) CPP (France) and in Germany upon a mere "suspicion" of the commission of certain enumerated crimes. § 100a (para. 1) StPO (Germany) (Appendix, 247). Spanish law requires only that there be "evidence that the discovery of the proof of an important fact or circumstance in the case can be obtained by these means." § 579(1) LECr (Spain) (Appendix, 261). Although the U.S. Supreme Court in Berger v. New York, 388 U.S. 41 (1967), once indicated that the "probable cause" standard for wiretaps was higher than for normal searches, courts nevertheless tend to apply an identical standard. LA FAVE ET AL, supra note 87, at 268–69. The U.S. wiretap statute also has something akin to an "indispensability" requirement. 18 U.S.C. § 2518(1)(c).

intentional crimes punishable by more than five years imprisonment, or other dangerous crimes, whereas house searches are not thus restricted.[107]

The fifteen day limit, subject to extensions, provided by Italian law is shorter than the thirty day limit in U.S. law[108] and the longer periods allowed by other European laws.[109] Clearly the shorter period of intervention allowed by statute, the greater will be the judicial control of the investigative measure, as extensions must be approved by a new reasoned order.[110]

Although there can, of course, be no right to be present or represented by counsel when an order to intercept confidential communications is issued or renewed due to the secret nature of the investigative act, there is concern in Europe that there be effective judicial control of the results of the eavesdropping and, where possible, defense participation.

Decision of June 25, 1993 (Spanish Supreme Court)[111]

Criminal procedure is directed towards the verification of that which has happened in reality so that the value judgment delivered by the judicial organs is based on facts and circumstances, the exactitude and veracity of which can withstand confrontations with the exculpatory allegations of the person who has been charged.

However (...), the truth which one pretends to ascertain in criminal procedure can only be achieved within the requirements, suppositions and limitations established by the judicial order. Actual truth may not

---

107. In France, wiretapping is possible in relation to crimes punishable by two years or more of imprisonment. § 100 (para. 1) CPP (France). Germany's statute includes a catalogue of serious crimes with no reference to possible punishment. § 100a StPO (Germany) (Appendix, 247). While the Spanish statute does not include a catalogue of crimes which may be investigated through the secret interception of communications, the Spanish Supreme Court has ruled that it must be a grave crime or one that causes an important deterioration of social life (such as crimes committed by public officials. Decision of June 18, 1992 (Spanish Supreme Court), cited in DE URBANO & TORRES, *supra* note 81, at 231.

108. 18 U.S.C. § 2518(5).

109. Three months in § 579(3) LECr (Spain) (Appendix, 261) and § 100b(2) StPO (Germany) (Appendix, 247) and four months in § 100-2 CPP (France).

110. *See* Lambert v. France, 30 E.H.R.R. 346 (2000), in which the French wiretapping statute was held to violate Art. 8 ECHR because it did not require a new judicial authorization for extensions.

111. RJ 1993, No. 5244, 6702, 6703, 6707–08.

be obtained at any price. Not everything is lawful in the discovery of the truth.

[The Court elaborates on the standard of probable cause for a wiretapping warrant and the fact that it extends to this type of case.]

From the examination of the procedures in this case one comes to the conclusion that there was no judicial control of the form in which the telephonic interceptions authorized in the warrant of November 29, 1989, were carried out to the point that the magistrate who decided on the intervention never found out about the results thereof.

The technology of telephonic intervention and its continued monitoring make it difficult for the magistrate to constantly pay attention to the form in which they are carried out. The courts lack material capacity to install the eavesdropping devices and to realize an integral control of the conversations engaged in and thus they must entrust its implementation to the units of the judicial police as they are currently configured, without any dependence on the judicial organs.

But in no case can one entrust the technical manipulation and selection of the conversations to the police who materially realize the telephonic intervention. The system of eavesdropping and the technology employed must be known by the investigating magistrate who must warn those charged with the monitoring of the obligation to respect the integrity of the tape recordings with the goal that they may later be listened to and that their selection may take place at a hearing with all the interested parties. The recording must be permanent and include all of the conversations which developed using the intercepted telephone number, and once they have been produced some technical procedure must be employed which would make difficult or prevent their later manipulation (...).

The transcription of the content of the tapes was carried out in the presence of a judge and with the intervention of the parties affected. The magistrate should provide for transcription of that which he considers of interest for the processing of the case in a form analogous to that established in § 586 LECr for the opening of postal correspondence, and reject all that which lacks relevance for the goals of the investigation, taking special care to destroy all which makes reference to intimate conversations of no interest to the investigation. In the instant case it was the police—following instructions of the Chief Prosecutor of the Court of Appeal—who proceeded to select the passages and transcribe their content, destroying all they deemed irrelevant to the goals of the investigation

This procedural act, as has already been noted, is in every case within the competence of the judicial organ which carries out the investigation and which should be identical with that which authorizes the telephonic intervention, and should be carried out in a hearing in the presence of all the parties, including, of course, the person who was the object of the investigation, so that an adversarial debate may be established which gives the person affected the possibility of defending herself, all without any detriment that could negate the authenticity of the recordings. (...)

The system of values established by our Constitution situates in first place the liberty and security of citizens, building respect for their validity and full effectiveness into the basis and foundation of the political order and social peace. Privacy is a manifestation of the free development of the personality and constitutes a frontier delimiting the area inaccessible to interference by others, whether from the acts of private citizens or state authorities. The violation of this fundamental right converts the person into a fragile and transparent being in relation to the informational voracity of the public authorities. The constitutional text only permits interference in the privacy of communications when a judicial decision dictated during the course of a criminal investigation authorizes it respecting the prerequisites and legal guarantees established by procedural laws.

Note the limitations on the search for truth placed on criminal investigators and the special importance given to privacy for the free development of the personality.

Questions

1. What differences are there between the American wiretapping regulations and those in the Italian statute and the Spanish case law?

2. Why do the Spanish insist on an adversary proceeding to inspect and sift through recordings of wiretaps and other intercepted communications?

3. Should the courts trust the police or prosecutor with custody of evidence seized secretly from criminal suspects?

4. Should our right to privacy as citizens in a democracy be a limitation on the powers of the government to discover the truth in criminal proceedings?

5. Is privacy necessary for the "free development of the personality?" Is the free development of the personality guaranteed or protected anywhere in the U.S. Constitution?

Relevant U.S. Case Law

Olmstead v. United States, 277 U.S. 438 (1928)

Berger v. United States, 388 U.S. 41 (1967)

Katz v. United States, 389 U.S. 347 (1967)

Selected Readings

David Banisar & Simon Davies, *Global Trends in Privacy Protection: An International Survey of Privacy Laws, Data Protection and Surveillance Laws and Developments*, 18 J. MARSHALL J. INFO & COMPUTER L. 1 (1999).

Edward A. Tomlinson, *The Saga of Wiretapping in France: What it Tells Us About the French Criminal Justice System*, 53 LA. L. REV. 1091 (1993).

2. Right to Privacy in the Identity of One's Conversation Partners

Decision No. 81 of March 11, 1993 (Italian Constitutional Court)[112]

During the course of a criminal trial, initiated as a result of the opposition by the accused Viele Soccorsa against the penal order of conviction with which she stood accused, *inter alia*, of the offense of molestation or harassment of persons committed by means of the telephone and against the motion of the public prosecutor to produce at trial a tabulation containing indications of the hour and the day on which calls were effectuated from the telephone number registered to the accused or at least accessible to her, directed to another number registered to the aggrieved party and complainant, the accused's defense has alleged the procedural irregularity and, hence, the inadmissibility of such a means of proof, due to it having been acquired by the public prosecutor during the course of the preliminary investigation without the particular precautionary guarantees secured in the criminal procedure code for telephonic interceptions. (...)

---

112. 38 GIUR. COST. 731, 733–34, 736, 738.

As this Court has stated for some time (...), within Art. 15 Const. "two distinct interests find protection: that inherent in the freedom and secrecy of communications recognized as being innate in the rights of personality defined as being inviolable in Art. 2 Const., and that connected with the need to prevent and repress criminal offenses, that is to say, an interest which is also an object of constitutional protection." (...)

[A description ensues of §266 et seq. CPP (Italy) which regulates wiretapping.]

The special guarantees provided in the norms just mentioned for the protection of the secrecy and freedom of telephonic communication reflect the constitutional requirements pursuant to which the absolute duty to prevent and repress criminal offenses should be carried out with the absolute respect for the particular provisions which aim to protect the interest in the inviolability of the secrecy and freedom of communications, which is strictly connected to the protection of the essential nucleus of human dignity and the full development of the personality within social formations (Art. 2 Const.).

In other words, the particular rigor of the guarantees included in the aforementioned provisions are intended to confront the formidable intrusive capacity inherent in the technical means usually adopted for the interception of telephonic communications, to the end of safeguarding the inviolable dignity of the human being from irreversible and irremediable injuries.

[The Court then notes that §§266–271 CPP (Italy) only apply to the content of conversations and not the way or time at which they take place.]

For the reasons now expostulated one cannot but agree with the judge below when he affirms that Art. 15 Const., in the absence of the guarantees provided above, precludes the divulgation or, moreover, the cognition by third parties of information or notes capable of identifying the exterior data of telephone conversations (the authors of the communications, the time and place thereof), from the moment when, having been made the object of a specific constitutional right to the protection of the private sphere pertaining to the freedom and secrecy of communications, one entrusts their diffusion, in principle, to the exclusive discretion of the interested subjects.

More precisely, the recognition and the constitutional guarantee of the freedom and secrecy of communications carries with it the assurance that the subject who is the holder of the corresponding right can freely choose the means of correspondence, each of which has different prerequisites for confidentiality, due either to their technical or ju-

ridical profiles. And there is no doubt that, once a person has chosen
to use the telephonic medium, that is to say, the use of an instrument
which technically assures a more extensive secrecy than that attributable to other means of communication (postal, telegraphic, etc.), one
must, pursuant to Art. 15 Const., recognize the right to maintain the
secrecy not only of the data which could lead to the identification of
the subjects of the conversations, but also that relative to the time and
place of the communicative intercourse. At the same time, still pursuant to Art. 15 Const., one cannot deny that the recognition of such
a right is concomitantly tied to the guarantee consisting in the duty,
charged to all those who for professional reasons come to know of the
content and the exterior data of communications, to maintain the
most rigorous confidentiality as to the aforementioned elements. If
this guarantee were not in fact made, the content of the right which
Art. 15 Const. intends to secure as the inviolable patrimony of every
person in relation to any form of communication would be empty,
the more so if the latter requires for its proper realization a consistent
organization of technology and human beings.[113]

Questions

1. Do you believe that the identity of one's conversation partners and the
means one uses to communicate deserve the same protection as the contents
of the communications themselves?

2. Should there be a distinction between the simultaneous interception of
communications and government access to stored communications?

Relevant U.S. Case Law

Smith v. Maryland, 442 U.S. 735 (1979)

---

113. The German Supreme Court has also ruled that "the concept of 'telecommunications' in §§ 100a, 100b StPO includes not only the content of the telephone conversations engaged in, but also "events necessarily directly connected with the act of
telephoning, such as, for instance, the choice of the conversation partner," and, thus,
pen register information. BGHSt 35, 32 at 33–35. The U.S. Supreme Court has
ruled, however, that callers have no reasonable expectation of privacy under the
Fourth Amendment in the numbers they call. Smith v. Maryland, 442 U.S. 735
(1979).

3. *Informant-Citizen Taping and Interception of Communications*

Decision of June 14, 1960 (German Supreme Court)[114]

Human dignity is inviolable (Art. 1(1)(1) Const.). Everyone has the right to freely develop one's personality as long as he does not violate the rights of others and does not infringe upon the constitutional order or moral law. (Art. 2(1) Const.). Similarly, Art. 8 ECHR (...), guarantees everyone a right to respect for his private and family life. Thus, contrary to an earlier theory, the right to free self-determination of the personality is recognized as a basic value of the legal order. Like the previously legally recognized copyright of written works (...), now the human being's right to his spoken word is also included in the content of this general right of personality. Every articulation of one's thoughts communicates at times already through its content (more or less), but always characteristically through the voice—the personality of the speaker. Thus he himself and alone determines who may hear his words and whether they should be preserved or extinguished with the memory of the listener. Also to him alone is reserved the decision whether his words and his voice should be recorded on tape or another recording device and whether, how, and to whom it should be replayed. For word and voice of a human being are detached from him on a tape recording and have become an autonomous object. A piece of his personality appears thus as an alienable thing. It would undermine one's dignity if others could take control of attributes of one's personality and use them as they please. It would also constrict the individual in the free expression of his thoughts, hinder his natural way of speaking, indeed, it would restrict him in a human development laid out in a long, gradual maturing process, and would poison in the end the relationships of human beings with one another if everyone had to live with the stifling awareness that his every word, a perhaps thoughtless or uncontrolled utterance, could be captured, preserved and retrieved at a given moment to bear witness against him with its content, expression or sound—and, where possible, bear false witness, if, by using technological capabilities, the content is distorted, the form of expression changed and the sound of the voice altered. It therefore violates the realm of personality of the speaker and the right to his own words when someone engages in conversation with him and secretly preserves it on a

---

114. BGHSt 14, 358, 359–60, 364–65.

tape recording; and no less when someone without the consent of the speaker passes it along through the tape recording. (...)

It is a principle of due process in the criminal trial that the word of the defendant may not bear witness against him when it is obtained through lack of respect of his personality, then it must not be permitted that an utterance obtained from him under the same conditions through technological means stands up against him through his own voice; and even less when, as here, it is uncertain whether the tape recording (and which of the three) proves the crime with which the defendant has been charged, and when it is therefore in the realm of possibility that hearing the tape recording again will violate the general personality right of the defendant. Of course, this legal interpretation has the consequence that important means for solving crimes, and at time the only ones, must remain unused. That must, however, be accepted. It is furthermore not a principle of the code of criminal procedure that the truth must be investigated at any price (...).[115]

The German Supreme Court here relates this type of invasion of the privacy of one's thoughts and utterances to the privilege against self-incrimination. Have you heard any similar ideas in American Supreme Court opinions?[116] The Const. (Germany) is even violated if a private citizen does the recording.[117]

Decision of July 5, 1988 (Italian Supreme Court)[118]

In the evening of November 23, 1981 in Moncalieri, the industrialist Paolo Alessio was kidnapped. He was released on May 25 of the succeeding year in the territory of Tarano Castello in Cosenza following a payment of a ransom of 4,200,000,000 Lira. The Court of Torino, in a

---

115. The German Constitutional Court has refused to extend such protection to business conversations in a case involving tax evasion, noting that "highly personal things, which could be attributed to the inviolable sphere of intimacy, were not uttered." BVerfGE 34, 238, 247–48. The Spanish Constitutional Court has come to a similar conclusion. 158 BJC 90, 94.

116. *See* United States v. White, 401 U.S. 745 (1971) (Harlan, Concurring; Douglas, Dissenting).

117. The U.S. Fourth Amendment is normally only applicable if there is state action. Some courts, however, have excluded evidence collected by citizens in violation of the U.S. federal wiretapping law even though they acted independently of any state actors. In re Grand Jury, 111 F.3d 1066 (3rd Cir. 1997); Chandler v. Simpson, 125 F.3d 1296 (9th Cir. 1997); Berry v. Funk, 146 F.3d 1003 (D.C.Cir. 1998).

118. Cass. penale No. 953, 1043, 1044, 1050 (1989).

judgment of January 20, 1987, found Domenico Belfiore, Mario Ursini, Placido Barresi, Renato Angeli, Tommaso De Pace and Vincenzo Pavia guilty of kidnaping a person with intent to commit extortion as well as various connected offenses (...).

At the trial in first instance, Francesco Miano testified as to numerous conversations relating to various criminal episodes, which he recorded in jail in the Summer of 1983. Among these conversations were those that related to the kidnapping of Alessio as a result of the declarations of the same Francesco Miano which he recorded in jail in the Summer of 1987. The court, having ascertained the existence of the relevant reel (...) at the office of the public prosecutor, ordered its transcription by technical experts (...). The Court of Appeal declared the recording to be non-usable, deeming it illicit because provisions in the prison regulations prohibit the use of recording devices.

[The public prosecutor appealed. A discussion of Art. 5 Const. and the law regulating wiretapping ensued.]

From the direct application of Art. 15 Const., there follows the unlawfulness of any type of interception of private communications by third persons who clandestinely, by listening or recording, capture the conversations of their interlocutors, from whom one must presume their lack of agreement except in case of a renunciation, in fact, of confidentiality. The interception is unlawful in itself, without any reference to the content of the conversations, which could not have any character of confidentiality and could involve the private sphere of the same interlocutors or of other persons. (...)

Recordings of conversations which come into being on the initiative of one interlocutor and without the knowledge of another remain outside of the ambit of this norm, and also of ordinary legislation. In this case the (constitutional) right to respect for one's privacy free of foreign interferences is not being violated, but only the right (non-constitutional) to confidentiality, that is, of non-diffusion of information by the person for whom it is destined and who has legitimately acquired it. Because the right to secrecy of conversations operates only in relation to foreign third parties, these last recordings are not unlawful and can be used for evidentiary purposes (...).

In the instant case under examination, the constitutional protection is applicable even if the recording of the colloquies has been materially effectuated by one of the interlocutors. True, the Court of Torino has established with the contested order, with reasons and beyond reproach, that the police, after they had entrusted a prison informant with the recording, not only refurnished him from time to time with necessary reels and recovered by hand that which was recorded without the same informant having listened, but also indicated to him the prisoners from whom he should receive information and admissions (...). According to the trial court, the initiative for the recordings and their execution arose, therefore, through activity of the police and were intentionally preordained for the secret interception on the part of the same police of conversations damaging to unwitting interlocutors (...), the informant being used by the police as a mere material instrument interposed to follow the conversations of those he gained knowledge of, without impediments or delay, by direct and exclusive listening. The judges on appeal, therefore, having evaluated the specific procedure for tape recording the aforementioned colloquies, have correctly excluded the hypothesis of a recording on the part of one of the interlocutors, considering that the introduction into the jail of a mobile device on the person of a prisoner is not dissimilar to the installation of a fixed device in the interior of the jail. The facts of this case constitute a violation of the secrecy of communications because the recorder was not used by the informant to document the declarations received, but constituted a form of intrusion by the police into conversations between its informant and the interlocutors and a means of procuring documentary evidence, extracting from the live voice of the latter admissions and information to use against them and others and thus transforming the suspect accusatory declarations of their own informant into confessions of fact by his interlocutors or attributions of responsibility to others. Thus, one derives from the challenge the declaration of non-usability of the reel with the colloquies between Miano and the defendants Belfire, Barresi and Ursini and the relative transcriptions, it being evidence prohibited by the legal order and not able, through an artifice, to undermine the constitutional guarantees of protection of the person.

Note the helpful distinction here between a constitutional right to privacy in conversations, for instance, within the home, and a non-constitutional right not to have private conversations divulged (or perhaps tape recorded).[119]

---

119. Spanish courts have held that it is not a violation of Art. 18(3) Const. (Spain), which protects the privacy of communications, if a conversation is recorded by a participant. But if a conversation is intimate and it is divulged, the right to the protection of personal dignity, protected by Art. 10 Const. (Spain) would be violated. Decision of June 29, 1993 (Spanish Supreme Court), RJ 1993, 8484; Decision No. 114 of November 29, 1984 (Spanish Constitutional Court), STC 114/1984, cited in DE URBANO & TORRES, *supra* note 81, at 207–08. Art. 10 Const. (Spain) provides: "personal dignity and the inviolable rights which are inherent therein, such as the

But observe how the Italian Supreme Court treats police-induced tape recording of a suspect's conversations not only as a violation of the right to personality, but also as a secret means of inducing a suspected to incriminate himself without legal protections.[120]

Decision of October 8, 1993 (German Supreme Court)[121]

A police official, who in the framework of a criminal investigation follows a telephone conversation with a second receiver, does not, as a rule, act unlawfully, if the user of the telephone line who offers him the chance of listening in permits it; this also applies when he listens to the conversation unbeknownst to the other participant. (...)

The protection of the secrecy of telecommunications does not go beyond the realm of secrecy which is determined by the participants according to their discretion. The constitutional guarantee of this secrecy limits none of the participants in the communication in his right to alone decide whether and to what extent he will keep the communication closed or will grant access thereto to a third party. His participation is not an intervention into the secrecy of telecommunications. This also applies when the third party participates without the consent and knowledge of the other communication partner. Whether and, in an appropriate case, when the secret inclusion of a third party which is kept secret from the partner might be impermissible from another legal perspective need not be discussed in this context (...).

[I]n light of the development in the telecommunications realm, everyone who uses a telephone must take into account that devices permitting other persons to hear have been connected to telephone outlets and are used; a person should also not trust that this is not the case when his conversation partner does not mention that such a device has been hooked up (...). This is especially true ten years later at the time of the case now under discussion. Since then there has been further development. To an even greater extent than before, supplementary devices are being used which allow third parties to listen in on conversations. The German Federal Post Office—TELEKOM and pri-

---

free development of the personality ... are fundamental to the political order and to social peace."

120. The German Supreme Court has also suppressed tape recordings made by a police informant at the suggestion of the police, though the defendant willingly engaged in the taped conversations. BGHSt 31 304, 308.

121. BGHSt 39, 335, 338–39, 344–45.

vate firms offer numerous telephone apparatuses with such a supplementary function, whereby, to be sure, the second telephone receiver has been largely replaced by loudspeakers or amplifiers which are integrated into the telephone apparatus and make the voice of the conversation partner audible for people who are in close proximity (...).

That the second receiver used in the instant case did not belong to a private line but to the telephonic apparatus of an agency does not justify another conclusion. It is also insignificant that the person listening in here was not a private person but a police official who was investigating a criminal case. For, from the point of view of the right to personality and the protection of privacy, the only issue is that the participant in the telephone conversation simply must reckon with the existence and the use of a device for listening in. If listening in to a telephone conversation by a private person does not impact on the personality right of the conversation partner, then it should make no difference when applied to the same conduct by a police official, even when it is aimed at solving a crime. For the same reason there exists no police "informational intervention" in relation to the conversational partner of the user of the telephone line, which would, according to the interpretation advocated in the literature, require a statutory foundation for its implementation (...).

For a finding of a violation of the right to personality there is therefore only room when the conduct of the participant who lets a third party listen in is based on deception, the content of the conversation has a confidential character, or—to the extent this does not apply— the conversational partner expressly declares, that he places a value on confidentiality. (...) This was not the case.

Questions

1. Do you believe that the distinction made by German courts between merely overhearing private conversations and secretly tape recording them is a valid one?

2. Would fear of tape recording chill open speech and hamper the development of the human personality? Should we care about this?

3. Do you believe police use of wired informants to penetrate private spaces should be treated the same as wiretapping and should thus require judicial authorization?[122]

---

122. Germany law regulates the use of undercover police informants to a much greater extent than does U.S. law. Police must get an order from the public prosecu-

4. Should citizens always have to assume the risk that a partner in a telephone conversation may be a police informant or might be allowing police to overhear the call?

Relevant U.S. Case Law

On Lee v. United States, 343 U.S. 747 (1952)

Lewis v. United States, 385 U.S. 206 (1966)

Hoffa v. United States, 385 U.S. 293 (1966)

United States v. White, 401 U.S. 745 (1971)

C. The Limits on Police Undercover Activity in the Proactive Investigation of Crime

Teixeira de Castro v. Portugal (European Court of Human Rights) (June 9, 1998)[123]

[Two plain-clothes officers approached V.S. who was suspected of petty drug trafficking. V.S. agreed to help the police find a supplier of heroin. He led them to the defendant, who had no previous criminal record. The defendant was contacted by V.S. and went to J.P.O.'s house to procure heroin. When defendant turned the heroin over to V.S. he was arrested.]

Mr. Teixeira de Castro complained that he had not had a fair trial in that he had been incited by plain-clothes police officers to commit an offence of which he was later convicted. He relied on Article 6(1) [ECHR], of which the part relevant in the present case reads as follows: "In the determination of (...) any criminal charge against him, everyone is entitled to a fair (...) hearing (...) by [a] (...) tribunal." He maintained that he had no previous convictions and would never have committed the offence had it not been for the intervention of those "*agents provacateurs*". In addition, the police officers had acted on their own initiative without any supervision by the courts and without there having been any preliminary investigation. (...)

---

tor for a police officer to work undercover and they must get judicial authorization for an undercover police officer to focus his/her investigative activity on a particular suspect or to enter a private dwelling. *See* § 110b StPO (Germany). *See also*, in general, §§ 110a, 110b, 110c, 110d StPO (Germany).

123. 28 E.H.R.R. 101, 113–116 (1999).

The use of undercover agents must be restricted and safeguards put in place even in cases concerning the fight against drug trafficking. While the rise in organised crime undoubtedly requires that appropriate measures be taken, the right to a fair administration of justice nevertheless holds such a prominent place that it cannot be sacrificed for the sake of expedience. The general requirements of fairness embodied in Article 6 apply to proceedings concerning all types of criminal offence, from the most straight-forward to the most complex. The public interest cannot justify the use of evidence obtained as a result of police incitement. (...)

In the instant case it is necessary to determine whether or not the two police officers' activity went beyond that of undercover agents. The Court notes that the Government have not contended that the officers' intervention took place as part of an anti-drug-trafficking operation ordered and supervised by a judge. It does not appear either that the competent authorities had good reason to suspect that Mr. Teixeira de Castro was a drug trafficker; on the contrary, he had no criminal record and no preliminary investigation concerning him had been opened. Indeed, he was not known to the police officers, who only came into contact with him through the intermediary of V.S. and F.O.

Furthermore, the drugs were not at the applicant's home; he obtained them from a third party who had in turn obtained them from another person. Nor does the Supreme Court's judgment of 5 May 1994 indicate that, at the time of his arrest, the applicant had more drugs in his possession than the quantity the police officers had requested thereby going beyond what he had been incited to do by the police. There is no evidence to support the Government's argument that the applicant was predisposed to commit offences. The necessary inference from these circumstances is that the two police officers did not confine themselves to investigating Mr. Teixeira de Castro's criminal activity in an essentially passive manner, but exercised an influence such as to incite the commission of the offence.

Lastly, the Court notes that in their decisions the domestic courts said that the applicant had been convicted mainly on the basis of the statements of the two police officers.

In the light of all these considerations, the Court concludes that the two police officers' actions went beyond those of undercover agents because they instigated the offence and there is nothing to suggest that without their intervention it would have been committed. That intervention and its use in the impugned criminal proceedings meant that, right from the outset, the applicant was definitively deprived of a fair trial. Consequently, there has been a violation of Article 6(1).

The Eur. Ct. HR holds that Mr. Teixeira de Castro was denied a procedural right to a fair trial, in that the police acted on their own without judicial control in initiating their contacts with him. This should be compared with American doctrine, which treats so-called "entrapment" as a complete excuse in the material criminal law for the commission of a crime, when otherwise all material elements of the crime have been proved, rather than a constitutional protection against police overreaching.[124]

Questions

1. Would Mr. Teixeira de Castro have benefited by the entrapment defense had the incident happened in the U.S.?

2. Should judicial authorization be required before undercover police or their informants target someone to induce them to commit a crime?

Relevant U.S. Case Law

Sorrells v. United States, 287 U.S. 435 (1932)

Sherman v. United States, 356 U.S. 369 (1958)

United States v. Russell, 411 U.S. 423 (1973)

Hampton v. United States, 425 U.S. 484 (1976)

Jacobson v. United States, 503 U.S. 540 (1992)

Selected Readings

Jacqueline E. Ross, *Impediments to transnational cooperation in undercover policing: a comparative study of the United States and Italy*. 52 Am. J. Comp. L. 569 (2004).

---

124. Justice Rehnquist of the U.S. Supreme Court once indicated that police conduct could be so egregious in inducing a person to commit a crime that it could violate the Due Process Clause of the Fourteenth Amendment. United States v. Russell, 411 U.S. 423 (1973). However he later retreated from this position. Hampton v. United States, 425 U.S. 484 (1976).

Jacqueline E. Ross, *Tradeoffs in undercover investigations: a comparative perspective*, 69 U. Chi. L. Rev. 1501 (2002).

Undercover: Police Surveillance in Comparative Perspective (Cyrille Fijnaut & Gary T. Marx eds 1995).

D. Seizure and Reading of Private Writings

Entick v. Carrington
(English Court of Common Pleas 1765)[125]

Papers are the owner's goods and chattels: they are his dearest property; and are so far from enduring a seizure, that they will hardly bear an inspection; and though the eye cannot by the laws of England be guilty of a trespass, yet where private papers are removed and carried away, the secret nature of those goods will be an aggravation of the trespass, and demand more considerable damages in that respect.

The special sanctity of one's personal papers, which entitled them to more protection than other property, was recognized in 18th Century England and in late 19th Century America,[126] but has been all but abandoned in U.S. law today.[127] European law usually prohibits the seizure of writings of the defendant to persons who would otherwise be privileged to refuse to testify about such communications.[128] In England the seizure of "items subject to legal privilege" and "excluded material," which relates to "personal records" relating to one's "physical or mental health" or "spiritual counseling," among other things,[129] is prohibited. Compare the following German case with the old approach of Entick v. Carrington:

---

125. 19 Howell's State Trials, *supra* note 16, at 1066.

126. Boyd v. United States, 116 U.S. 616 (1886).

127. Fisher v. United States, 425 U.S. 391 (1976); Doe v. United States. 465 U.S. 605 (1984).

128. *See* §97 StPO (Germany), which prohibits the seizure of communications from the suspect which are in the hands of those who have a privilege not to testify against the suspect. This includes a broad list of family members, such as one's fiancé, spouse, ex-spouse, relatives of the immediate family and in-laws, §52 StPO (Germany), as well as priests, defense lawyers, notaries, accountants, tax-consultants, doctors, pharmacists, midwifes, social workers in various capacities (such as drug programs), and journalists, §53 StPO (Germany).

129. *See* §§10, 11(1)(a), 12 PACE (England) (Appendix, 234).

Decision of February 21, 1964
(German Supreme Court)[130]

The defendant was convicted of perjury.

The superior court[131] based its conclusions to a great extent on the content of a diary of the defendant which had been sent by a third party to the law enforcement agency (...).

[The Court cites language relating to an earlier decision involving secret tape recording.[132]]

These principles must surely apply when someone keeps opinions, feelings, and experiences to himself without, with rare, self-determined exceptions, allowing them to come to the attention of others. In conversations everyone intends, after all, a goal of announcing something, even if only in a limited way to one's conversational partners. Intimate writings are from the outset, as a rule, not intended to be brought to the attention of others. If their compiler had to fear that they would be read or even used against his will, this could substantially hamper the free development of his personality. Everyone must be free to memorialize at his discretion feelings, views and experiences without the suspicion and the fear that such writings could be impermissibly used. Here he can have different kinds of interests worthy of protection. A writer can, for instance, intend to use such writings literarily under the most intimate of circumstances. A psychologist can through observations of himself or others draw conclusions which will be scientifically applied. Someone can, after lengthy observations of her own feelings, experiences, peculiarities or reactions, or those of others, gradually strive towards self-perfection. It could also be that someone achieves through such written assertions or outpourings an inner struggle with himself or the relaxation of inner tensions, especially when he does not have the opportunity for confidential conversation or does not seek it. According to their content, the writings of the defendant could also be looked at in this way. In this and similar cases a need to prevent the usability of such intimate papers under certain legal circumstances which will be clarified is legally worthy of protection and shall be recognized.

---

130. BGHSt 19, 325, 326, 327–28.

131. I will use the term "superior court" to refer to courts of first instance for the trial of serious crimes (felonies) and the term "municipal court" for lower investigative courts or courts of first instance for the trial of minor crimes (misdemeanors or infractions). *See* the Glossary, for the names of the courts in the respective countries.

132. *See* Decision of June 14, 1960 (German Supreme Court), *supra* at 72.

Note that there are still some areas in Germany into which the government may not penetrate. Even where writings may be seized, the law in Germany and Spain specifically prevents the police from actually inspecting or reading them and provides for the presence of the suspect during such seizure and perusal.[133]

Questions

1. Should personal confidential writings be admissible evidence against their author in a criminal action?

2. Is this tantamount to compelling a person to be a witness against herself?

3. Is it a problem of the privilege against self-incrimination if a person chooses not to write a diary for fear it could be used against them in some future criminal case? Would such a decision be damaging to the constitutionally protected right to freely develop one's personality?

Relevant U.S. Case Law

Boyd v. United States, 116 U.S. 616 (1886)

Fisher v. United States, 425 U.S. 391 (1976)

Andresen v. Maryland, 427 U.S. 463 (1976)

United States v. Doe, 465 U.S. 605 (1984)

---

133. *See* § 110 StPO (Germany) and § 573 LECr (Spain) (Appendix, 260). This is much like the procedure used when reviewing recordings made following judicially authorized wiretaps. *See* Decision of June 25, 1993 (Spanish Supreme Court), *supra*, at 66.

Chapter Four

The Defendant as a Source of Evidence: The Privilege against Self-Incrimination

I. Police Interrogations Before the Initiation of Criminal Proceedings

A. Privilege against Self-Incrimination and Right to Counsel during Police Interrogation

1. The Requirement of Admonitions ("Miranda Rights")

Decision of October 29, 1992 (German Supreme Court)[134]

[The defendant was convicted of murder, rape and false imprisonment.]

As defense counsel asserts in referring to the judgment reasons, the defendant, who was in investigative detention on the other case which was the object of his conviction, was brought to the police station for interrogation in the morning of May 17, 1990. There "he was advised of his rights as an accused. He said he was ready to give a statement, but asked first to speak with defense counsel. This request was refused by KHK N. with the rationale that he himself must know if he wants to give a statement or not and the defense lawyer cannot deprive him of this decision. In addition, N. explained that the defendant would be interrogated 'until clarity reigns.' The defendant no longer insisted on further consultation with his defense counsel." The defendant then gave a statement about the case; the police officials then conducted a view of the scene with him and thereafter he was interrogated in writing. At that

---

134. BGHSt 38, 372, 372–73.

time he gave first a general, and later a detailed confession. He retracted this confession in a letter to his defense counsel on May 19, 1990, in which he explained that he confessed only due to "psychic torture."

The accused may not be denied further consultation with his defense counsel. Pursuant to § 137(1)(1) StPO the accused may "during any stage of the proceedings" take advantage of the assistance of counsel. § 136(1)(2) StPO (in connection with § 163a(4) StPO)[135] seeks to secure with the therein prescribed instruction that the accused, especially before his first interrogation, is aware of the possibility of consultation with defense counsel. It is correct, to be sure, that only the accused alone can make the decision whether or not he will give a statement. The consultation with defense counsel shall allow him the possibility to discuss this highly important question for his defense with defense counsel. If the accused asks to speak with defense counsel after the instruction and before the interrogation, then the interrogation must be immediately interrupted for this purpose (...); the attempt of an accused who finds himself in official custody to make contact with defense counsel may not be hindered or made more difficult (...). The police officials violated this duty because they denied the accused contact with defense counsel — whose name was known to them — continued the interrogation and furthermore explained that they would continue the interrogation "until clarity reigned."

Interrogations have always been the main method of ascertaining the truth in inquisitorial systems, which even allowed torture into the 19th Century to obtain admissions of guilt. In this area the "principle of material truth" collides with the right to due process or fair procedures in which the suspect is treated as a human being with inherent human dignity.

Note the absolute right to consult with counsel "during any stage of the proceedings." The provisions of § 163a(4) StPO (Germany) in conjunction with § 136(1) StPO (Germany) also require that criminal suspects be advised of the right to counsel and the right to remain silent before being interrogated, which, since the landmark U.S. Supreme Court decision of *Miranda v. Arizona*,[136] are known as "*Miranda* rights." In Germany, however, the accused has no right to have his or her lawyer present during police questioning. This is strictly within the discretion of the police.[137]

---

135. See Appendix, 249)

136. 384 U.S. 436 (1966)

137. Huber, *supra* note 67, at 121. Cf. California v. Prysock, 451 U.S. 1301 (1981) and Duckworth v. Eagan, 492 U.S. 195 (1989), in which the U.S. Supreme

Decision of May 21, 1996 (German Supreme Court)[138]

The superior court convicted the defendant of, *inter alia*, murder.

His appeal in cassation is without merit.[139]

The superior court could use the statements of the defendant in his first police interrogation of March 12–13, 1995.

During the interrogation, of course, he invoked his right to refuse to give a statement before having consulted with defense counsel a total of three times after a procedurally correct instruction about his rights as an accused (…). He found himself ready, however, after a short pause in the interrogation, to first give information about his person and finally also about the case, after he was unable to reach a defense lawyer because the interrogation was being conducted at night. Indications that the defendant's free determination of his will had been influenced by the interrogating official through force or deception are not apparent. Especially any evidence of excessive fatigue of the then accused is absent (…) or that he was prevented from summoning a lawyer (…).

§ 137(1)(1) StPO has also not been violated. A prohibition against interrogating an accused who is ready to give testimony does not follow from the right of the accused at every stage of the proceedings to summon defense counsel only because he asked for one at an earlier point in time. While it is generally maintained in the literature that an interrogation should be interrupted when the accused utters a wish to first speak with counsel (…), the interrogation may nevertheless be continued after a certain period for reflection. The contrary view, which draws its support from the context of the provisions dealing with the interrogation of suspects is not convincing (…). The accused who is

---

Court held it was permissible to advise a suspect that he or she would not be able to consult with court-appointed counsel in police custody prior to arraignment.

138. BGHSt 42, 170, 171, 173–74.

139. Many continental European systems distinguish between two types of review of judgments and decisions made by trial courts: that of "appeal" and "cassation." We will adopt this terminology and use the term "appeal" to refer to a review procedure, similar to what Americans would call a trial *de novo*, in which the appellate court may conduct an entirely new appraisal of the facts and enter a new judgment which replaces that of the trial in first instance. "Cassation," on the other hand, is a more limited review based primarily on the record of the trial in first instance and dedicated exclusively to questions of law. If successful it will usually lead to a reversal of the lower court's judgment and a new trial. The American "appeal" is thus more similar to the European "appeal in cassation."

instructed in a procedurally correct manner would have had little difficulty enforcing his rights under § 137(1)(1) StPO if he would have refused to give further statements during his interrogation.

In the U.S., the police may not return to interrogate a suspect after she has invoked the right to counsel during custodial interrogation unless the suspect herself reinitiates the contact with the police.[140]

Germany is not alone on the European continent in guaranteeing that criminal suspects will be advised of the right to remain silent and the right to counsel before being interrogated by police. Such a regime is statutorily rooted in Spain[141] and enjoys constitutional status in Russia.[142]

Italian law has taken an innovative approach by allowing police to question defendants to gather "information," while, at the same time, prohibiting the use of virtually any statements taken in the absence of defense counsel.

§ 64(3)(a,b)(3-bis) CPP (Italy)

(3) Before beginning the interrogation, the person must be informed that

(a) her declarations may always be used against her;

(b) (...) she has the right not to respond and that, even if she does not respond, the proceedings will continue their course; (...)

(3bis) The failure to observe the provisions of paragraph 3, subsections a and b will render the declarations by the person interrogated non-usable.

§ 350 CPP (Italy)

1. The officials of the judicial police (...) gather summary information useful for the investigation of the suspect, who has neither been

---

140. Edwards v. Arizona, 451 U.S. 477 (1981). American law is not so strict when a suspect has merely invoked the right to silence and will, under some circumstances, allow the police to return and make another attempt to get a statement. Michigan v. Mosley, 423 U.S. 96 (1975). In Russia, police may not make a second attempt to interrogate a suspect a who invokes her right to silence, unless the suspect freely initiates contact. § 173(4) UPK (Russia).

141. § 520(2)(a–c) LECr (Spain) (Appendix, 259–60)

142. Art. 51 Const. (Russia) guarantees the privilege against self-incrimination. All citations from KONSTITUTSIIA ROSSIYSKOY FEDERATSII. KOMENTARIY (B.N. Topornin ed. 1994). The Russian Supreme Court has ruled that suspects must be advised of the constitutional right to remain silent before being questioned and § 47(6) UPK (Russia) embodies the equivalent of *Miranda* rights. Stephen C. Thaman, *Miranda in Comparative Law*, 45 ST. LOUIS U. L. J. 581, 597 (2001).

arrested or detained pursuant to § 384 [i.e., taken into custody in other than flagrant situations].

2. Before gathering the summary information, the judicial police invite the suspect to name a defense counsel or, where this is not done, to proceed according to the provisions of § 97(3) [relating to official appointment of defense counsel].

3. The summary information shall be gathered in the obligatory presence of the defense lawyer, whom the judicial police must give timely notice. Defense counsel is obliged to be present when the act is conducted.

4. If defense counsel cannot be located or does not appear, the judicial police shall request the public prosecutor to proceed according to § 97(4) [relating to official appointment of defense counsel].

5. At the scene, or during the commission of the crime, the officials of the judicial police may, even in the absence of defense counsel, gather from the suspect, even if she has been arrested *in flagrante* or detained pursuant to § 384, information and tips useful in immediately achieving the goals of the investigation.

6. No record or use may be made of the information and tips gathered in the absence of defense counsel at the scene or during the commission of the crime pursuant to paragraph 5.

7. The judicial police may also receive spontaneous declarations from the suspect, but their use at trial is not permitted, except pursuant to the provisions of § 503(3).

Unlike in Germany, the suspect in Italy has the absolute right to have a lawyer present during all conversations with the police and a statutory exclusionary rule applies to any statements which intentionally or unintentionally are heard by the police. Russian law has strengthened the right to counsel in 2001 by also providing for the inadmissibility of any statement taken by police in the absence of counsel, even if defendant allegedly waived the right to counsel, if the defendant retracts his confession at trial.[143]

As on the European continent, English law gives a person in police detention the right to "consult a solicitor privately at any time."[144] While certain exceptions exist in emergency situations, if "delay will involve an immediate

---

143. *See* § 175(4) UPK (Russia).

144. § 58(1) PACE (England) (Appendix, 236). A "solicitor" is a lawyer who handles all pretrial aspects of a case, but usually does not appear in court as defense counsel. The case is usually argued by a "barrister" who is hired by the solicitor.

risk of harm to persons or serious loss of, or damage to, property,"[145] the right to consult with a solicitor is strengthened by the institution of a regime of "duty solicitors" who are always present in the jailhouse and are available to those who wish to consult with them prior to talking to the police.

Now let's look at the content of the warnings given to English suspects before interrogation:

§§ 10.1, 10.5 Code of Practice C. PACE (England)

10.1 A person whom there are grounds to suspect of an offence must be cautioned before any questions about an offence, or further questions if the answers provide the grounds for suspicion, are put to them if either the suspect's answers or silence, (i.e. failure or refusal to answer or answer satisfactorily) may be given in evidence to a court in a prosecution. (...)

10.5 The caution (...) should (...) be in the following terms:

"You do not have to say anything. But it may harm your defence if you do not mention, when questioned something which you later rely on in court. Anything you do say may be given in evidence."

Note how the English "caution" differs from the U.S. *Miranda* warnings. If a suspect remains silent during police interrogation, her silence may be used against her if she attempts to introduce exculpatory evidence at trial which she should have known of at the time of police questioning.

Questions

1. Why do we insist on advising criminal suspects of the right to remain silent even though it may hinder the search for truth in the investigation of the case?

2. Do you believe police should be allowed to interrogate criminal suspects without defense counsel being present?

3. Do you think criminal cases can be effectively investigated in Italy where the suspect's statement may not be used against him?

4. Should a suspect's silence be used as possible evidence of guilt, as it may in England?

---

145. §6.6(b)(i) PACE (England), Code of Practice C (Appendix, 236–37). Compare this language with the "public safety" exception to the giving of *Miranda* warnings articulated in New York v. Quarles, 467 U.S. 649 (1984).

Relevant U.S. Case Law

Miranda v. Arizona, 384 U.S. 436 (1966)

Michigan v. Mosley, 423 U.S. 96 (1975)

Edwards v. Arizona, 451 U.S. 477 (1981)

California v. Prysock, 451 U.S. 1301 (1981)

Oregon v. Bradshaw, 462 U.S. 1039 (1983)

New York v. Quarles, 467 U.S. 649 (1984)

Duckworth v. Eagan, 492 U.S. 195 (1989)

2. When Must Police Give a Suspect the Miranda-Type Admonitions?

Decision of February 27, 1992
(German Supreme Court)[146]

The defendant, who had no prior criminal record or prior vehicular infractions, drove an automobile at night under the influence of a blood alcohol content of .167%. He lost control of the car, which was left behind severely damaged, and left the scene. The witness R., a police official, found the defendant's driver's license in the car which had been in the accident. About a half hour after the accident, R. met the defendant, who was walking on a street leading away from the scene of the accident. Upon being questioned, the defendant first responded with a false name ("La." instead of "Li.") and an incorrect place of residence. R. suspected that the defendant was the person depicted on the driver's license he had found and confronted him with this fact. The defendant admitted this. "Asked about the traffic accident," the defendant denied he had driven the vehicle involved in the accident; he had been a passenger, but he did not want to name the name of the driver or say anything about how the accident happened. The defendant maintained that he had drunk two glasses of beer after the accident.

[The court then describes how the defendant remained silent at trial, and was convicted of drunk driving and how the court found that defendant had not been truthful in the statements he gave to R. on the road after the accident.]

The court of appeal holds that the advice according to §§ 136(1)(2), 163a(4)(2) StPO should "in any case," i.e. at the latest, have been given

---

146. BGHSt 38, 214, 215, 218

before the pedestrian was "spoken to about the accident." The court of appeal meant the official's question as to whether the defendant had driven the accident vehicle. This is apparent from the fact that the defendant, "spoken to about the accident," immediately denied that he had been the driver. The court of appeal evaluates the situation in which the official "spoke" to him about the traffic accident as if he was questioned as an accused within the meaning of §§ 136(1)(2), 163a(4)(2) StPO. In view of the previous events, including the introductory conversation with the official, this legal evaluation by the court of appeal is reasonable. It is therefore accepted by the Chamber. Thus, the Chamber assumes that the admonition according to §§ 136(1)(2), 163a(4)(2) StPO should have been given, but was not.

Note how soon the German *Miranda* warnings apply, even in the investigation of a drunk driving incident before the suspect is taken into custody. In the United States, the *Miranda* warnings would not have applied in such a situation for the defendant was not in custody.[147] English "cautions" must also be given to out-of-custody suspects when "on an objective test, there were grounds for suspicion, falling short of evidence which would support a prima facie case of guilt, not simply that an offence had been committed, but committed by the person who was being questioned."[148] Although it was the inherent coercive nature of police custody that inspired the introduction of the *Miranda* admonitions, the U.S. Supreme Court later spawned a doctrine which recognizes that a person can be in jail or interrogated in a police-dominated atmosphere, but still not be "in custody" such that admonitions of the right to counsel and silence must be given.[149]

Decision of May 31, 1990 (German Supreme Court)[150]

The fact that the police officials interrogated the defendant on November 6, 1988, as a witness and not immediately as an accused, does not constitute a circumvention of §§ 163a(3), 136 StPO. As to the issue of when the transition from an interrogation of a witness to that of an accused should take place depends on the strength of the suspicion (...). It is within the duty-bound discretion of the law enforce-

---

147. *See* Berkemer v. McCarty, 468 U.S. 420 (1984)

148. Regina v. Nelson and Rose [1998] Crim. L. R. 814, 815. This standard appears to be similar to that of "reasonable suspicion" enunciated in Terry v. Ohio, 392 U.S. 1 (1968).

149. Oregon v. Mathiason, 429 U.S. 492 (1977); California v. Beheler, 463 U.S. 1121 (1983); Yarborough v. Alvarado, 541 U.S. 652 (2004).

150. DER STRAFVERTEIDIGER (StV) Vol. 8, 337, at 337–39.

ment authorities to determine whether they have found that such a level of suspicion of punishable conduct has been reached, that they are pursuing him as an accused and interrogate him as such (...). An admonition pursuant to § 136 StPO and a corresponding interrogation as an accused is triggered when the suspicion already present at the beginning of the interrogation has so thickened, that the interrogated person can seriously be considered to be a perpetrator of the investigated crime (...). In this regard a very careful consideration is required in cases of the particularly serious charge of commission of a homicide. The law enforcement authorities exceed the limits of the discretion accorded them only when they fail to make the transition from a witness interrogation to an interrogation of an accused despite a serious suspicion (...).

In the instant case, there existed at the beginning only a suspicion that the defendant had had contact with the deceased on the day of the killing. The suspicion was confirmed only during the interrogation. Only towards the end of the interrogation—after the pause at 11:25 p.m.—did the defendant admit that he had accidentally found the body. This was finally the cause for placing the defendant under arrest. In this manner of procedure one cannot discern an improper use by the law enforcement authorities of their authorized discretion during the interrogation of someone suspected of having committed a crime.

It is important to emphasize that post-inquisitorial systems still require witnesses to answer truthfully to questions posed them by criminal investigators, whether police, prosecutors or investigating magistrates. The right to remain silent belongs only to suspects or accuseds. It is on this lacuna between the status of witness and suspect that continental European jurisprudence focuses a great deal of attention. When does a witness become a suspect protected by the privilege against self-incrimination and absolved from the duty to speak the truth upon penalty of perjury? It is in this area that Italian law again imposes a radical exclusionary rule:

§ 63 CPP (Italy)

1. If a person who is neither a defendant nor an accused makes declarations before a judicial authority or the judicial police from which emerge indicia of guilt on his part, the authority at the proceedings shall interrupt the examination, inform her that, as a result of such declarations an investigation can be carried out against her and invite her to name defense counsel. The preceding declarations may not be used against the person who gave them.

2. If the person should have been questioned as a defendant or accused from the beginning, his declarations may not be used.

Questions

1. Should *Miranda*-type warnings only be applicable to criminal suspects when they have been arrested or are in custody? Why?

2. Should *Miranda*-type warnings only protect against the inherent coercive nature of police custody or should they protect broader social and personal interests? If so, what are they?

Relevant U.S. Case Law

Beckwith v. United States, 425 U.S. 341 (1975)

Oregon v. Mathiason, 429 U.S. 492 (1977)

California v. Beheler, 463 U.S. 1121 (1983)

Berkemer v. McCarty, 468 U.S. 420 (1984)

Yarborough v. Alvarado, 541 U.S. 652 (2004)

3. The Problem of Undercover Interrogation

Having observed that *Miranda*-like warnings are required even when the suspect is not in custody, we will now explore what happens when police officers engage in the equivalent of interrogation of suspects when working undercover in the field.

Regina v. Bryce (English Court of Appeals) (1992)[151]

[An undercover policeman using the name "Pearson" called the defendant, arranged to buy a stolen car, and elicited incriminating statements from him. The conversations were admitted at trial and the defendant was convicted.]

This appeal is based upon the same two grounds which founded the submissions before the learned judge.

The first raises again the question as to what evidence can be admitted of conversations between a suspect and an undercover police officer, an

---

151. [1992] All ER, 569, 571–72.

issue recently addressed by this court in *R. v. Christou* (...). There a jeweller's shop (Stardust Jewellers) was set up, manned by two undercover officers, Gary and Aggi, and fitted with video cameras and sound recorders. The object was to recover stolen property, brought in by thieves or handlers, and to obtain evidence against them. It was argued that Code C [PACE] applied to the conversations between suspects and the undercover officers, so that a caution should have been given.

This court rejected the argument for reasons set out as follows (...):

"In our view, although Code C extends beyond the treatment of those in detention, what is clear is that it was intended to protect suspects who are vulnerable to abuse or pressure from police officers or who may believe themselves to be so. Frequently, the suspect will be a detainee. But the code will also apply where a suspect, not in detention, is being questioned about an offence by a police officer acting as a police officer for the purpose of obtaining evidence. In that situation, the officer and the suspect are not on equal terms. The officer is perceived to be in a position of authority; the suspect may be intimidated or undermined. The situation at "Stardust Jewellers" was quite different. The appellants were not being questioned by police officers acting as such. Conversation was on equal terms. There could be no question of pressure or intimidation by Gary or Aggi as persons actually in authority or believed to be so. We agree with the learned judge that the code simply was not intended to apply in such a context. In reaching that conclusion, we should ourselves administer a caution. It would be wrong for police officers to adopt or use an undercover pose or disguise to enable themselves to ask questions about an offence uninhibited by the requirements of the code and with the effect of circumventing. Were they to do so, it would be open to the judge to exclude the questions and answers under § 78 [PACE]."

Here Mr. Thomas [for the defense] argues that what took place offended against the final caveat in the passage cited. He submits the evidence that the appellant turned up in a stolen car at Smithfield as a result of a telephone call was admissible. However, the conversation on the telephone and at Smithfield should, he submits, have been excluded because "Pearson" asked questions which were in the nature of an interrogation. They deprived the appellant of his right not to incriminate himself by answering questions which, had they been put by a police officer acting overtly as such, would have required a caution under the code. In particular, Mr. Thomas points to the question and answer on the telephone: "*Pearson.* How warm is it? *Paul.* It is a couple days old" and the question and answer at Smithfield: "*Pearson.* How long has it been nicked? *Paul.* Two to three days."

Those questions went to the heart of the vital issue of dishonesty. They were not even necessary to the undercover operation, which was designed to provide evidence of the appellant in possession of a recently stolen car offering it for sale at a knock-down price. Moreover, the second question simply invited the appellant to repeat his answer to the first in more specifically incriminating terms.

On the voir dire "Pearson" was asked in cross-examination what he would have done had the appellant said the car was not stolen. He replied:

"If he had said, 'It is not stolen', I would have asked other questions, Sir. What are you doing selling a motor car like that? What is wrong with it? Is it an import? Has it come from abroad?"

In our judgment, that series of questions by an undercover officer would clearly ofend against the caveat this court stated in *R v. Christou*. It would blatantly have been an interrogation with the effect, if not the design, of using an undercover pose to circumvent the code.

II. The Prevention of Involuntary Confessions

§ 136a StPO (Germany)

(1) The suspect's freedom to determine and exercise his will shall not be impaired through maltreatment, fatigue, physical intervention, the administration of substances, through torture, deception or hypnosis. Coercion may only be applied to the extent allowed by the law of criminal procedure. The threat of a measure which is not applicable according to its rules, or the promise of a benefit not provided by law are prohibited.

(2) Measures which impair the suspect's capacity for memory or the capability of exercising insight are not permitted.

(3) The prohibitions of paragraphs 1 and 2 apply regardless of the consent of the suspect. Statements made as a result of the violation of this prohibition may not be used, even if the suspect agrees to said use.[152]

Note the unconditional exclusionary rule in § 136a(3) StPO (Germany), if the above provision is violated. In the U.S., if a statement is rendered "involuntary" by police interrogation practices under a general appraisal of the "to-

---

152. Cf. § 64(3) CPP (Italy).

tality of the circumstances," then the U.S. Supreme Court will find a violation of "due process" and will also prevent the use of the statement at trial.[153]

Decision of February 16, 1954
(German Supreme Court)[154]

"The dignity of the person is inviolable. It is the duty of all state power to recognize and protect it." (Art. 1(1) Const.) This guiding principle of the Constitution applies in an unrestricted manner also to a person suspected of having committed a crime. (...)

The ascertainment of the truth, the main duty of the court in a criminal proceeding, must also take place in a just manner exclusively as prescribed by these and other provisions. The accused is a participant in, not the object of, a criminal proceeding. The law subjects him to necessary investigations and limitations only within the given framework. It limits his physical freedom to the extent he must be made available for the proceeding and be prevented from obstructing the investigation into the responsibility of the accused (...), and further, to the extent that a physical examination of him can reveal facts which relate to a circumstance or facts of a physical nature, clues or foreign substances, and can contribute to solving the crime (...).

The accused's freedom of decision as to how to answer the charge remains by law inviolable at every stage of the proceedings. He need not respond to the charge nor contribute to the resolution of the matter (...); he might also have reasons therefor which are worthy of acceptance. The act must also be solved without any contribution by him in a just manner. These principles of the constitution and the law of criminal procedure have their roots in the fact that even someone suspected of a crime and subject to punishment confronts society always as a responsible, ethical personality; if his guilt is proved he should and must, as punishment, be made to bow before the law which was violated; his personality, however, must not be sacrificed beyond these lawful limitations to the certainly important public interest in fighting crime. (...)

Correspondingly, it is up to him during the interrogation to decide as to the "whether" and "how" of his response to every question, without unconscious utterances of his personality thus becoming perceivable

---

153. Oregon v. Elstad, 470 U.S. 298 (1985). On the "voluntariness" test in general, *see* LA FAVE ET AL, *supra* note 87, at 315–22.

154. BGHSt 5, 332, 333–35.

in ways other than in normal situations. He is no longer free to do this when questioned in a polygraph examination. (...)

Such a view into the soul of the accused and his unconscious emotions violates his freedom to determine and exercise his will (§ 136a StPO) and is inadmissible in criminal proceedings. For the preservation and development of the personality there exists a spiritual inner space which is necessary to life and may not be sacrificed and that must remain inviolable in criminal proceedings.

Note how, in this old German case, the ascertainment of the truth, the quintessential principle of the inquisitorial trial, may not be pursued in any way, even with the otherwise non-coercive use of a lie-detector, which may undermine the suspect's freedom to determine and exercise his will.[155]

Decision of April 28, 1987 (German Supreme Court)[156]

[The defendant was in custody, suspected of involvement in a robbery. Police encouraged Y., another detainee, to find out if the defendant was involved, and placed him in defendant's cell for this purpose. Feeling he would benefit by working for the police, Y. tried without success to pry information from the defendant. Y. then claimed he was planning an escape and asked defendant's help, claiming he would take the blame for the robbery defendant was suspected of. Defendant then made incriminating statements to Y. and these were used at trial.]

These statements were acquired in violation of §§ 136a, 163a(4)(2) StPO. The law enforcement organs undermined the defendant's freedom to determine his will through impermissible coercion.

The aforementioned provisions, of course, have direct application only to interrogations. However they are also correspondingly applicable to a case in which law enforcement agencies use prohibited means to exert influence over the accused in order that he make particular statements as to an act, which had already occurred at the time of the utterance, to a private person, who will thereafter be questioned as a witness. (...). This is the case here.

---

155. Although polygraph evidence is generally inadmissible in the U.S., it is primarily because of its lack of reliability and not because it violates the human dignity of the subject. *See,* United States v. Scheffer, 523 U.S. 303 (1998).

156. BGHSt 34, 362, 363–64.

The defendant was in investigative detention. Its goal is (...) to guarantee the conduct of orderly criminal proceedings and to secure a subsequent execution of sentence (...). It may not be misused in order to influence the testimonial behavior of the accused, especially to induce him to make no use of his right to remain silent (...).

This, however, happened here. The defendant was locked in a cell with another person under investigative detention, who had been commissioned by the police to pump him about the hold-up. The responsible police and justice agencies have thereby intentionally subjected him to influences on his freedom to determine his will as to whether to give a statement about the act. The otherwise permissible coercive measure of investigative detention was used for an end that violates procedural law. That is a coercive influence on the prisoner that is not covered by the law of criminal procedure and is therefore impermissible (...).

In Germany pretrial detention may not be used to induce a suspect to utter self-incriminating statements. According to the *Miranda* decision, custody is coercive in itself and the U.S. Supreme Court has recognized that statements induced by police jail plants could be coerced, or "involuntary" under the due process test.[157] However, in a case remarkably similar to the above German decision, the U.S. Supreme Court held that the questioning of a suspect by an undercover police officer in his cell, masquerading as an inmate planning an escape, is not "interrogation," because the suspect does not realize he is speaking to a police officer, and therefore not governed by the *Miranda* rules, nor is it considered to be an unlawful use of custody to induce self-incrimination.[158]

Decision of November 25, 1997
(Court of Appeal of Frankfurt/Main, Germany)[159]

[The accused was suspected of repeated arsons in Z from February 18, 1991, through November 2, 1996. Anonymous callers mentioned him as a suspect and said they had seen him at the scene when fires were being extinguished.]

Before the accused gave a blanket confession there existed only a preliminary suspicion and no reasonable suspicion against him: for up

---

157. Arizona v. Fulminante, 499 U.S. 279 (1991).
158. Illinois v. Perkins, 496 U.S. 292 (1990).
159. StV 3/98, 119, 120–21.

to this point there existed only statements of witnesses, who generally suspected him of the arsons without giving concrete information in this respect, or, in some cases, had seen him in close proximity to the places where the fires occurred. That the general suspicions, indeed, only amounted to rumors, and that the reported presence of the accused on four occasions at the scene of the fires after their outbreak or during their extinguishment constitutes, due to the fact that he lived nearby, negligible, if any circumstantial evidence which would never have sufficed for a conclusion of probable cause required for the issuance of an arrest warrant, goes without saying. Although the interrogating officials understood this, they aroused in relation to the accused the impression that his earlier presence at all of the fire scenes had been confirmed by witnesses, which was actually, as has been shown, not the case. Moreover, they told the accused that they would refer the case to the public prosecutor and that under the circumstances he would have to reckon with an arrest warrant "due to his dangerousness and the danger of repetition." The accused, who had no criminal record, could only understand from these explanations that the existing evidence sufficed in order to cause the issuance of an arrest warrant and his being held in investigative detention: for it is unlikely that the accused, as a person inexperienced in dealings with law enforcement organs, would be capable of recognizing the lacking substance of the assertions and evaluations of the interrogating officials and to draw the appropriate consequences for his procedural situation.

Although the circumstance that the accused at the particular time of his interrogation had neither been advised of his right to remain silent, nor of his right to consult with defense counsel, speaks for the fact, that the accused at the time of giving his blanket confession was not clear about the complete procedural situation and therefore, in connection with the utterances of the interrogating officials, which did not coincide with the actual facts, proceeded from the fact that his plight was hopeless and could only be improved through a confession. It is thus evident, taking into consideration the concrete state of the evidence and the situation of the interrogation as depicted in the dossier, that this was not, as is maintained in the pleadings of the public prosecutor before the court of appeal, only the case of a reference by the interrogating officials to procedurally appropriate consequences, but rather an impermissible exertion of influence over the accused's conceptual understanding.

The English legislator has meticulously regulated police interrogation not only in relation to the aforementioned regime of duty solicitors and cautions, but also with detailed rules relating to the conditions under which a suspect may be interrogated, with provisions relating to the amount of rest a suspect must be given, mandatory breaks in the questioning, food, etc.[160] The following case illustrates how English law differentiates between statements resulting from "oppression" and those produced through non-oppressive means likely to render them unreliable:

Regina v. Fulling (English Court of Appeal) (1987)[161]

[Defendant claimed a detective told her that her lover had had an affair with another woman in the jail in which she was incarcerated. She got very upset. She claimed the detective then asked her to give a statement. She gave one, claiming she thought she would be released. The detective denied any of the foregoing.]

Bearing in mind that whatever happens to a person who is arrested and questioned is by its very nature oppressive, I am quite satisfied that in [§ 76(2)(a) PACE], the word oppression means something above and beyond that which is inherently oppressive in police custody and must import some impropriety, some oppression actively applied in an improper manner by the police. I do not find that what was done in this case can be so defined and, in those circumstances, I am satisfied that oppression cannot be made out on the evidence I have heard in the context required by the statutory provision. I go on to add simply this, that I have not addressed my mind as to whether or not I believe the police or the defendant on this issue because my ruling is based exclusively upon the basis that, even if I wholly believed the defendant, I do not regard oppression as having been made out. In those circumstances, her confession—if that is the proper term for it—the interview in which she confessed, I rule to be admissible. (...)

§ 76(2) distinguishes between two different ways in which a confession may be rendered inadmissible: (a) where it has been obtained by oppression; (b) where it has been made in consequence of anything said or done which was likely in the circumstances to render unreliable any confession which might be made by the defendant in consequence thereof. Paragraph (b) is wider than the old formulation, namely that

---

160. *See* §§ 12.2, 12.4, 12.6, 12.8 Code of Practice C. PACE (England) (Appendix, 237–38).

161. [1987] 1 Q.B. 426, 429–30, 432.

the confession must be shown to be voluntary in the sense that it was not obtained by fear of prejudice or hope of advantage, excited or held out by a person in authority. (...)

This in turn leads us to believe that "oppression" in § 76(2)(a) should be given its ordinary dictionary meaning. The *Oxford English Dictionary* as its third definition of the word runs as follows: "Exercise of authority or power in burdensome, harsh, or wrongful manner; unjust or cruel treatment of subjects, inferiors, etc.; the imposition of unreasonable or unjust burdens." One of the quotations given under that paragraph runs as follows: "There is not a word in our language which expresses more detestable wickedness than oppression."

We find it hard to envisage any circumstances in which such oppression would not entail some impropriety on the part of the interrogator. We do not think that the judge was wrong in using that test. What, however, is abundantly clear is that a confession may be invalidated under § 76(2)(b) where there is no suspicion of impropriety. No reliance was placed on the words of § 76(2)(b) either before the judge at trial or before this court. Even if there had been such reliance, we do not consider that the policeman's remark was likely to make unreliable any confession of the appellant's own criminal activities, and she expressly exonerated — or tried to exonerate — her unfaithful lover.

Questions

1. Which test of voluntariness, the German or the English, places more restrictions on police use of deception, threats, promises or coercion?

2. Which is closer to the test used in U.S. courts?

3. Which of the tests do you think best balances the interests in uncovering crime with that of protecting the dignity and free will of the suspect?

Relevant U.S. Case Law

United States v. Henry, 447 U.S. 264 (1980)

Oregon v. Elstad, 470 U.S. 298 (1985)

Kuhlmann v. Wilson, 744 U.S. 436 (1986)

Illinois v. Perkins, 496 U.S. 292 (1990)

Arizona v. Fulminante, 499 U.S. 279 (1991)

III. The Formal Interrogation of the Accused during the Preliminary Investigation

Would having a pretrial judicial interrogation of the accused avoid all of the negative aspects of custodial police interrogation which the decision in *Miranda v. Arizona* was designed to mitigate?[162]

In French and Spanish law it is still asserted that the accused has a right to be interrogated as often as he or she pleases.[163] It is often the case in Europe that the accused, after having consulted with counsel, recants his police confession and asserts his innocence. European authorities thus see the investigating magistrate as a protection for the accused to correct involuntary or untrue assertions made in police custody.[164] In most jurisdictions defense counsel only has an absolute right to be present, however, when the accused is interrogated by the public prosecutor or the judge of the investigation.[165] Note, finally, how the Italian legislator has explicitly tried to reinvent judicial interrogations as a tool for the protection of the accused instead of a vehicle for gathering further incriminating evidence:

§ 65 CPP (Italy)

1. The judicial authority shall advise the accused in a clear and precise form of the act attributed to her, informs her of the elements of evidence which exist against her and, if it will not prejudice the investigation, tells her the sources of this information.

2. The accused is then invited to explain to the extent she deems it useful for her defense and direct questions may be asked of her.

3. If the accused refuses to respond, this is noted in the file (...).

---

162. Several noted U.S. scholars have advocated such a position. *See* Yale Kamisar, *On the "Fruits" of Miranda Violations, Coerced Confessions, and Compelled Testimony*, 98 MICH. L. REV. 929, 931–32 (1995), for a discussion of this literature.

163. E.g. §§ 396 (para. 1), 400 LECr (Spain) (Appendix, 259).

164. French jurisprudence has held that the investigating magistrate must interrogate the accused at least once "to protect the defendant." PRADEL, *supra* note 31, at 357. The French see the involvement of an independent judge as a much better safeguard than an abstract right of silence. Vogler, *supra* note 48, at 31.

165. Cf. §§ 168(c)(1), 163(3) StPO (Germany).

Questions

1. Do you believe judicial examination of the accused would eliminate the abuses often found in police interrogations?

2. Why do you think many countries allow police interrogations even though investigating magistrates or judges of the investigation are available to examine the accused?

3. Should interrogations only be a weapon of defense for the accused, as is theoretically the case in Italy, or also a means of gathering incriminating evidence?

Selected Readings

Mark Berger, *Europeanizing Self-incrimination: the Right to Remain Silent in the European Court of Human Rights*, 12 Col. J. Eur. L. 339 (2006).

R.H. Helmholz et al, The Privilege Against Self-Incrimination (1997).

Peter Mirfield, Silence, Confessions, and Improperly Obtained Evidence (1998).

Stephen C. Thaman, *Miranda in Comparative Law*, 45 St. Louis U. L. J. 581 (2001).

Raymond J. Toney, *English Criminal Procedure Under Article 6 of the European Convention on Human Rights: Implications of Custodial Interrogation*, 24 Hous. J. Int'l L. 411 (2002).

Gordon Van Kessel, *European Perspectives on the Accused as a Source of Testimonial Evidence*, 100 W. Va. L. Rev. 799 (1998).

Michael Zander, *You Have No Right to Remain Silent: the Abolition of the Privilege Against Self-Incrimination in England*, 40 St. Louis U. L. J. 659 (1996).

Chapter Five

Determining the Admissibility of Evidence at Trial

I. Exclusion of Illegally Gathered Evidence

A. From Nullities to Non-Usability

Post-inquisitorial European systems traditionally treated errors in the carrying out of procedural acts, even if they would today constitute violations of fundamental constitutional rights, as procedural "nullities," that is, void of any legal force.

§ 170 CPP (France)

In all matters, the investigating magistrate, the public prosecutor, the parties, or the represented witness may, during the preliminary investigation, submit to the chamber of investigation motions seeking the annulment of a procedural act or document.

§ 171 CPP (France)

There is a nullity when a failure to recognize a substantial formality contained in a provision of the present Code or any other provision of criminal procedure has infringed on the interests of the party to which it applies.[166]

---

166. Cf. § 177 CPP (Italy).

§ 174 (para. 3) CPP (France)

The annulled acts or documents are withdrawn from the investigative dossier and filed with the clerk of the Court of appeal (...). It is prohibited to derive any information against the parties from the annulled acts or documents or parts of the acts or documents, upon the pain of disciplinary proceedings against the lawyers or judges.

Note how the investigative dossier functions as the receptacle for all probative evidence and suppression is understood in terms of removing the tainted item from the dossier

Decision of July 9, 1993 (Spanish Supreme Court)[167]

[Victoria U.C. and Ana S.J. were convicted of violations of the narcotics laws based on evidence seized in a search pursuant to a warrant at which the clerk of the court was not present in violation of statute.]

As this Chamber has repeatedly said (...), pursuant to the important decision of the Constitutional Court (...), and the provisions of § 11.1 LOPJ,[168] which prohibit according any effect to evidence obtained directly or indirectly in violation of fundamental rights and liberties, there is no doubt in our positive law, that when a search of an individual's dwelling is carried out in violation of the provisions of Art. 18.2 Const., the evidence thus obtained is radically nullified.

Traditionally the doctrine in such cases would concede relevance to the results of illegally acquired evidence, because in the weighing of the interests at stake it was deemed that the public interest, derived as it is from the necessity that the final judgment in a criminal case must correspond to material truth, must prevail over that which is considered to be a violation of an individual right.

However, when these personal rights are incorporated into the political life of states in a manner that, transcending their merely subjective or individual character, they constitute essential elements of the judicial order in that they are conceived as keystones for the organization of a truly human, just and peaceful coexistence (...), then the perspective changes in light of the fundamental character which is attached to such rights, the protection of which acquires, in addition,

---

167. RJ 1993, No. 6060, 7682, 7682–83.

168. Ley Orgánica 6/1985, de 1 de julio, del Poder Judicial (Law on the Judicial Power), all citations from LEY DE ENJUICIAMIENTO CRIMINAL Y OTRAS NORMAS PROCESALES, *supra* note 20, at 245–404. See (Appendix, 264).

international status due to the obligation contracted by some states, like Spain, through agreements negotiated with others, in order to obtain an indispensable dissuasive effect among its possible violators. To the end of preventing eventual violations of this sort, it becomes necessary to declare evidence thus obtained to be radically a nullity, and, because of this, without any effect in the trial (…).

Thus, when the origin of the evidence's illegality is found in a violation of a fundamental right, there is no doubt but that such evidence lacks validity in the proceedings and that the judges and courts must treat it as non-existent at the time they construct the factual basis to support a judgment of guilt.

(…) [A]n act of entry and search of the dwelling of the accused has been deemed to be a nullity because entry was gained therein without the authorization of the judge or the owner and it was not a case of a flagrant crime, thus constituting a violation of the right to the inviolability of the dwelling of Art. 18.2 Const., and there have been repeated similar pronouncements in this Chamber in similar cases (…)

But this is not what happened in the present case in which there existed a judicial decision upon police request, by which the entry in the dwelling was authorized precisely due to suspicions that narcotic substances would be found there, for which we must conclude that the requirements of Art. 18.2 [Const.] were complied with, actually making the entry constitutionally legal without the consent of the owner in the absence of a flagrant crime. (…)

Judicial authorization existed and there appears to be no defect at all on its face which could invalidate it. The fact that in the later execution of the authorized act the clerk of the court was missing, violating the provisions of § 569(IV) LECr, does not affect the validity of the previous judicial decision which was dictated after an examination of the reasons adduced by the officials who requested it, having found that the formulated petition was reasonable. It thus seems evident that this act of the judicial authority is not made ineffective in its intrinsic substance and validity due to what occurred thereafter in completing the authorized act, although the later defect was of such importance, as undoubtedly the absence of the clerk of the court is, in the act that followed.

It is well-known that the clerk of the court is the only official competent to give full faith and credit to judicial acts (…), and since the entry and search of a home is a judicial act, although neither the investigating magistrate himself, nor a different magistrate performed the act and the act is performed by another authority or an agent of the judicial police through delegation as provided by §563 LECr. (...)

The first consequence derived from such norms is that which underlies the legal requirement of the presence of the clerk of the court, or of an official who legally replaces him, in this class of judicial actions.

The second is that his absence prevents the document which must be completed in said act from being considered as it would have been had the clerk of the court acted therein, that is, as a document authenticated by the public judicial authority of an official who, in the exercise of his duty, exudes the character of authority (...).

From the above one can deduce precisely the effect which the absence of the clerk of the court carries with it in this type of investigative act: the record created does not constitute documentary evidence which, as preconstituted, could have an effect in the trial, and it does not serve to prove the reality of that which occurred during the execution of the search nor, for that matter, with respect to the case which concerns us, can it serve to prove the fact of the discovery of the toxic drugs.

Thus, the invalidation of this concrete means of proof was not caused, as was said earlier, by violation of a constitutional right, which would bring with it the complete lack of effect of the act of the entry and search in conformity with the provisions in the aforementioned §11.1 LOPJ, and with the resulting impossibility of proving this radically nullified act by other evidentiary procedures. The constitutional violation, in order to definitively deter the act which ignores the fundamental right from acquiring any effect, so as to achieve the necessary dissuasive effect in relation to its perpetrators, as was articulated earlier, produces the consequence of complete invalidity, which does not occur in other situations, such as that which now concerns us, in which the invalidity refers to a concrete means of proof and not to the act of the search itself, which is procedurally a nullity, but constitutionally valid, so that its results can be accredited by other means (...)

In the present case evidence was taken at the trial consisting in the declaration of the defendant Ana, who always claimed that the safe found was the property of Victoria, and the testimony of seven witnesses, four police officials, a daughter of Ana, who referred to the fact of the discovery of the safe and its opening, by blows of a hammer, due to the fact that the key was not found, in the presence of all, with the result being the discovery in its interior of 71 bindles of heroin, undoubtedly destined for trafficking.

Note the difference between a mere "nullity" and a violation of a fundamental constitutional right. For our purposes, we will treat "nullities," unless otherwise specified, as formal errors in the collection of evidence which do not involve infringements of constitutionally protected rights of the defendant. Though the report documenting the results of the search is inadmissible as it was not prepared by the authorized official, the clerk of the court, the fact of the search and seizure may be proved by other means, because it was based on a proper judicial warrant. The witness testimony constituted a source of proof of the investigative act independent of the report which was prepared in violation of the statute.[169]

The Italian CPP differentiates between "nullities" and "non-usability" of evidence:

§ 191 CPP (Italy)

1. Evidence acquired in violation of prohibitions established by law may not be used.

2. Non-usability may be raised *ex officio* at any stage or level of the procedure.[170]

If evidence is declared to be "non-usable" in Italy, exclusion is required. Errors in the gathering of evidence leading to "non-usability" may not be "sanitized" or corrected as can some "nullities." Implicit in "non-usability" is a double sanction: the act of gathering the evidence is voided, as is any attempt to utilize the vitiated evidence at trial or in the court's judgment reasons.[171]

---

169. In other words, a statutory error in the execution of an otherwise valid search warrant does not lead to a suppression of the fact of the search and seizure. The U.S. Supreme Court recently came to a similar conclusion, when it decided that a violation of the statutory duty imposed upon the police to knock and announce their authority to search before serving a search warrant, though constitutionally required by its previous decision in Wilson v. Arkansas, 514 U.S. 927 (1995) would not lead to suppression of the evidence gathered pursuant to the search. Hudson v. Michigan, 126 S.Ct. 2159 (2006).

170. Cf. Art. 50 Const. (Russia) and § 75(1) UPK (Russia) (Appendix, 258). The exclusion of evidence illegally acquired is constitutionally required in Russia. Russian courts have in the past excluded evidence whether it was gathered in violation of a mere statutory norm or a fundamental constitutional right of the defendant. Stephen C. Thaman, *The Resurrection of Trial by Jury in Russia*, 31 STAN. J. INT'L L. 61, 90–94 (1995).

171. Elizabeth M.T. Di Palma, *Riflessioni sulla sfera di operatività della sanzione di cui all'art. 191 c.p.p.*, in PERCORSI DI PROCEDURA PENALE. DAL GARANTISMO INQUISITORIO A UN ACCUSATORIO NON GARANTITO 116–117 (Vincenzo Perchinunno ed. 1996). For the difference between "prohibitions in the collection of evidence" and

B. The Proportionality Test of Exclusion

In the analysis of the Spanish Supreme Court in the previous case, when a violation does not affect fundamental rights, then the inquisitorial principle of material truth prevails and the evidence will be admitted. In the following two cases, however, the German Supreme Court engages in balancing the seriousness of the violation of the defendants' rights against the seriousness of the state interest in convicting and punishing the alleged criminal conduct. The first case is a continuation of the case noted earlier that dealt with *Miranda*-like warnings in the context of a drunk-driving stop.[172]

Decision of February 27, 1992
(German Supreme Court)[173]

The Chamber shares the interpretation of the submitting court of appeal that the violation by a police official of the duty to advise pursuant to §§ 136(1)(2), 163a(4)(2) StPO provides the basis for a prohibition in the use of evidence upon which the appeal in cassation filed by the defendant can fundamentally rely. (...) The Chamber deviates thereby from its earlier case law (...).

The Code of Criminal Procedure makes no conclusive regulation of prohibitions on the use of evidence (...). The question as to whether a prohibition on the gathering of evidence brings with it a prohibition on the use of the evidence must be separately decided as to each provision and for each case on its facts. (...) Thus, the case law has affirmed a prohibition on use after certain procedural errors, for example, in the case of a deficient instruction as to a privilege against testifying pursuant to § 52 StPO (...) or an unlawful failure to notify defense counsel before an imminent interrogation pursuant to § 168c(2) StPO (...). In these cases no indication can be gleaned from the law as to whether a prohibition on use exists or not. In addition, the case law has derived prohibitions on use directly from decisions relating to constitutional values in the area of protection of the right to personality (...). In other cases the case law rejected a prohibition on use, for example, in relation to a violation of the provision of § 81a StPO which requires doctors to take blood samples (...).

"prohibitions in the use of evidence" in the German doctrine, *see* Roxin, *supra* note 32, at 164.

172. *See supra*, at 91.

173. BGHSt 38, 214, 218–22, 224–25, 228–30.

The decision as to whether or not there will be a prohibition on use is made on the basis of a comprehensive balancing (...). The weight of the procedural violation as well as its importance for the legally protected sphere of the affected party must be considered and placed in the balance, as well as the consideration that the truth may not be investigated at any price (...). On the other hand, one must consider that prohibitions on use impede the possibilities of determining the truth (...) and that the state, according to the case law of the Constitutional Court, must constitutionally guarantee an administration of justice which is capable of functioning, without which justice cannot be realized (...). If the procedural provision which has been violated does not, or not primarily, serve to protect the defendant, then a prohibition on use will be unlikely; (...) On the other hand, a prohibition on use is appropriate when the violated procedural provision is designed to secure the foundations of the procedural position of the accused or defendant in a criminal prosecution (...).

The principle, that no one must testify against himself in a criminal proceeding, that is, that everyone has a right to remain silent, belongs to the recognized principles of criminal procedure (...). It has found a positive expression in Art. 14(3)(g) of the International Covenant on Civil and Political Rights[174] (...). The recognition of this right to remain silent reflects the respect given to human dignity (...). It protects the personality rights of the accused and is a necessary component of a fair trial (...).

At the time of the first interrogation by the police the accused is, compared with the circumstances at trial, not to a lesser, but rather to a greater extent in danger of unthinkingly incriminating himself (...). While the defendant can calmly prepare himself for his testimonial behavior at trial and seek legal counsel, and at trial, moreover, has a defense counsel at his side, the first police interrogation usually finds the accused unprepared, without anyone to counsel him, cut off as well from familiar surroundings, and also not seldom confused by the events and pressured or afraid due to the unaccustomed surroundings. The defendant can, also with the help of his defense counsel, smooth out statements given at the trial, while the first statements to the police are often deprived of such possibility of influence and can, even with a change in testimonial behavior, develop a factual impact which has significant importance for the further course of the trial. (...)

---

174. Adopted Dec. 16, 1966, *entered into force* March 23, 1976, G.A. Res. 2200A (XXI), 21 U.N. GAOR Supp. (No. 16) 52, U.N. Doc. A/6316 (1967) (hereafter ICCPR).

Whoever at the beginning of the interrogation knew, even without instructions, that he did not have to give a statement, is, however, not worthy of protection to the same extent as the person who was unaware of his right to silence. To be sure, he must be admonished pursuant to §§ 136(1)(2), 163a(4)(2) StPO. However, the prohibition on use will exceptionally not apply then. The balancing of the values leads to the result, that the interest in proceeding with the trial in such a case should be accorded priority. If the trial judge, preferably through free evaluation of the evidence, comes to the conclusion that the accused knew of his right to silence at the beginning of the interrogation, then he may use the content of the statements which the accused made to the police without the instructions in formulating the judgment. Otherwise he must heed the prohibition on use.

[The Court then looks at comparative sources, discussing the rules applied in France, Italy, England and Denmark. It then emphasizes the importance of *Miranda v. Arizona* but notes that it would not apply to the facts of the instant case.]

Note the importance that a court from a post-inquisitorial country attaches to the right to remain silent even where the violation, that of asking a suspect whether he was the driver of a car and had anything to drink, was certainly not egregious. Once a German court determines that a right is fundamental, such as the right to remain silent, then it will engage in further balancing, to determine whether the seriousness of the charged crime will outweigh the violation and nevertheless allow use of the tainted evidence. Recall the perjury prosecution which relied on entries in the defendant's diary, discussed, *supra*.[175] After the German Supreme Court emphasized the *per se* protected nature of diary entries based in the citizen's right "to free development of the personality," it engaged in this further balancing:

Decision of February 21, 1964 (German Supreme Court)[176]

However not all limitations in the area of evidence law result in a prohibition of use. Sometimes the law expressly mandates a prohibition of use (i.e., § 136a StPO). In other cases, in which evidentiary prohibitions exist or should be recognized in accordance with constitutional principles, a case-by-case test is necessary to determine whether a violation of an evidentiary prohibition should result in a prohibition

---

175. *See supra*, at 82.
176. BGHSt 19, 325, 331–34.

of use. In the case of the aforementioned intimate writings, however, the personality can only be effectively protected if a prohibition of their use is recognized, regardless of whether the writings came to the attention of the law enforcement agency through state action or private intervention. In cases like this absolutely no intrusion in the private sphere shall take place, so that it is of no legal significance in which way the writings come to the attention of the agency against the will of their author.

Such an evidentiary and use prohibition can only be justified to the extent that one is dealing with utterances, the relevance of which is based in content which is expressive of the personality of the author. Here, in the case of diaries with a very personal content, no further elaboration is necessary. If, however, a criminal prepares writings about his crimes and victims, (...) or a foreign agent about his acts of espionage, there is no room for protection of the personality. The development, not the disintegration of the personality, is protected by the constitutional rights. Also business writings and those that address themselves merely to events of an external nature and are not connected to the sphere of the personality, are not subject to evidentiary and use prohibitions. (...)

A prohibition of use can also only be recognized, however, in the context of a balanced relationship between the personal, constitutionally guaranteed interest in the protection of one's own private sphere and the state interest in the prosecution of crime. (...)

If the accusation is less weighty, then the personality interest of the author of the writings will often prevail. In cases of probable cause that a serious attack on life, other important legal interests, or the state, or other serious attacks on the legal order have been committed, then the protection of the private life-sphere must give way. The balancing must be undertaken while taking into consideration the interest in criminal prosecution in light of the importance of the constitutional right, whereby the alleged wrongful act, to the extent it can be judged, must also be considered.

The judgment must therefore be reversed. The superior court may not use the diaries as evidence in the new trial. No evidence may be taken concerning their content in other ways, such as by examination of persons who have knowledge of their content as witnesses.[177]

Note how the German approach balances the strong government interest in solving and prosecuting serious crimes against the citizenry's strong inter-

---

177. The German Supreme Court allowed diary entries to be used, however, in a brutal murder case. BGHSt 34, 397.

est in protecting valuable civil rights. In serious cases there can be an incursion into protected constitutional rights without exclusion of the evidence being a remedy.

C. Case-by-Case Fairness Test: The English Approach

Regina v. Samuel (English Court of Appeal) (1987)[178]

[The accused was interviewed four times without access to counsel in violation of § 58 PACE. The admissions were introduced into evidence and he was convicted of robbery.]

The means adopted by [PACE] to ensure that persons in police detention are not denied the right given to them by, inter alia, § 58(I), are twofold. First, if the right is denied, that can lead to the exclusion of evidence obtained at unlawful interviews conducted after the denial either by the exercise of the judge's power under § 78(I) or, where the prosecution fails to satisfy the court that the denial was not oppression or a part of oppressive conduct, under § 76. In this case counsel for the appellant did not and does not submit that the refusal of access, although an impropriety, amounted to oppression. (...)

§ 78, under the heading "Exclusion of Evidence", provides:

> "(1) In any proceedings the court may refuse to allow evidence on which the prosecution proposed to rely to be given if it appears to the court that, having regard to all the circumstances, including the circumstances in which the evidence was obtained, the admission of the evidence would have such an adverse effect on the fairness of the proceedings that the court ought not to admit it." (...)

It is undesirable to attempt any general guidance as to the way in which a judge's discretion under § 78 or his inherent powers should be exercised. Circumstances vary infinitely. Counsel for the Crown has made the extreme submission that, in the absence of impropriety, the discretion should never be exercised to exclude admissible evidence.

We have no hesitation in rejecting that submission, although the propriety or otherwise of the way in which the evidence was obtained is something which a court is, in terms, enjoined by the section to take into account.

---

178. [1988] 2 All ER 135, 145–47.

This court is always reluctant to interfere with the exercise of a judge's discretion, but the position is different where there was no discretion to exercise in the judge's ruling and all the court has is an indication of how the judge would have exercised it. This is particularly so in this case, where, on the § 58(8) point, the judge failed properly to address his mind to the point in time which was most material and did not in terms give considerations to what his decision would have been had he ruled in favour of the defence on this more fundamental issue before him.

In this case this appellant was denied improperly one of the most important and fundamental rights of a citizen. The trial judge fell into error in not so holding. If he had arrived at correct decisions on the two points argued before him he might well have concluded that the refusal of access and consequent unlawful interview compelled him to find that the admission of evidence as to the final interview would have "such an adverse effect on the fairness of the proceedings" that he ought not to admit it. Such a decision would, of course, have very significantly weakened the prosecution case (...). In those circumstances this court feels that it had no alternative but to quash the appellant's conviction on count I in the indictment, the charge of robbery.

§ 78 PACE (England) displaces the old case law in England which did not provide for suppression of illegally gathered evidence other than in cases of involuntary confessions.[179] Note that in the case of confessions, § 78 can be the basis of exclusion when an "oppression" analysis under § 76 PACE (England) would be unsuccessful.

D. Presumption of Innocence and Equality of Arms: The Spanish Approach

Decision No. 49 of March 26, 1996 (Spanish Constitutional Court)[180]

[Police got an order to wiretap one person on suspicion of drug trafficking, renewed the order, and then began listening to conversations

---

179. Stephen Seabrooke & John Sprack, Criminal Evidence and Procedure: The Statutory Framework 139 (1996). Since official abolition of torture all European countries have an ironclad exclusionary rule applying to involuntary confessions.

180. 180 BJC 133, 137–38.

of another person relating to bribery. A search warrant later issued based on the conversations about bribery without letting the magistrate know of the eavesdropping on the second person.]

The object of the present constitutional appeal consists in determining if the judgments contested violate the right of the petitioner to the presumption of innocence guaranteed by Art. 24.2 Const. To this end it is necessary to analyze, with hindsight, if the evidence upon which the lower courts and court of cassation based their conclusions relative to the guilt of the petitioner as the perpetrator of a crime constitute incriminating evidence sufficient to deem that said constitutional presumption has been controverted, as the public prosecutor maintains, or if, on the contrary, as the petitioner adduces, the evidence upon which the aforementioned judicial organs relied has its origin in a violation of the fundamental rights to a trial with all the guarantees and to secrecy of communications recognized, respectively, in Arts. 24.1 and 18.3 Const; that is, the evidence which was used by the police, behind the back of the magistrates, to investigate a crime with which the petitioner was not charged. (...)

On repeated occasions we have said, in relation to the presumption of innocence, that the function of this Court consists in verifying whether there exists sufficient evidentiary activity from which the guilt of someone could be deduced. It constitutes an indispensable necessity for the protection of the right, that the judgment of conviction is based on true evidence, presented at trial with due procedural guarantees, evidence which may rationally be considered as incriminating, and from which results the guilt of the defendants (...)

Our case law has also established an absolute prohibition of the use of evidence obtained in violation of fundamental rights, such that the means of proof may neither be given any value, nor be admitted, if they were obtained in violation of fundamental rights (...). The inadmissibility of prohibited evidence due to a violation of fundamental rights is derived directly from the Constitution because of the collision it causes with the right to a trial with all the guarantees and the equality of the parties (Arts. 24.2 and 14 Const.) and is based, as well, in the preferred position of fundamental rights in the legal order and their affirmed condition of being inviolable (Art. 10.1 Const.). (...)

... [G]iven the inadmissibility of evidence obtained in violation of fundamental rights, its procedural reception implies an ignorance of the proper "guarantees" of the trial (Art. 24.2 Const.), implying also an unacceptable institutional confirmation of the inequality between the parties at the trial (Art. 14 Const.), an inequality which has been procured in an illegal manner benefiting whoever has gathered evidentiary instruments in violation of the fundamental rights of the other. The concept of "relevant means of evidence," which appears in the same Art. 24.2 Const., serves, as well, to incorporate, in its essentially technical and procedural content a substantive facet as well, thanks to which an evidentiary instrument thus obtained could never be considered "relevant." (...)

We have seen in the above cases that evidence seized in violation of fundamental rights may not be used in formulating the reasons for a judgment of guilt. Spanish jurisprudence sees this as a violation of the presumption of innocence, for such a presumption may only be rebutted with legally gathered evidence. Its use also violates the principle of equality of arms for the prosecuting parties can benefit from illegality, whereas the defense may not. Note as well that illegally seized evidence is no longer considered to be relevant.

Art. 24(2) Canadian Charter of Rights and Freedoms[181]

"[W]here ... a court finds that evidence was obtained in a manner that infringed or denied any of the rights or freedoms guaranteed by this Charter, the evidence shall be excluded if it is established that, having regard to all the circumstances, the admission of it in the proceedings would bring the administration of justice into disrepute."

Compare the Canadian language with the "judicial integrity" argument for the exclusion of evidence obtained in violation of the U.S. Fourth Amendment which was originally part of the jurisprudence of the U.S. Supreme Court.[182] Compare the German, Spanish, English and Canadian approaches with the current U.S. test, which is based solely on deterrence of police lawlessness and allows admissibility of evidence if the officer who conducts the illegal search was acting in good faith.[183]

---

181. http://laws.justice.gc.ca/en/Charter/index.html For balancing tests used to determine the "interests of justice" in other common law countries, for New Zealand, see Richard Mahoney, *Abolition of New Zealand's Prima Facie Exclusionary Rule*, [2003] CRIM. L. REV. 607–17, and for Australia, see Craig M. Bradley, *Mapp Goes Abroad*, 52 CASE WESTERN RES. L. REV. 375, 379 (2001).

182. Mapp v. Ohio, 367 U.S. 643, 659 (1961).

183. United States v. Leon, 468 U.S. 897 (1984); Arizona v. Evans, 514 U.S. 1 (1995).

Questions

1. Which approach to the exclusion of evidence achieves the best balance between the protection of the rights of the citizen (and suspect or accused) and the need for effective law enforcement?

2. Which method of balancing do you think is more just, that which takes into consideration the seriousness of the violation perpetrated by the police (constitutional right or mere statutory provision) or the seriousness of the crime being investigated (as in Germany)?[184]

3. Are there certain violations of rights which should trigger absolute prohibitions on admissibility?

4. Are their certain crimes where the police should be in no way deterred from pursuing their investigation?

5. Should deterrence of police violations of protected rights be the sole reason for excluding illegally seized but otherwise relevant and admissible evidence?

6. Do courts become accomplices in the illegality when they allow illegally seized evidence to be admitted and used to rebut the presumption of innocence?

Relevant U.S. Case Law

Weeks v. United States, 232 U.S. 383 (1914)

Mapp v. Ohio, 367 U.S. 643 (1961)

United States v. Leon, 468 U.S. 897 (1984)

Arizona v. Evans, 514 U.S. 1 (1995)

Hudson v. Michigan, 126 S.Ct. 2159 (2006)

E. Fruits of the Poisonous Tree

Decision of June 5, 1995 (Spanish Supreme Court)[185]

[The Court held that a judicial wiretap order was deficient due to lack of reasonable suspicion.]

---

184. The U.S. Supreme Court has prohibited searches of dwellings under exigent circumstances when only a petty crime is being investigated, Welsh v. Wisconsin, 466 U.S. 740 (1984).

185. RJ 1995, No. 4538, 6058, 6060.

It is beginning with these premises that one must analyze the viability of the indicated reasons. And in relation to them it is clear that such police investigations and the judicial decisions which authorize them are void and may not constitute evidentiary support in the trial of guilt, which, among other things, the well-constructed reasoning of the judgment now being contested does not do. The problem is another and consists in the determination of the indirect effect of such evidentiary illegality based in the reflexive effect established in the aforementioned § 11.1 LOPJ in applying the doctrine referred to in the Anglo-Saxon realm as the rotten or *tainted fruit* or, generically, the doctrine of the "fruit of the poisonous tree" which this Chamber, in a repeated body of doctrine (...) has followed (...). (1) There is no contamination of the remaining evidence if it is possible to establish a causal disconnection between the evidence which form the basis for the conviction and that which was illegally obtained; (2) This disconnection always exists in cases known in North American jurisprudence as "independent source" (...).

All in all, therefore, a declaration of nullity lacks autarchy. If it contaminates the remaining evidence it leads to acquittal by applying the fundamental right of the presumption of innocence established in Art. 24.2 Const., inasmuch as there does not exist incriminating evidence which can be the basis for a pronouncement of guilt. If it does not produce this effect, the consequence is none other than that of determining if the unaffected evidence taken into consideration by the trial judge can be deemed appropriate and sufficient to find that the interim truth of non-culpability, in which the presumption of innocence consists, has been enervated. (...)

Note how the U.S. doctrines of "fruit of the poisonous tree" and "independent source" have found their way into the jurisprudence of the high courts of Spain.

Decision of February 22, 1978
(German Supreme Court)[186]

[A wiretap aimed at uncovering membership in a criminal organization revealed the commission of other offenses which cannot be the subject of a wiretap order. Defendant was interrogated after proper

---

186. BGHSt 27, 355, 357–58.

admonitions and was confronted with the tape of the intercepted conversations. He made admissions.]

In making limitations it must be recognized, that a prohibition on the use of evidence limits one of the important principles of criminal procedure, namely that the court investigate the truth and thus that the taking of evidence *ex officio* extend to all facts and evidence that are of importance. As against this principle, the prohibition on the use of evidence is an exception which must be accepted in the individual case (...). That is of substantial importance for the question of how far the prohibition on use must reach. The surveillance of telecommunications pursuant to § 100a StPO constitutes not only an intervention into the telecommunications, but also into the private sphere of the given participant. Thus, in the opinion of the Chamber such tape recording should not be used to confront the suspect and the statements acquired should not be used. This also applies when the person affected has been instructed as to his right to remain silent pursuant to §§ 136(1), 163a(4) StPO. Even during a voluntary statement an accused is no longer free in his decision, whether and how to address individual points with which he is confronted on the basis of the tape recording.

If he mentions during the interrogation circumstances and facts which do not arise from the tape recording and with which he could not therefore have been confronted, these statements may be used, of course, in further proceedings. They contain an autonomous process of knowledge and do not rest on the breaking of the protection of the secrecy of telecommunications permitted by § 100a StPO and Art. 10 Const. The tape recording is therefore only the external reason for the interrogation, but the later statement is the actual piece of evidence as to which the original tape recording no longer has any determining influence. The protection of the secrecy of telecommunications no longer plays a role. As the Supreme Court already explained (...), not every procedural error which leads to a prohibition on use of evidence will always, without more, result in a complete laming of the criminal proceedings. Otherwise a confession given at trial could never even be used in a case which was originally prosecuted based on a tape recording. The investigative agencies are not prohibited from following clues learned from a tape recording and investigating on that basis (...).

If the accused, on the other hand, once gave a statement influenced by having been confronted with the tape recording, then later statements that are still influenced by the confrontation may also not be used. As a rule, a later statement can only be used (...) on which the tape recording no longer has an effect because, for example, a long period of time has elapsed and the interrogated person is no longer confronted with the tape recording or the earlier non-usable interrogations."

Note that the German court allows police to follow leads derived from an unlawful wiretap as long as they pertain to "catalogue offenses." It will not, however, allow police to confront a suspect with an illegal wiretap and use the statement gathered in response thereto. The Court applies "independent source" analysis in relation to statements which are no longer affected by the illegal tape recording. The thought processes therein generated do not relate back to the primary illegality.

Regina v. McGovern (English Court of Appeal (1990)[187]

M has been convicted of manslaughter on the grounds of her diminished responsibility. (...) Following her arrest she was interviewed on two occasions. On the first occasion she was interviewed without a solicitor being present and the second occasion in the presence of a solicitor. (...)

On appeal it was held that the first confession was made in consequence of M being denied access to a solicitor and was for that reason likely to be unreliable. Had a solicitor been present the interview would have been halted when M became emotionally upset. The interview was held quickly and without the formalities of the code because the police were anxious to discover the missing woman, but this heightened the risk of the confession being unreliable. The second interview took place the following day in compliance with the provisions of the code and in the presence of a solicitor. However that confession was a direct consequence of the first. Moreover the appellant's solicitor was not informed that the appellant had been wrongly denied access when M was brought to the police station. If the solicitor had known that, she would have realised immediately that the first confession was suspect and in all probability would not have allowed the second interview to take place.

Held, that the earlier breaches of the Act and the Code rendered the contents of the second interview inadmissible also. The court added that one cannot refrain from emphasising that when an accused person has made a series of admissions as to his or her complicity in a crime at a first interview, the very fact that those admissions have been made are likely to have an effect upon the person during the

---

187. [1991] Crim. L. R. 124, 124–25.

course of a second interview. Accordingly, if it be held, as it is held here, that the first interview was in breach of the rules and in breach of § 58 [PACE], it seems to the court that the subsequent interview must be similarly tainted.

Both confessions should have been excluded under § 76 PACE. The result of that evidence being excluded is that there was no reliable evidence against M and accordingly the appeal was allowed and the conviction quashed.

In the U.S. the *McGovern* case might have come out differently. First, the police are relieved of the necessity of advising a suspect of *Miranda* rights, included the right to counsel, when public safety issues, such as the finding of a dangerous weapon or a missing person are involved.[188] Secondly, a statement taken after proper admonitions of the right to silence and counsel is not necessarily treated as being the "fruit of the poisonous tree" of an earlier statement taken in violation of the *Miranda* requirements.[189]

Decision of March 27, 1996 (Italian Supreme Court)[190]

The proceedings were initiated following the seizure of around 31 grams of cocaine recovered from the dwelling of the defendant on August 13, 1994, during the course of a dwelling search executed without authorization of the competent judicial authority. (...)

The court of appeal of Bologna, while recognizing that the arguments presented by the defense in relation to the legality of the search were well-founded (...), because reasons for particular urgency did not exist such as to justify the failure to acquire previous authorization of a competent magistrate, nevertheless deemed the evidence of the seizure of the drugs during the course of the search to be usable in order to prove the commission of the offense. (...)

The search, having been executed illegally in the dwelling of Sala Giorgio on August 13, 1994, was concluded with the discovery and seizure of around 31 grams of cocaine because the conditions were present for the application of § 253(1) CPP [requiring seizure of the *corpus delicti* of crimes].

Well, if it is true that the illegality of the search for evidence of the offense committed, when it assumes the dimensions which result from a

---

188. New York v. Quarles, 467 U.S. 649 (1984).

189. Oregon v. Elstad, 470 U.S. 298 (1985); Missouri v. Seibert, 542 U.S. 600 (2004).

190. GIUST. PENALE 138, 140, 144–45 (1997).

manifest violation of norms created to protect subjective rights which are the object of specific constitutional protections, will generally diffuse its invalidating effects to the results which said search permitted to happen, it is also true that where that search, regardless of how effectuated, concludes with the discovery and seizure of the *corpus delicti* of the offense or things related thereto, and the same procedural code considers that the method by which such a seizure comes about is completely irrelevant: in relation to such a specific situation, even when created in an illegal manner, the seizure represents an "obligatory act," the omission of which would expose its perpetrators to specific penal responsibility. (...)

If one accepts the opposite conclusion demanded by the appellant, one would come to the absurdity of permitting the judge to confiscate the *corpus delicti* and, at the same time, to not take account of it in the concluding decision of the trial. (...)

In conclusion, therefore, the seizure of the drug in the instant case was legally executed, concerning as it does a procedure imposed by law and, once executed, it not only may not be revoked, but also preserves its complete validity along with all of its effects in the procedure in which it was conducted.

The same goes for the testimonial declarations made by the officials and agents of the judicial police who conducted that seizure: this act carried out by them represents nothing other, as has already been stated, than the results of the fulfillment of a duty imposed on them by law and in relation to the execution of that obligation, they may legally offer the contribution attributable to their direct participation in the procedure of acquiring the *corpus delicti*, something which due to its intrinsic illegality is subject to obligatory confiscation.

Thus, the judgment contested, having legitimately used the evidentiary results which were acquired and expressed an exhaustive evaluation of their content, withstands the arguments adduced by the defendant on appeal.

The opinion advocated in the above case, that a seizure of contraband mandated by law is independent of the initial constitutional illegality of a warrantless search of a dwelling in the absence of exigent circumstances, reflects the prevailing view of the Italian Supreme Court.[191] It is interesting that

---

191. Dec. 5.26.94, No. 204, GIUST. PENALE 368 (1995); Dec. 4.24.91, No. 1006, CASS. PENALE 1879 (1992). At least one panel of the Italian Supreme Court has held that the otherwise legal seizure of contraband is the fruit of a constitutionally defective search which turned it up, and provides for its suppression. Dec. 3.13.92, No.

the court does not explain why evidence has to be admissible in court just because its seizure in the narrowest sense was lawful. This would obviously mean that the only evidence suppressible in Italian courts would be evidence which was neither contraband, nor evidence proving the commission of a crime. This would render § 191 CPP itself a "nullity" which may as well be removed from the Italian code. Do you think this is what the Italian legislator had in mind when it enacted § 191 CPP?

Questions

1. To what extent should an initial illegal act by the police render subsequent evidence collected by them inadmissible?

2. If the police violate an important constitutional right, such as that which protects the privacy of dwellings or communications, should they be able to use the evidence they seize as a direct result thereof? Should they be able to use leads from the evidence illegally seized to continue their investigation?

3. If the police violate a suspect's right to remain silent by failing to advise her of the right to silence or the right to counsel, should they be able to use the ensuing statements for leads in developing their case? Should they be able to use physical evidence seized as a direct result of information contained in the illegal statement?[192] Should they be able to re-interrogate the suspect (following proper warnings) after they have induced her to "let the cat out of the bag?"

Relevant U.S. Case Law

Nardone v. United States, 308 U.S. 338 (1939)

Wong Sun v. United states, 371 U.S. 471 (1963)

240, CASS. PENALE 393 (1993). The German Supreme Court also does not suppress physical evidence which has been acquired pursuant to a warrantless search, if there was probable cause for the search and a magistrate would have authorized it if asked. *See* Stephen C. Thaman, *Wahrheit oder Rechtsstaatlichkeit? Die Verwertung von verfassungswidrig erlangten Beweisgegenständen im Strafverfahren*, in MENSCHENGERECHTES STRAFRECHT. FESTSCHRIFT FÜR ALBIN ESER ZUM 70. GEBURTSTAG 1041, 1047 (Jörg Arnold et al. eds. 2005).

192. A plurality of the U.S. Supreme Court recently ruled that physical evidence found as a result of a statement which was taken in violation of the *Miranda* rules is nonetheless admissible at the defendant's trial. United States v. Patane, 542 U.S. 630 (2004).

Michigan v. Tucker, 417 U.S. 433 (1974)

Nix v. Williams, 467 U.S. 431 (1984)

Oregon v. Elstad, 470 U.S. 298 (1985)

Murray v. United States, 487 U.S. 533 (1988)

Missouri v. Seibert, 542 U.S. 600 (2004)

United States v. Patane, 542 U.S. 630 (2004)

II. Admissibility of Evidence and the Right to Confrontation

A. The Transformation of the Inquisitorial "Written" Trial

The "right to be confronted with the witnesses against him" contained in the Sixth Amendment of the U.S. Constitution is increasingly recognized in continental European criminal procedure. Much progress has been made since inquisitorial times, when the criminal trial was based "partly in the darkness of the torture chamber and partly on the green file table before learned men in wigs" who "never actually sat face to face with the accused" and judged "based on the dead writings of torture and witness transcripts."[193]

Decision of July 18, 1884 (French Supreme Court)[194]

Considering that it follows from the contested decision that the municipal court in which the judgment was upheld had written statements of two witnesses, who had not yet been heard in court, read, in order to make other testimony more intelligible, and this reading took place when these witnesses were not present at the hearing;

Considering that this method of proceeding does not have the same shortcomings before the municipal court and would not produce the same effects as if it had been conducted before the jury court where the trial should be essentially oral;

---

193. Gustav Radbruch, *Zur Einführung in die Carolina*, in Die Peinliche Gerichtsordnung Kaiser Karls V. von 1532 (Carolina) 22 (5th ed. 1996).

194. No. 242, Crim. 404, 405 (1884).

Whereas, without doubt, the trial is oral in the municipal court, but it does not exclusively have this character (...) [for] the reading of transcripts which often relate to the declarations of witnesses precedes the hearing of the witnesses; whereas the judges may rely on means of proof other than transcripts and witness testimony as long as they are submitted for debate at the hearing and may draw their exhibits from the documents collected during the written investigation; whereas no provision of law prevents this possibility, from which it follows that, in the instant case, by authorizing the reading of two written depositions in the absence of the witnesses who had made them, the contested decision did not violate the substantial rules of criminal procedure;

Note how the French Supreme Court in this old case differentiates between the rules for trials before the municipal court (*tribunal correctionnel*) staffed solely by professional judges and that before the jury court which was introduced following the French Revolution and brought with it the principles of the oral trial and immediacy.[195]

Kostovski v. The Netherlands (European Court of Human Rights) (November 20, 1989)[196]

On 8 August 1981 the applicant escaped from Scheveningen prison together with one Stanley Hillis and others; he remained on the run until the following April.

On 20 January 1982 three masked men conducted an armed raid on a bank in Baarn and made off with a substantial amount of currency and cheques.

[Suspicion focused on Kostovski, Hillis and others. They were tried in both the district court and the court of appeal on the basis of anonymous witnesses' statements to the investigating magistrates which were read in court. The witnesses had requested anonymity due to fear of reprisals.]

The Dutch Code of Criminal Procedure (CCP) came into force on 1 January 1926. The citations appearing in the present judgment are taken from the CCP as it stood at the time of the applicant's trials (...)

Under § 338 CCP, a finding that the accused has been proved to have committed the acts with which he is charged may be made by a judge

---

195. Even today witnesses are seldom called to testify in trials in French non-jury courts and statements made during the preliminary investigation are routinely read in open court in lieu of live testimony. PRADEL, *supra* note 31, at 646.

196. 12 E.H.R.R. 434, 436, 441–44 (1990).

only if he has been so convinced through the investigation at the trial, by the contents of "legal means of evidence." The latter consist, according to § 339 CCP, exclusively of (i) what the judge has himself observed; (ii) statements made by the accused; (iii) statements made by a witness; (iv) statements made by an expert; (v) written documents.

Evidence in the third category is defined in § 342 CCP, which reads:

"1. A statement by a witness is understood to be his statement, made in the investigation at the trial, of facts or circumstances which he himself has seen or experienced.

2. The judge cannot accept as proven that the defendant has committed the act with which he is charged, solely on the statement of one witness."

§§ 280 and 281–295 CCP contain various provisions concerning the examination of witnesses at the trial, of which the following are of importance in the context of the present case. (...)

§§ 284, 285 and 286 CCP make it clear that the accused is entitled to put questions to a witness. As a general rule witnesses are examined first by the president of the court; however, a witness who has not been heard during the preliminary investigation and has been called at the request of the defence will be examined first by the accused and only afterwards by the president (§ 280(3) CCP). In any event, § 288 CCP empowers the court "to prevent a question put by the accused, counsel for the defence or the public prosecutor from being answered."

§ 295 CCP provides for an exception to the rule in § 342 CPP (...) that witnesses should be heard at the trial. It reads:

"An earlier statement by a witness who, having been sworn in or admonished to speak the truth in accordance with § 216(2), has died or, in the opinion of the court, is unable to appear at the trial shall be considered as having been made at the trial, on condition that it is read aloud there."

In connection with witnesses unable to appear at the trial, § 187 CCP provides:

"If the examining magistrate is of the opinion that there are grounds for assuming that the witness or the expert will not be able to appear at the trial, he shall invite the public prosecutor, the defendant and counsel to be present at the hearing before him, unless, in the interest of the investigation, that hearing cannot be delayed." (...)

In the Netherlands, the procedure in a criminal case follows in actual practice a course that is markedly different from that suggested by the provisions referred to (...) above. This is to a considerable extent due to a leading judgment delivered by the Supreme Court on 20 December 1926, the year in which the CCP came into force. That judgment (...) contains the following rulings each of which is of importance in the context of the present case:

"(a) for a statement by a witness to be considered as having been made at the trial under § 295 CCP (...), it is immaterial whether or not the examining magistrate has complied with § 187 CCP (...);

"(b) a deposition by a witness concerning what he was told by another person (hearsay evidence) may be used as evidence, albeit with the utmost caution;

"(c) it is permissible to use as evidence declarations made by the accused or by a witness to a police officer, as recorded in the latter's official report."

These rulings permit the use, as "legal means of evidence" within the meaning of §§ 338 and 339 CCP (...), of depositions made by a witness not at the trial but before a police officer or the examining magistrate, provided they are recorded in an official report which is read aloud in court. The rulings have had the effect that in practice the importance of the investigation at the trial—which is never conducted before a jury—has dwindled. In the great majority of cases witnesses are not heard at the trial but either only by the police or also by the examining magistrate.

The law does not make the presence of counsel for the defence obligatory during the investigation by the police. The same applies to the preliminary investigation by the examining magistrate (...). Nowadays, however, most examining magistrates invite the accused and his counsel to attend when they are hearing witnesses.

Compare the Dutch procedure used in the *Kostovsky* case with the procedure used in French courts staffed with professional judges described in the 1884 case which preceded it. Despite the presence of a code of criminal procedure which guaranteed a right of the defendant to confront witnesses during the preliminary investigation for those statements to be admissible at trial in the case of the witness's unavailability, the Dutch Supreme Court interpreted these protections out of the code and returned to the inquisitorial approach which makes all documents in the investigative dossier admissible in court and usable by professional triers of fact in the process of "free evaluation of evidence."

Before returning to *Kostovsky* in the section dealing with anonymous witnesses, we will look at how the European Court of Human Rights has triggered changes in the "written" trial before the French professional courts:

Delta v. France (European Court of Human Rights) (December 19, 1990)[197]

At 6:40 p.m. on 29 March 1983 a girl of 16, Miss Poggi, and a friend of the same age, Miss Blin, were in a Paris underground station when two coloured men accosted them. One of the men snatched a gold chain and crucifix which Miss Poggi was wearing round her neck and ran towards the exit.

The two girls immediately went to the central police station of the 12th District, and at 7 p.m., as a result, Mr. Delta was arrested by Police Constable Bonci, accompanied by the two girls, in a building by the exit from the underground. The victim and her friend immediately said they recognised him. A search of the applicant and subsequently of the premises, however, yielded nothing. (...)

On 5 May the court passed a sentence of three years' imprisonment on him. (...)

Moreover, in a judgment dated 22 October 1983 Delta (...) was sentenced to two years' imprisonment by the Paris Court of Appeal for robbery (...).[198]

Although they had been duly summoned by the prosecution, the two girls did not attend the trial and gave no reasons for their failure to do so. The court did not take any steps to have them brought before it (...).

Mr. Delta complained that he had not had a fair trial. He relied on paragraphs 1 and 3(d) of Article 6 of the Convention:

"1. In the determination of (...) any criminal charge against him, everyone is entitled to a fair (...) hearing (...) by [a] tribunal (...).

"3. Everyone charged with a criminal offence has the following minimum rights: (...)

(d) to examine or have examined witnesses against him and to obtain the attendance and examination of witnesses on his behalf under the same conditions as witnesses against him."

The Paris Criminal Court and Court of Appeal had allegedly convicted him on the strength solely of statements made to the police by persons—the victim of a robbery, Miss Poggi, and a friend of hers,

---

197. 16 E.H.R.R. 574, 576–77, 585, 587 (1993).

198. A full trial *de novo* is held before the French Court of Appeal upon appeal of a judgment issuing from a court staffed solely by professional judges. PRADEL, *supra* note 31, at 732–46.

Miss Blin—whom neither his lawyer nor he himself had been able to examine or have examined before either of those two courts or, because of recourse to the direct committal procedure, before an investigating judge. They had thus, he claimed, deprived him of the opportunity to impugn the statements of the two persons concerned. The only witness heard at the trial was the police constable who had arrested Mr. Delta and taken the initial statements of Miss Poggi and Miss Blin; but he had not witnessed the attack in the underground and was not an *officier de police judiciaire*. In sum, the applicant claimed that he had been tried exclusively on the basis of written evidence, in accordance with a practice of taking hearsay evidence from policemen. (...)

In principle, the evidence must be produced in the presence of the accused at a public hearing with a view to adversarial argument. This does not mean, however, that in order to be used as evidence statements of witnesses should always be made at a public hearing in court: to use as evidence such statements obtained at the pre-trial stage is not in itself inconsistent with paragraphs 3(d) and 1 of Article 6, provided the rights of the defence have been respected. As a rule, these rights require that an accused should be given an adequate and proper opportunity to challenge and question a witness against him, either at the time the witness makes his statement or at some later stage of the proceedings (...).

Accordingly, neither the applicant nor his counsel ever had an adequate opportunity to examine witnesses whose evidence, which had been taken in their absence and later reported by a policeman who had not witnessed the attack in the underground, was taken into account by the courts responsible for trying the facts—decisively at first instance and on appeal, as the file contained no other evidence. They were therefore unable to test the witnesses' reliability or cast doubt on their credibility.

In sum, the rights of the defence were subject to such restrictions that Mr. Delta did not receive a fair trial. There has accordingly been a breach of paragraph 3(d) of Article 6 taken together with paragraph 1.

Recall from Chapter Two that, while police are authorized to interview witnesses during the police inquest, such evidence is usually not admissible at trial unless the statements have been reaffirmed during the formal preliminary investigation in front of a judge with guarantees of the right to confrontation by the defendant or defense counsel. We will now discuss how these principles play out in modern European jurisprudence.

B. Admissibility of Statements of Unavailable Witnesses

Decision of March 5, 1993 (Spanish Supreme Court)[199]

The judgment of the superior court condemned Manuel S.M. and Nicolás T.M. as perpetrators of a felony of robbery to five years prison. (...)

The defense maintains in the first place that the victim of one of the acts, Laurent D., did not appear at the trial and did not ratify [his statement] during the preliminary investigation. It also alleges that the superior court considered the declaration of two police officers offered by the public prosecutor after the formulation of his provisional pleadings. (...)

The declaration of a single witness who only declared before the police and who did not ratify his declaration before the investigating magistrate cannot be used by the trial court although he disappeared and presumably no longer can be found on Spanish territory, for it was not confirmed at any judicial instance which could have considered his statements. Thus, to the extent that, pursuant to § 297 LECr[200] it only constitutes a crime report which must be proved (...), it cannot be used as evidence of the act by the superior court.

In this case it remains in any case to determine if the declaration at the trial by the police officer who prepared the police report could convert this declaration into a document usable as evidence. The response must be in the negative. The LECr does not establish the value of the declaration of a hearsay witness. In § 710 [LECr] it only talks of what circumstances such witnesses may testify to. This chamber has held, for its part, that the evidentiary value of such testimony is very diminished and that it may thus only be considered in very exceptional circumstances to the extent that the exclusively exceptional use is compatible with the principles of an oral trial and immediacy (...) and without the considerable reduction of the right of the defendant to question the prosecution and defense witnesses causing prejudice. Among these exceptional circumstances is indicated the need to combat organized crime.

In the instant case the hearsay witness ended up being the only evidence which the superior court had at its disposition because the other police officer did not appear.

---

199. RJ 1993, No. 1840, 2400, 2400–01.
200. See § 297 (para. 1) LECr (Spain) (Appendix, 258)

Note that, as in *Delta*, the hearsay testimony was the only proof available tending to incriminate the defendant. In such cases the defendant must be guaranteed the right of confrontation before the investigating magistrate. The witness's statement to the police must be "ratified" during a formal examination in the presence of the defense. It must be "anticipated" and preserved in the sense of §§ 392(1), 401(103,5), 403 CPP (Italy).[201]

Compare the approaches of the European Court of Human Rights and Spain with the following case from England, the cradle of the Common Law and the hearsay rule:

Regina v. Cole (English Court of Appeal) (1989)[202]

On 25 July 1989 in the Crown Court at Kingston before Judge Hamilton the defendant was convicted of assault occasioning actual bodily harm and was sentenced to 12 months' imprisonment. (...)

[Defendant was accused of assaulting Ronald Barham at a stadium after the latter had gotten into an altercation with defendant's daughter. Defendant claimed self-defense and was supported by his daughter and her friends. A security guard supported Barham's account of an unprovoked assault. Another security guard, Mr. Luff, gave a statement to police supporting Barham's account. Luff died before trial.]

The sole ground of appeal was based upon the alleged wrongful admission in evidence of the statement of Mr. Luff.

So far as we are aware, this is the first occasion upon which this court has had to consider the meaning and effect of the sections contained in Part II of the Criminal Justice Act 1988 under which the issue in this appeal is to be decided. The particular provision under which the judge ruled that Mr. Luff's statement should be admitted was § 26 of the Act of 1988, of which the heading and provisions are as follows:

"*Statements in documents that appear to have been prepared for purposes of criminal proceedings or investigations.*

"26. Where a statement which is admissible in criminal proceedings (...) appears to the court to have been prepared (...) for the purposes—(a) of pending or contemplated criminal proceedings; or (b) of a criminal investigation, the statement shall not be given in evidence in any criminal proceedings without the leave of the court, and the court shall not give leave unless it is of the opinion

---

201. *See supra*, Ch. 2, III.B.3.
202. [1990] 1 W.L.R. 866, at 867, 869–71, 875, 877.

that the statement ought to be admitted in the interests of justice; and in considering whether its admission would be in the interests of justice, it shall be the duty of the court to have regard—(i) to the contents of the statement; (ii) to any risk, having regard in particular to whether it is likely to be possible to controvert the statement if the person making it does not attend to give oral evidence in the proceedings, that its admission or exclusion will result in unfairness to the accused or, if there is more than one, to any one of them; and (iii) to any other circumstances that appear to the court to be relevant." (...)

It is necessary to refer briefly to the law as it was before Part II of the Act of 1988 came into force in order to explain the relevance of certain authorities to which we were referred. (...)

The conditions to be satisfied [under prior law] include the following:

"(a) The deposition must be the deposition either of a witness in respect to whom a conditional witness order (...) has been made (...) or of a witness who is proved at the trial by the oath of a credible witness to be dead or insane, or so ill as not to be able to travel, or to be kept out of the way by means of the procurement of the accused or on his behalf; (b) It must be proved at the trial (...) that the deposition was taken in the presence of the accused and that the accused or his counsel or solicitor had full opportunity of cross-examining the witness (...)."

Upon the introduction of "new style" committals the accused of course had in many cases no opportunity of cross-examining the witness (...).

The provisions of § 13(3) created a statutory discretion, or were enacted with reference to a common law discretion to refuse to admit a statement made potentially admissible by the subsection. (...)

The overall purpose of the provisions was to widen the power of the court to admit documentary hearsay evidence while ensuring that the accused receives a fair trial. In judging how to achieve the fairness of the trial a balance must on occasions be struck between the interests of the public in enabling the prosecution case to be properly presented and the interest of a particular defendant in not being put in a disadvantageous position, for example by the death or illness of a witness. The public of course also has a direct interest in the proper protection of the individual accused. The point of balance, as directed by parliament, is set out in the sections.

It is not of course the case that these provisions are available only to enable the prosecution to put evidence before the court. A defendant also may wish to make use of the provisions, in order to get before the jury documentary evidence which would not otherwise be admissible. (…)

Thus the weight to be attached to the inability to cross-examine and the magnitude of any consequential risk that admission of the statement will result in unfairness to the accused, will depend in apart upon the court's assessment of the quality of the evidence shown by the contents of the statement. Each case, as is obvious, must turn upon its own facts. The court should, we accept, consider whether (…) the inability to probe a statement by cross-examination of the maker of it must be regarded as having such consequences, having regard to the terms and substance of the statement in the light of the issues in the case, that for that reason the statement should be excluded.

In considering a submission to that effect the court is entitled, and in our view required, to consider how far any potential unfairness, arising from the inability to cross-examine on the particular statement, may be effectively counter-balanced by the sort of warning and explanation in the summing up described by Lord Griffiths and in fact given by the judge in this case. The court will also, for example, consider whether, having regard to other evidence available to the prosecution, the interests of justice will be properly served by excluding the statement. (…)

We conclude that the judge did not err in law by having regard to the likelihood of it being possible for the defendant to controvert the statement of Mr. Luff by himself giving evidence and by calling the evidence of other witnesses.

Note how the English courts appear to leave the introduction of the hearsay testimony of unavailable witnesses whom the defendant has had no chance to confront or cross-examine to the sound discretion of the trial judge. Although the U.S. Federal Rules of Evidence provide for similar discretionary use of hearsay testimony if it reveals indicia of trustworthiness[203] the U.S. Supreme Court has recently clamped down on the use of any prior "testimonial" statements taken by the police during police investigations unless the defendant had a right to confront the witness and cross-examine her when the prior statement was taken.[204] Hearsay statements are considered to be "non-testimonial" if made during or immediately after a flagrant crime to report it to the police, or in answer to police questions in relation to an emergency situation.[205]

---

203. *See* Fed. Rules of Evidence, Rule 807.
204. Crawford v. Washington, 541 U.S. 36, 52–53 (2004).
205. Davis v. Washington, 126 S.Ct. 2266, 2273–74 (2006).

Questions

1. Why did the French feel it was more permissible to read written statements before a court composed exclusively of professional judges than before a jury court?

2. Do you think the Spanish courts would have admitted Mr. Luff's statement in the *Cole* case? Would the European Court of Human Rights have found a violation in *Cole*?

3. How do you explain the fact that a Common Law country like England perhaps admits more hearsay in violation of the right of confrontation than some formerly inquisitorial countries?

4. Would American courts have admitted either Mr. Luff's statement in the *Cole* case or the statement in the Spanish case?

5. Should the fact that hearsay statements, where admissible, should be treated with caution, justify the violation of the right of confrontation?

6. In an adversary trial, should one side in the dispute, the prosecution and the judicial police, be able to prepare written evidence and documents in secrecy and use them in court against the other side, the defense?

Relevant U.S. Case Law

Crawford v. Washington, 541 U.S. 36 (2004)

Davis v. Washington, 126 S.Ct. 2266 (2006)

C. Admissibility of Prior Statements to Impeach or Contradict a Testifying Witness

Decision No. 52 of February 23, 1995 (Spanish Constitutional Court)[206]

[In his declaration to the police, Mr. Juan José de los Santos Moreno incriminated the defendant as one of the perpetrators of a robbery, explaining in detail his version of the events of the day of the crime. The defendant made no statement. Mr. de los Santos Moreno retracted his statement before the investigating magistrate and indicated that the defendant was not involved in the robbery. At trial he re-

---

206. 167 BJC 145, 148, 149.

peated this statement and maintained that his original statement to the police was false.]

It is evident in the first place that declarations of a co-accused in the police station may be considered neither as exponents of anticipated nor preconstituted evidence, and this not only because their reproduction at trial is neither impossible nor difficult—in fact, Mr. Juan José de los Santos Moreno appeared personally at trial where he had the opportunity to declare about all the relative extremes of the charges—but fundamentally because they were not effectuated in the presence of a judicial authority, the only organ which, blessed institutionally with independence and impartiality, can assure the truth of the testimony and its eventual evidentiary efficacy. (...)

In the instant case the incriminating declaration made before the police by the co-accused Mr. Juan José de los Santos Moreno was not ratified in the presence of a judge but denied in such a way that the judge who pronounced judgment should have abstained from considering such a declaration as incriminating evidence in that it did not comply with the conditions of § 714 LECr[207] and did not have the character of anticipated or preconstituted evidence. In order for such a statement to have been incorporated in the trial, thus acquiring the value of incriminating evidence, it would have been necessary for the co-accused to ratify it before the investigating magistrate—thus making the use of the mechanism foreseen in § 714 LECr possible—or the police officials before whom such testimony was made should be called as witnesses in the trial observing the principles of confrontation and immediacy.

Decision of November 3, 1982
(German Supreme Court)[208]

The superior court sentenced the defendant to four years imprisonment for encouragement of prostitution in conjunction with pimping and infliction of bodily injury and also ordered preventive detention. (...)

The defendant rightfully objects that the statement of the witness Sabine E., which she made on December 18, 1980, in the municipal court F., was used in the judgment although he was not notified of the date of the examination.

The defendant—then the accused—was provisionally arrested the day before in F. and was in police custody there when the examination

---

207. See Appendix, at 261.
208. BGHSt 31, 140, 140–42.

of the witness took place. He was not notified of the time of the examination. It is not apparent from the file why notice was not given. In the trial on August 6, 1981, the witness stated that she unjustifiably incriminated the defendant. When confronted with it, however, she admitted that she did testify before the judge of the investigation as indicated in the transcript. (...)

This procedure was legally in error.

If a witness is examined by a judge in the preparatory proceeding, then the accused must as a principle be notified of the time of questioning (§ 168c(5, sent. 1, (2) StPO). The law here does, however, allow for exceptions. (...) For excluding the accused there is no support in the present case. The fact that he had been provisionally arrested does not affect his right to be present because the examination of the witness was set in the courthouse of the same place where he was in police custody (§ 168c(4) StPO). Notification can otherwise be denied if it would endanger the success of the investigation. (§ 168c(5, sent. 2) StPO). This, however, requires a corresponding decision by the judge of the investigation and the reasons must be entered into the record.

Questions

1. Would the prior statements of the witnesses in the Spanish and German cases above have been admissible if the cases had been tried in U.S. courts.[209]

2. What do you think accounts for the stricter approach of these European courts?

D. Anonymous Witness Testimony

Kostovski v. The Netherlands (European Court of Human Rights) (November 20, 1989)[210]

The CCP contains no express provisions on statements by anonymous witnesses.

However, with the increase in violent, organised crime a need was felt to protect those witnesses who had justification for fearing reprisals, by granting them anonymity. In a series of judgments the Supreme Court has made this possible.

---

209. *See* Federal Rules of Evidence 801(d)(1).
210. *See supra*, at 126. 12 E.H.R.R. at 444, 446, 447–49 (1990).

[Summary given of Dutch Law from 1938 through the *Kostovski* case which allowed the introduction of written testimony of anonymous witnesses who had been questioned in the absence of the defense by the police and/or investigating magistrate.]

The essence of Mr. Kostovski's claim was that he had not received a fair trial. In this connection he relied mainly on the following provisions of Article 6 of the Convention.[211]

[The court then summarizes the right to confrontation, see *Delta*, *supra*, at 129–30.]

Yet such an opportunity [to confront the witnesses] was not afforded to the applicant in the present case, although there could be no doubt that he desired to challenge and question the anonymous persons involved. Not only were the latter not heard at the trials but also their declarations were taken, whether by the police or the examining magistrate, in the absence of Mr. Kostovski and his counsel. Accordingly, at no stage could they be questioned directly by him or on his behalf. It is true that the defence was able, before both the Utrecht District Court and the Amsterdam Court of Appeal, to question one of the police officers and both of the examining magistrates who had taken the declarations. It was also able, but as regards only one of the anonymous persons, to submit written questions to him/her indirectly through the examining magistrate. However, the nature and scope of the questions it could put in either of these ways were considerably restricted by reason of the decision that the anonymity of the authors of the statements should be preserved.

The latter feature of the case compounded the difficulties facing the applicant. If the defence is unaware of the identity of the person it seeks to question, it may be deprived of the very particulars enabling it to demonstrate that he or she is prejudiced, hostile or unreliable. Testimony or other declarations inculpating an accused may well be designedly untruthful or simply erroneous and the defence will scarcely be able to bring this to light if it lacks the information permitting it to test the author's reliability or cast doubt on his credibility. The dangers inherent in such a situation are obvious.

Furthermore, each of the trial courts was precluded by the absence of the said anonymous persons from observing their demeanour under questioning and thus forming its own impression of their reliability. The courts admittedly heard evidence on the latter point and no doubt—as is required by Dutch law—they observed caution in eval-

---

211. *See Delta, supra*, at 129.

uating the statements in question, but this can scarcely be regarded as a proper substitute for direct observation.

It is true that one of the anonymous persons was heard by examining magistrates. However, the Court is bound to observe that—in addition to the fact that neither the applicant nor his counsel was present at the interviews—the examining magistrates themselves were unaware of the person's identity, a situation which cannot have been without implications for the testing of his/her reliability. As for the other anonymous person, he was not heard by an examining magistrate at all, but only by the police.

In these circumstances it cannot be said that the handicaps under which the defence laboured were counterbalanced by the procedures followed by the judicial authorities.

The Government stressed the fact that case-law and practice in the Netherlands in the matter of anonymous evidence stemmed from an increase in the intimidation of witnesses and were based on a balancing of the interests of society, the accused and the witnesses. They pointed out that in the present case it had been established that the authors of the statements in question had good reason to fear reprisals.

As on previous occasions, the Court does not underestimate the importance of the struggle against organised crime. Yet the Government's line of argument, whilst not without force, is not decisive.

Although the growth in organised crime doubtless demands the introduction of appropriate measures, the Government's submissions appear to the Court to lay insufficient weight on what the applicant's counsel described as "the interest of everybody in a civilised society in a controllable and fair judicial procedure." The right to a fair administration of justice holds so prominent a place in a democratic society that it cannot be sacrificed to expediency. The Convention does not preclude reliance, at the investigation stage of criminal proceedings, on sources such as anonymous informants. However, the subsequent use of anonymous statements as sufficient evidence to found a conviction, as in the present case, is a different matter. It involved limitations on the rights of the defence which were irreconcilable with the guarantees contained in Article 6. In fact, the Government accepted that the applicant's conviction was based "to a decisive extent" on the anonymous statements.

The Court therefore concludes that in the circumstances of the case the constraints affecting the rights of the defence were such that Mr. Kostovski cannot be said to have received a fair trial. There was accordingly a violation of paragraph 3(d), taken together with paragraph 1, of Article 6.

On the issue of the extent the participatory rights of the defendant in criminal proceedings may be restricted in order to encourage the participation of victims and witnesses in such proceedings by granting them anonymity, note in the following case how the European Court of Human Rights attempts to maximize such citizen participation without stripping the defendant of the right to confrontation.

Doorson v. The Netherlands European Court of Human Rights (March 26, 1996)[212]

In August 1987 the prosecuting authorities decided to take action against the nuisance caused by drug trafficking in Amsterdam. The police had compiled sets of photographs of persons suspected of being drug dealers. These were shown to about 150 drug addicts in order to collect statements from them. However, following a similar action in 1986 when drug addicts who had made statements to the police had been threatened, it turned out that most of those to whom photographs were shown were only prepared to make statements on condition that their identity was not disclosed to the drug dealers whom they identified. (...)

A number of drug addicts subsequently stated to the police that they recognised the applicant from his photograph and that he had sold drugs. Six of these drug addicts remained anonymous; they were referred to by the police under the code names Y.05, Y.06, Y.13, Y.14, Y.15 and Y.16. The identity of two others was disclosed, namely R. and N. (...)

[Defendant was convicted and appealed for a trial *de novo* before the Amsterdam Court of Appeal.]

On 14 February 1990 the investigating judge heard the witnesses Y.15 and Y.16 in the presence of the applicant's lawyer. (...)

The lawyer was given the opportunity to put questions to the witnesses but was not informed of their identity. The identity of both witnesses was known to the investigating judge.

---

212. 22 E.H.R.R. 330, 333, 336–37, 358–59 (1996).

Both witnesses expressed the wish to remain anonymous and not to appear in court. Witness Y.16 stated that he had in the past suffered injuries at the hands of another drug dealer after he had "talked" and feared similar reprisals from the applicant. Witness Y.15 stated that he had in the past been threatened by drug dealers if he were to talk. He further stated that the applicant was aggressive. The investigating judge concluded from the reasons given that both witnesses had sufficient reason to wish to maintain their anonymity and not to appear in open court.

Y.15 and Y.16 were extensively questioned, both by the investigating judge and by the applicant's lawyer. The latter inquired, inter alia, into their reasons for testifying against the dealer who they both said sold good quality drugs and asked them whether they were being paid for giving evidence. Neither Y.15 nor Y.16 refused to answer any of the questions put by the applicant's lawyer. They both stated that they had bought drugs from the applicant and that they had seen him selling drugs to others. They again identified him from the police photograph and gave descriptions of his appearance and dress. (...)

It is true that Article 6 does not explicitly require the interests of witnesses in general, and those of victims called upon to testify in particular, to be taken into consideration. However, their life, liberty or security of person may be at stake, as may interests coming generally within the ambit of Article 8 of the Convention. Such interests of witnesses and victims are in principle protected by other, substantive provisions of the Convention, which imply that Contracting States should organise their criminal proceedings in such a way that those interests are not unjustifiably imperiled. Against this background, principles of fair trial also require that in appropriate cases the interests of the defence are balanced against those of witnesses or victims called upon to testify. (...)

The maintenance of the anonymity of the witnesses Y.15 and Y.16 presented the defence with difficulties which criminal proceedings should not normally involve. Nevertheless, no violation of Article 6(1) taken together with Article 6(3)(d) of the convention can be found if it is established that the handicaps under which the defence laboured were sufficiently counterbalanced by the procedures followed by the judicial authorities.

In the instant case the anonymous witnesses were questioned at the appeals stage in the presence of counsel by an investigating judge who was aware of their identity, even if the defence was not. She noted, in the official record of her findings dated 19 November 1990, circumstances on the basis of which the Court of Appeal was able to draw conclusions as to the reliability of their evidence. In this respect the present case is to be distinguished from that of Kostovski. Counsel was not only present, but he was put in a position to ask the witnesses whatever questions he considered to be in the interests of the defence except in so far as they might lead to the disclosure of their identity, and these questions were all answered. In this respect also the present case differs from that of Kostovski.

While it would clearly have been preferable for the applicant to have attended the questioning of the witnesses, the Court considers, on balance, that the Amsterdam Court of Appeal was entitled to consider that the interests of the applicant were in this respect outweighed by the need to ensure the safety of the witnesses.

Questions

1. Do you agree with the compromise reached by the European Court of Human Rights?

2. Do American courts engage in any similar balancing of the right to confront witnesses with the interest in protecting their anonymity or avoiding a face-to-face confrontation with the defendant?[213]

Relevant U.S. Case Law

Smith v. Illinois, 390 U.S. 129 (1968)

Coy v. Iowa, 487 U.S. 1012 (1988)

Maryland v. Craig, 497 U.S. 836 (1990)

---

213. In the U.S. it is not possible for a crucial prosecution witness to testify anonymously at trial. Smith v. Illinois, 390 U.S. 129 (1968). The U.S. Supreme Court has disallowed separating the defendant from a witness by using a screen, Coy v. Iowa, 487 U.S. 1012 (1988), a practice used in Spain, but has allowed the use of closed-circuit television which enables the defendant to see the witness while testifying in room separate from him. Maryland v. Craig, 497 U.S. 836 (1990). The identity of an undercover informant used during the investigation must even be revealed if he or she could be a material witness to defendant's guilt or innocence. Roviaro v. United States, 353 U.S. 53 (1957). While a witness's identity may be kept secret during the police inquest in France, any deposition during the preliminary examination is a nullity if the person's identity is not disclosed. PRADEL, *supra* note 31, at 349–50.

E. The Admissibility of Hearsay as Corroborative Evidence

Decision of March 31, 1989 (German Supreme Court)[214]

The superior court acquitted the defendant of the charge of having participated as a co-perpetrator in a bank robbery of the *Kreissparkasse* in D, which was committed on March 27, 1986, with use of handguns.

The public prosecutor directs its cassation against this judgment. (…)

The appellate remedy is successful.

The objection proves well-founded, that the superior court violated its duty to determine the truth (§ 244(2) StPO). The appellant rightfully complains that the penal chamber failed to examine public prosecutor D. and master detective H. as witnesses as to the statement that an anonymous informant made during their interrogation of him.

The penal chamber cannot be affirmed in its decision that the examination of the two witnesses was inadmissible.

That the witnesses were only going to state what a third person whom they questioned told them about the case during the examination does not prevent its admissibility. A hearsay witness is admissible evidence under the Code of Criminal Procedure; in principle there are no objections to questioning interrogators about statements that an informant made to them. (…) This applies when such evidence should substitute for the immediate questioning of the informant, in any case, if this witness is unavailable to the court.

This was the case here. The penal chamber was prohibited from examining the informant, because it had no knowledge of his identity and the public authorities refused to give information as to his identity or to give the interrogators permission which would have made it possible to reveal the identity of the informant. Thus the informant was "barred" from being a witness who could be examined in court.

The informant is, however, not always unavailable if the public authorities refuse to "release" him. The court need not, without more, concur with the declaration of a bar made by public authorities. It

---

214. BGHSt 36, 159, 160–61, 164–66.

must, moreover, make all necessary efforts under the circumstances of the case to eliminate the contravening obstacle to the questioning of the informant. (...) Thus it must not satisfy itself with the declaration of the bar of a subordinate public authority but must seek a decision by the superior governmental authority, (...) which should present legal reasons for the refusal. (...)

These prerequisites existed here. The declarations of a bar came from the highest state government authorities. They contained, respectively, reasons from which was evident why the identity of the informant in the opinion of the public authorities could not be revealed. (...)

The examination by the interrogators was thus admissible, and was therefore required in order to clarify the facts.

That the penal chamber—as it emphasized in its judgment reasons—could not, on the one hand, acquire any direct personal impression of the anonymous informant and on the other hand could not adopt the judgment of the credibility from the interrogators, does not contradict this. (...) This predicament, which every court, as a rule, in such or similar manner, confronts when it can only examine a hearsay witness, was in the instant case not a sufficient reason to refuse to examine the two witnesses. (...)

In the instant case the penal chamber should have seen itself compelled, under all of the points of view under consideration, to examine both interrogators. The subject of proof was of substantial importance: it was a question of the introduction of an "extrajudicial confession," that the defendant, according to the statements of the informant, made to him. The interrogators were a public prosecutor and a police official, that is, persons who are familiar with investigations in criminal cases due to their profession. They would not only have taken reports in conservation, but would have conducted a formal interrogation and made transcripts of the examination which would serve them as supports for their memory as to the course and results of the examination. It could also be excluded that they—not lastly on the basis of their professional experience in examining witnesses—would make observations about the testimonial conduct of the informant which would be capable of giving the court a factual basis for judging the credibility of the informant. Clearly the state of the evidence was not such that the statements of the informant were the only incriminating evidence against the defendant. In the judgment reasons a sequence of other indications are listed and discussed which could point to the identity of the defendant as a perpetrator; they were also evaluated as incriminating evidence by the court (...).

This circumstantial evidence did not suffice for the chamber to justify a guilty verdict. It if had, in addition, included the statements of the informant mediated by the interrogators, then a substantially different picture would be generated: it would then not be a long shot, that the penal chamber, especially in the event of agreement of the details described by the informant with the details of the execution of the act which were determined—would have come to a conviction as to the identity of the defendant as a perpetrator.

Compare the German approach to hearsay with that of the European Court of Human Rights in the *Kostovski, Doorson,* and *Delta* cases. Note the German Supreme Court's emphasis on the fact that the proposed hearsay testimony would not have been the only incriminating evidence, although the other evidence would have been insufficient for a judgment of guilt. In the cases of the European Court the hearsay evidence was always the only evidence of certain crucial elements of the prosecution's case. In all cases the emphasis is on the fact that a judgment of guilt cannot rest alone on hearsay statements where the defendant has no right to confront the witness. It appears that hearsay is still admissible in Europe as long as it is inherently reliable and corroborated by other evidence. The principle of free evaluation of evidence tends to favor more inclusive rules and is in tension with the right to confrontation which would tend to exclude hearsay.

Chapter Six

Procedural Economy: Avoiding the Trial with All Its Guarantees

I. Different Procedures for Different Substantive Crimes: Avoiding Trials with Lay Participation

Concerns of procedural economy and predictability of decision making have always led courts, prosecutors and the defense to experiment with ways of simplifying trials, if the results they desired could be obtained. Since the early 19th Century, French prosecutors have manipulated the jurisdiction of cases by charging a case, that would otherwise be a serious felony subject to the jury court or *cour d'assise*, as a lesser crime subject to the municipal courts in which professional judges alone were the triers of fact.[215] In England there are certain types of lesser felonies called "either-way" offenses which can be tried either in the jury court, the *Crown Court*, or in the *Magistrates' Court*, usually composed of three lay part-time judges where the maximum sentence which may be imposed is substantially lower. Thus, the defendant who goes to trial in the *Magistrates' Court* is more likely to be convicted, but also more likely to get a milder sentence. The procedure in "either-way" cases is discussed in the following case:

---

215. This practice is called *correctionnalisation*, derived from the French name for the court without jury, the *tribunal correctionnel*. For a discussion and critique of this practice, *see* PRADEL, *supra* note 31, at 96–100.

Regina v. Canterbury et al.
(English Divisional Court) (1982)[216]

[In two consolidated cases defendants were charged with aggravated vandalism and disturbing the peace and requested trial by jury as they were "either-way" offenses. The prosecutor failed to proceed and recharged lesser offenses where only a summary trial in the Magistrates' Court without jury was possible.]

I am prepared to assume that there does exist in the justices an inherent power to act so as to prevent any flagrant abuse of the processes of this court, limited necessarily by any relevant statutory obligation. This power, if it exists, would have to be exercised by the justices very sparingly and only in the most obvious circumstances which disclose blatant injustice. There must be, somewhere, some limit as to what can be done before the court (...). [The Court then cites language from an earlier case:]

"The accused, a soldier, was alleged, during a barrack room quarrel, to have stabbed another soldier in the back with a bayonet, the injury being of so serious a nature that the doctors were of opinion that the injured man could not survive, and steps were taken to get his evidence by deposition. He, however, recovered, and at the trial before a court of summary jurisdiction, where the accused was charged (...) with 'wounding with intent to do grievous bodily harm,' the justices at the request of both the prosecution and the defence, allowed the charge to be reduced to one of 'unlawful wounding' and proceeded to deal with the case summarily. The accused pleaded guilty to the misdemeanour and the justices retired to their room to consider their sentence." (...)

"Here is a case in which a man's life has been seriously imperiled and if he had died, this applicant, the accused, would have been charged with murder. It was never intended that where a man, whether under the influence of drink or not, takes a bayonet and stabs a fellow soldier in the back, with the consequences which are disclosed in this case, justices should deal with such a case by reason of that section. For justices to exercise jurisdiction under that section by treating a case of this sort as nothing much more than common assault is a most extraordinary state of affairs. Justices should remember that they have to deal with matters of this sort judicially, and, although they must take into ac-

---

216. [1982] 1 Q.B. 389, 411–12, 414–15.

count what the prosecution and the defence say with regard to whether or not it is a proper case for the charge to be reduced, they are not bound to assent to dealing with the case summarily because the prosecution want to get the matter dealt with there and then, without the necessity of going to the assizes, where this case undoubtedly should have been sent."

It seems to me, however, that in this particular case it cannot be said that there was any abuse of the process of the court. (...) In deed, what the prosecution have done is to lower the nature of the case against the defendants and the possible consequential penalties. We have a Gilbertian result here of applicants complaining that they are now charged with lesser offences than those which they originally had to face. The prosecution, it is conceded, acted in accordance with the statutory provision and, in my judgment, there was nothing in the result which was unfair. (...)

Before parting with this case, I should say this. Providing that the offences are not grave ones and that the powers of the justices vis-á-vis sentence are appropriate, there is no reason why the prosecuting authority should not charge an offence which is not the gravest possible allegation on the facts. There may be many reasons for choosing a lesser charge—amongst other ones, speed of trial, sufficiency of proof, and trial summarily rather than on indictment. It is necessarily a matter of discretion and careful choice. It is not easy for a prosecuting authority to steer between Scylla and Charybdis, but it is a tolerably wide passage through which they have to navigate. Prosecuting authorities have the duty to exercise great care in selecting the proper charges to prefer in any case. (...) [I]f in reality the offence is nothing more than can properly be dealt with summarily by the justices, then it is proper so to charge it, despite the fact that the defendant may thereby lose his right to trial by jury if, indeed, it is, on balance, properly to be described as a loss at all. It is, however, to be hoped that, where proper, the lesser charges will be preferred at the outset, and the sort of discussion we have in these two matters may thereby be avoided.

There have always been a multiplicity of criminal procedures, of the ways society responds to crime. In ancient times, defendants were subjected to trials by ordeal, duel, and oath-helpers or compurgators,[217] and even to trial by self-help in flagrant cases. In early inquisitorial times, accusatorial procedure

---

217. Esmein, *supra* note 2, at 34–36.

remained for normal crimes involving victims, whereas inquisitorial procedure was reserved for more serious crimes and crimes against the state.[218]

In the 19th Century, reforms of the inquisitorial systems led to introduction of jury trials for the more serious crimes, but mixed courts or panels of professional judges were maintained for the trials of lesser crimes. We have seen in an 1884 French case[219] that procedures before professional courts retained much of their inquisitorial trappings, such as reading of documents from the preliminary investigation dossier. Thus the substantive nature of a crime and the gravity of the punishment determine the procedure to be followed. In general, the procedures for serious charges often involve popular participation in the determination of guilt and/or punishment and enhanced participation of the victim, defendant and the public by virtue of the greater publicity and immediacy of the taking of the evidence. The current trend is for infractions and misdemeanors punishable by less than a determinate number of years to be tried by a single professional judge.[220]

Questions

1. Is it fair to the defendant to intentionally charge a less serious crime than the one she arguably committed, and thereby deprive her of trial before a jury or mixed court with greater procedural guarantees? Is it fair to the victim? To society as a whole?

2. Is there any difference between a prosecutor charging a lesser crime that the defendant actually did not commit and the jury finding a defendant guilty of a lesser crime that the defendant actually did not commit after trial? Does this not violate the principle of material truth?

3. Is it fair to trade the right to jury trial (or trial before a mixed court) with its greater guarantees for a more summary trial with a lesser threatened punishment before a professional court?

4. Do these practices look a lot like plea bargaining?

---

218. One finds both accusatorial and inquisitorial procedures in the CONSTITUTIO CRIMINALIS CAROLINA (1532), *see supra*, note 4. THOMAS WEIGEND, DELIKTSOPFER UND STRAFVERFAHREN 85 (1989).

219. *Supra*, at 125.

220. Single judges handle all cases punishable by less than two years in Germany. § 25 Gerichtsverfassungsgesetz (Law on Court Organization) (hereafter GVG (Germany), all cites from STRAFPROZESSORDNUNG 207–47 (37th ed. DTV 2004); in Russia single judges hear cases punishable by less than ten years. § 30(2)(1) UPK (Russia).

II. Procedural Encouragement of Confessions to Avoid or Simplify the Trial

Confessions obtained by torture did not lead to any mitigation of sentence and, on the contrary, often led to the execution of the confessor because torture was not employed in misdemeanor, non-capital cases. Once torture was officially prohibited, confessions had to be induced through statutory mitigation of sentence for the remorseful accused who spared the investigating authorities the need to mount a full investigation or present a full case at trial.[221] One should ask whether such confessions, motivated perhaps by a desire for lenient treatment, are necessarily voluntary or always truthful. On the European continent, perhaps due to skepticism about the truthfulness of confessions arising from that area's inquisitorial past, defendants are often not allowed to make "guilty pleas" that result in an immediately binding judgment, as is possible in the U.S. and England.

Decision of August 28, 1997 (German Supreme Court)[222]

The superior court sentenced the defendant and the co-defendant E, as to whom the judgment is final, for aggravated robbery-like extortion in two cases to an aggregate imprisonment of twelve years. (...)

In imposing punishment it considered that the defendant's confession, among other circumstances, mitigated the punishment. In the judgment reasons the following is additionally expostulated in relation to both defendants: "Both the individual punishments as well as the aggregate punishment in this magnitude were agreed upon moreover in a public hearing with the defendants, defense counsel and the public prosecutor, along with a contemporaneous conditional dismissal of other charges within the context of a deal to terminate the proceedings."

[The Court summarizes the arguments of opponents of "deals" and their proponents and summarizes the case law which overwhelmingly supports procedural bargaining.]

The chamber is of the opinion, that the code of criminal procedure does not generally forbid agreements between the court and the pro-

---

221. Mirjan Damaska, *Negotiated Justice in International Criminal Courts*, 2 J. Int'l Crim. Just. 1019, 1020 (2004).
222. BGHSt 43, 195, 195–96, 202–10.

cedural participants, which concern themselves with the question of the magnitude of punishment upon the giving of a confession.

It is true, to be sure, that the German law of criminal procedure is designed in a way which is fundamentally inimical to settlements (...); it prohibits the free disposition of the court and the procedural participants over the state's right to punish, the adherence to procedural principles, the subjection to law and the principles of punishment (...).

On the other hand, the provisions of § 153a StPO, which make possible the conditional dismissal of the proceedings with the consent of the defendant and the public prosecutor, show that an agreement between the procedural participants—even as to the result and the termination of criminal proceedings—is not wholly alien to German criminal procedure. In addition, there are other provisions which allow for the consent of the affected party to a certain legal consequence and are therefore linked, as a rule, with a prognosis as to the result of the trial, a conversation about the factual and legal situation and an agreement between the parties (...).

It cannot therefore be deduced from the code of criminal procedure itself that deals as to the result of the trial are completely inadmissible (...). Deals, which have as their content the defendant's making of a confession in exchange for a promise of mitigation of punishment by the court, are moreover fundamentally possible; they do not at the outset violate constitutional or procedural principles. An agreement must be measured in each case, in its concrete formulation, against non-waivable principles of procedural and substantive criminal law; they must satisfy these principles not only with respect to their realization but also with respect to their content.

The point of departure for testing the admissibility of a deal is the general right of the defendant, derived from the principle of due process (Arts. 20(3), 2(a) Const.), to a fair trial with the interpretations which this principle has found in the procedural principles of the law of criminal procedure. This excludes from the outset a deal involving a guilt-finding. Its foundation must always and exclusively be the actual given facts of the case according to the conviction of the court; its evaluation and categorization from a criminal law perspective may not be the result of an agreement. A deal may also not result in a situation where the guilty judgment against the defendant is based, without more, on a confession arising from an agreement, without the court being convinced of its correctness. The court remains obligated to the command of ascertaining the truth. The credibility of the confession must therefore be examined; the taking of evidence to this end must not be omitted (...).

It is obvious that the defendant's free determination of his will must be maintained during the efforts of the participants to realize a deal and he must not be pressured to confess through threats of a higher punishment or through promises of a benefit not provided by law (...). During the settlement discussions, § 136a StPO must therefore be adhered to, along with the principle that no one is obligated to incriminate himself (*nemo tenetur se ipsum accusare*). The promise of a benefit not provided by law is not, however, *per se* present, when the court holds out to the defendant the prospect of a mitigation of punishment in the event of a confession (...).

On the other hand, it is not permissible for the court to condition the prospect of a more mitigated punishment on a promise by the defendant to waive appellate remedies. This signifies, on the one hand, an impermissible linkage of the right to appeal with the magnitude of the punishment on which it should have no influence. On the other hand, the defendant can waive appellate remedies at the earliest after the pronouncement of judgment (...); the court must therefore never demand of him that he surrenders this possibility of control before the conclusion of the trial and notice of the decision.

One of the substantial doubts as to the admissibility of deals results from the fact that they are often made outside of the trial (...).

This practice violates the principle of publicity (...), according to which the proceedings in the trial court (including the pronouncement of judgments and orders) is public. "The publicity of criminal proceedings belongs to the fundamental institutions of the state under the rule of law. The provisions relating thereto shall guarantee that the court adjudication be played out fundamentally with 'complete publicity' and not behind closed doors." (...). The principle of publicity seeks to guarantee the interest of the general public in information and the control of the administration of justice and thus promote trust in the adjudication of the courts. This control is, however, only possible when the public can view the important stages of the proceedings which lead to judgment (...). If a deal, however, is transferred out of the public trial, then the trial becomes a mere facade which veils any public view into the circumstances which lay at the foundation of the judgment.

An agreement between the court and the other parties which has as its object the defendant's admissions and the magnitude of the punishment must take place in the public trial—following deliberation by the entire panel of judges. This does not exclude the occurrence of preliminary discussions between the parties before or outside of the proceedings in order to clarify whether there is an interest in such discussions and the respective "bargaining positions;" the court must, however, then reveal the important content and the results of these discussions in the trial (...).

Public discussion during the trial guarantees, as well, the adherence to a further non-waivable criterion for an agreement to be admissible, namely, the inclusion of all the parties. Because such conversations are of important significance for the rest of the trial and the judgment, they must take place only with the knowledge and participation of all the parties and the persons responsible for deciding the case. A deal without the participation of the defendant himself or, similarly, without the lay assessors, is especially inadmissible.

It is important thereby that deals about the content and result of the proceedings do not take place under the cloak of secrecy and uncontrollability; they may not be conducted simultaneously, as an autonomous, informal procedure collateral to the actual trial, without gaining entry into the latter. Deals must therefore be revealed, their content must be subject to examination by all participants and also for the reviewing court. The result of the deal must—inasmuch as it concerns an important procedural event—be entered into the trial record (...). Only thus will later disputes about supposedly consummated deals be (...) avoided (...).

The court may not violate §§ 260(1), 261 StPO in the deal by making a binding promise as to the magnitude of the punishment to be imposed; for the court must decide the punishment in the judgment deliberations based on the material in the trial. This judicial decision making may not be anticipated through a fixing of a concrete punishment; binding the court to a particular procedural result before the conclusion of the trial is excluded (...). Such a self-binding includes at the same time a violation of substantive legal sentencing principles (...) because the court is no longer free in the judgment deliberations to assess the magnitude of the punishment based on the relevant sentencing criteria in relation to the guilt of the perpetrator.

It is acceptable, on the other hand, when the court, in the case of a credible confession made in the course of an agreement, sets a maximum punishment which it will not exceed (...). When the defendant makes a confession he limits his defense possibilities, namely, to a narrow area. He can then, as a rule, produce nothing further against his conviction and only attempt to influence the magnitude of the sentence to be imposed. It is therefore not improper for him to want to know, before making the confession, how the court will evaluate it in assessing punishment.

If the court, in accordance therewith, explains that the punishment in the event of the making of a confession will not exceed a particular limit, that the—usually very broad—range of punishment provided by law will thus be restricted in a particular way, then the decision of the court has not been anticipated. The determination of a concrete punishment after weighing all sentencing criteria is reserved for the judgment deliberations. Such a promise also does not eliminate the necessary impartiality and objectivity of the court; for the fact that the court has an opinion as to the possible result of the proceedings during the proceedings—in anticipation of the further course of the proceedings and the result of the deliberations—is not alien to the code of criminal procedure and lies at the root of the decision as to setting the case for trial or ordering pretrial detention.

The deal does not replace the judgment, which would be inadmissible and contradict the principles of the code of criminal procedure. Inasmuch as the court, because of the confession, reduces (at times substantially) the upper limit of punishment in contrast to those who deny the act, the punishment imposed in the judgment will often, to be sure, reach this limit. This does not, however, make the agreement inadmissible (...); for the court retains the power to impose a punishment which lies under this limit after the judgment deliberations. (...)

The agreement thus achieved remains subject to the condition that the judgment later announced must accord with the substantive law and be justifiable after considering all the circumstances.

The pronouncement of the punishment may not abandon "the foundations of a guilt-proportionate punishment." The court may in no case avoid these criteria in the hopes of encouraging a confession and fix a magnitude of punishment which does not reflect the wrongfulness of the act (...). Even when an agreement takes place which has as its object the confession of the defendant, the court must determine the magnitude of the punishment according to the general principles of sentencing and weigh all circumstances that speak for and against the defendant. The court is, however, not prevented from according to the confession of the defendant significance which mitigates the sentence, even when the defendant made the confession for tactical procedural reasons and obviously not due to insight into his guilt and remorse at the outset (...).

If an agreement has occurred in such a way in a public hearing including all parties, then the court is bound by it. This results from the principles of a fair trial, which include that the court may not act contrary to its own earlier explanations upon which a party has relied; the situation of trust which the court has thus created prevents it from deviating from its earlier explanation (...). If, however, grave new circumstances present themselves after the deal which were earlier unknown to the court and could influence the judgment, then the court may deviate from the settled deal. Such circumstances could, for instance, be that the act turns out to be a felony instead of a misdemeanor due to new facts or evidence (...) or that serious prior convictions of the defendant were unknown. In such a case the court must point to this possibility during the public trial and explain the circumstances. (...)

[The Supreme Court then reverses the conviction because the judge had set a firm sentence if the defendant confessed.]

Compare the emphasis on ascertaining the truth and verifying the truthfulness of the confession in the above case with the approach of the following case:

Decision of June 10, 1998 (German Supreme Court)[223]

[Defendant was charged with 247 counts of sexual assault on his daughter when she was between the ages of eleven and seventeen, including one rape and one sodomy.]

After the chamber indicated the prospect of an aggregate term of imprisonment of eight years in the event of a confession after a corresponding inquiry by defense counsel at the trial, the defendant allowed his defense counsel to declare that the charges in the accusatory pleading were, in essence, true. When questioned he himself stated that the charges were correct in the form in which they were charged. All agreed to refrain from questioning the victim who left the courtroom in an emotionally aroused state after the accusatory pleading was read.

The superior court found the defendant to be guilty in 245 cases of sexual abuse of wards, in 40 thereof in unity with sexual abuse of children and in one case in unity with rape, and, in addition, in two other cases of abuse of a ward; it sentenced him, as a consequence, to an aggregate term of imprisonment of eight years. (...).

The fact that the defendant only admitted the charges in the accusatory pleading in a superficial way did not have to prevent the court from believing the confession and basing its findings thereon. The principle of free judicial evaluation of the evidence also applies to the evaluation of a confession (...). The trial court, however, if it desires to base the conviction of the defendant on his admissions, must be convinced of their correctness; this was—as shown—here the case. When, and under which circumstances, it may or may not come to this conviction may not, in principle, be prescribed. This applies also

---

223. BGHSt NStZ 1999, 92, 93–94.

when there is a question whether or not a confession, based on the nature of its content, is sufficient for the proof of the charges in the accusatory pleading. The freedom of the trial court's evaluation reaches, however, its limits, where the defendant does not confirm the substantive presuppositions of the accusatory pleading as correct but rather limits himself to a position which includes a merely procedural admission or a formal acceptance of the charges; for such a position may, to be sure, be a piece of circumstantial evidence as such, but it cannot provide by itself alone the evidentiary basis for the matter if the statement's content lacks factual content which can support the conviction.

This was not the case here, however. The defendant, after the as yet uncertain declaration of his defense counsel that the charges in the accusatory pleading were "in essence" true, admitted after questioning that the charges were correct in the form in which they were charged. This related without doubt to the description of the acts as they were contained in the accusatory pleading, which was concrete enough in order to be confirmed through a simple affirmation that did not contain anything which the defendant was prevented from knowing.

The fact that the defendant first made his confession after the prospect of a particular measure of punishment was laid out, does not mean that the superior court was prevented from finding it to be believable. As the Supreme Court has already emphasized, an agreement as to the measure of punishment may not, however, result in a confession arising in such a manner being made the basis of a finding of guilt without the court being convinced of its correctness. The court remains obligated to the requirement of ascertaining the truth; the taking of evidence which becomes necessary to achieve this end should not be omitted (...). That the required review did not take place cannot itself lead to the conclusion that an express discussion including substantial arguments for judging the credibility of the confession is absent from the judgment reasons. For such a discussion is not always required; it is required only when circumstances exist which are capable of laying a foundation for doubt as to the correctness of the confession. (...)

The instant case offers, however, no particularities which—compared with the general danger of giving a false confession in order to receive benefits in the measure of punishment—could be a foundation for heightened doubts as to the correctness of the confession: the initiative came from defense counsel, who directed an inquiry as to the measure of punishment to the chamber; it gave him the desired answer and, in the case of a confession, named what was itself a serious punishment. In this course of events, concern that the defendant could have given a false confession in order to achieve a mitigated punishment did not arise; a discussion of this argument in the judgment reasons was not necessary.

If there was a lack of points of reference worthy of discussion which spoke against the credibility of the confession, then, on the other hand, circumstances were present which were capable of supporting the conviction as to its correctness. They are found in the conduct of the victim of the act, the collateral complainant, who left the courtroom at the time of the reading of the accusatory pleading in an emotionally aroused state and, after the confession of the defendant, declared that she never believed that her father would admit, that she forgave the majority and felt that he had changed and asked for the mildest possible punishment (…).

Note how the principle of the "free evaluation of evidence" forms the basis for a judge to use a superficial, perfunctory confession as the basis for a finding of guilt, even if the confession was motivated by the prospect of a reduced sentence. The principle of material truth can be interpreted quite flexibly, leading to results similar to those achieved by American plea bargaining.

III. Accepting the Prosecution's Pleadings: A Way around the Guilty Plea for Lesser Crimes

When they have not resorted to decriminalization, many European countries have developed special procedures for infractions or misdemeanors, especially those which are only punished by fines. Dismissals, conditioned on the defendant paying monetary penalties, making restitution, doing volunteer work, etc., procedures similar to what is called "diversion" in the U.S., are becoming increasingly popular for resolving such minor cases.[224] Prosecutors in many countries may now issue so-called "penal orders," in which they request a particular punishment (usually a fine) for the commission of the charged infraction or misdemeanor. The accused will then have a certain period of time to object to the prosecutor's order. If the time elapses without objection, the order becomes final and the fine becomes due. There is no trial, but the judge to whom the order is simultaneously sent, issues a judg-

---

224. *See* Thaman, *Plea-Bargaining, supra* note 10, at 964–66.

ment and theoretically has the possibility of rejecting the order if there appears to be an insufficient factual basis for conviction.[225]

The Italian CCP of 1988 introduced a procedure called "application for punishment on request of the parties" which originally provided for a discount of one-third in cases in which a maximum punishment of three years imprisonment was threatened.[226]

Decision No. 313 of July 3, 1990
(Italian Constitutional Court)[227]

In substance, both remitting [courts] lament that the agreement of the parties on the measure of punishment deprives the judge of any supervision of its congruity and of any possibility of expressing effective reasons for imposing it, given that they would be limited to the so-called "framework of legitimacy" and to the limits which were requested upon consent of the parties. (...)

Both, moreover, maintain that such a situation comes into conflict with Art. 101(1) Const. because the judge, instead of being subject only to the law, would be substantially bound by the will of the parties except in the control of the legitimacy of the juridical definition of the facts and attendant circumstances. In particular, the judge would remain deprived of the power of determining the punishment, not by virtue of predetermined rigorous criteria, but because of a discretionary power attributed to other subjects. (...)

In reality, the scope within which the agreement becomes possible is subject to rigorous conditions and the punishment must remain within the limit of two years of imprisonment. This means that the agreement is admissible only for those offenses which provide for a minimum amount of punishment, which may then be reduced, together with all other possible reductions, within the aforesaid limits.

---

225. *Id.*, at 969–71. *See* in particular, §§ 407, 408(2,3), 409(1) StPO (Germany) (Appendix, 251–52); §§ 459–460 CPP (Italy); §§ 524–528-1 CCP (France).

226. The procedure is now simply called "application for punishment" and, since 2003, applies to crimes punishable by up to five years. *See* § 444(1,2) CPP (Italy) (Appendix, 255). The Italians call this procedure the *patteggiamento* or "deal." Russia introduced a similar procedure in 2001 for cases punishable by up to five years, but in 2003 it was extended to cases punishable by up to 10 years. §§ 314–317 UPK (Russia).

227. 35 Giur. cost. 1981, 1988, 1990–93.

Equally predetermined is the necessity that conditions do not exist which could require an acquittal "on the basis of the file." If such exist, therefore, the power-duty of the judge trumps the will of the parties. (...)

In exercising control over the legal definition of the facts, the judge already not only evaluates the correctness of a logical-juridical operation. (...) Here, on the other hand, the judge develops his conviction directly from the results of the file and not from the way the parties have evaluated them, for he may respond that the legal definition to which the parties adhere is not that which is effectively derived from the results. And this is already an evaluation on the merits and an essential aspect of the subjugation of the judge only to the law. (...)

Thus, one may also imply that the judge, while always inspired to a correct evaluation of the results, not only has a power-duty to control—as has been said—the correctness of the circumstances which the parties have alleged, but may also freely refer to others, both mitigating and aggravating, and thus differentially condition the final act of balancing. (...)

It can thus also not be accepted that the judgment pursuant to § 444 CPP contains no reasons which express the conviction of the judge. The pronouncement of the disposition which has been requested by the parties is not effectively a giving of reasons—as the municipal court itself notes—but this does not signify that the duty of the judge relating to the giving of reasons is exhausted in the pronouncement.

In reality, the judge may not leave the appreciation of the correctness, or lack thereof, of the legal definition of the facts derived from the file results, without any justification in his judgment, for he is required to give the reasons why the mitigating or aggravating circumstances and the eventual predomination or equivalence of one aspect in relation to others, is or is not deemed to be plausible in the sense presented by the parties in their consensual request.

On the other hand, the general model of the judgment which the legislator delineates (...) provides for a "concise exposition of the reasons in fact and law upon which the decision is based." This concerns a requirement which is not excluded in the particular configuration of judgment provided in § 444 CPP, even if it is obviously minimized.

It is a case, therefore, of an order with reasons emitted by an ordinary judicial authority in the exercise of jurisdiction which ranges from the merits to legitimacy.

Now the complaint shall be examined, which alleges that the defendant is applying a punishment to himself, thus signifying a disposition of the right to personal liberty and defense in violation of Arts. 23, 24 of the Const., which are fundamental, non-disposable rights.

As was said above, the [contested provisions], rather than violating the parameters of Art. 101(1) Const., exclude the possibility of the judge taking no part in the determination of the punishment.

Here one must furthermore add that the direct ascertainment, aimed at excluding the existence within the contents of the file of elements which negate responsibility or punishability, integrates an important participation of the judge in the investigation of responsibility.

It should not be forgotten that, with a request for application of punishment, the defendant does not substantially deny his responsibility and knowingly waives any appellate remedy if the request is accepted (§ 448(2) CPP). Therefore, if there arises perplexity as to the effective meaning of his request, the judge has ample possibility to determine if it is sincere, and is able to summon the defendant to hear him personally: this is also a method of ascertainment. (...)

It is not exactly the case, therefore, that it is the defendant who imposes punishment upon himself and not the judge who does so. (...) [I]t is thus not the case of a defendant imposing something on himself, but only that of a request which is presented to the judge with the consent of the public prosecutor. It is thus obvious, on the formal level, that the request will have no effect on the personal liberty of the petitioner if the judges does not intervene, using the powers he possesses, with a judgment which concretely imposes the proposed punishment. (...)

However, one can absolutely not agree with the notion that the defendant "disposes" of his "non-disposable" personal liberty by personally placing limits on it.

When he asks for the application of a punishment, the defendant, in reality, only does so to reduce to the minimum a larger sacrifice of his liberty which he anticipates at the conclusion of an ordinary trial. And with respect to the defense, this possibility which the law offers to the defendant is an efficient instrument for him to achieve, with security, a minimal punishment by withdrawing himself from a risk of more serious penalties, thereby (...) benefiting from the conditional suspension.

Furthermore, one must avoid the danger of confounding the right to liberty and the right of defense with the absolute obligation of exercising them. The fundamental law guarantees the conditions for exercising the right of personal liberty and the right of defense in all of their legitimate aspects, but it neither mandates nor assumes that such exercise be obligatory.

Finally, it is also not clear why the remitting municipal court deems that in § 444 CPP there is a substantial reversal of the burden of proof which violates the presumption of innocence contained in Art. 27(2) Const.

To be sure, the initiative of the parties in the evidentiary realm is preponderant in the new procedural law, but this does not in fact change the principle, not even in the special procedure under examination, that the judge is required at the outset to examine *ex officio* if there exists in the file evidence that the act did not occur or the defendant did not commit it. Afterwards, if this first review is negative and if the defendant claims to have evidence which proves his own innocence, no one obliges him to request the application of punishment and he has at his disposition the guarantees of the ordinary procedure. In other words, whoever requests the application of punishment must state that he waives the right to avail himself of the power to dispute the accusation, and in the absence of such a waiver this would signify a violation of the principle of the presumption of innocence, which continues to play its role until a judgment becomes final.

The defendant, by accepting a discount of one-third on his sentence, does not really plead guilty but requests punishment within the reduced range without disputing guilt. It is still the judge who must evaluate the file, yet not for the purpose of finding guilt, but only for excluding innocence. Note the reticence in allowing the defendant himself to determine the outcome of the trial by pleading guilty. This procedure, however, is not conducted by the trial judge but by the judge of the investigation, who evaluates the results of the preliminary investigation contained in the investigative dossier and then imposes the reduced sentence or even acquits, if he/she finds that there is insufficient incriminating evidence in the file.

Decision of February 19, 1990 (Italian Supreme Court)[228]

[Defendants were found guilty following a "deal" of attempted arson and sentenced to two years imprisonment.]

---

228. Cass. penale, No. 15, 44, 45, 47 (1990).

It has been asserted that the judgment runs afoul of the model legislatively provided in the hypotheses of this particular special procedure in that the provision does not foresee that the judge, once he has accepted the request for application of punishment agreed upon by the parties, can affirm the responsibility of the defendants and issue a judgment of conviction.

They request, therefore, the annulment of the contested judgment and substitution, in lieu of the declaration of guilt and the conviction, of a more suitable expression, i.e., that actually consented to: an application of punishment. (...)

[A] conviction is, as it has been happily defined, "a judgment of positive and constitutive ascertainment," in which the judge ascertains the responsibility of the defendant and thence declares the consequences emanating from such jurisdictional ascertainment, with the consequence, which is also quite clear, that decisions cannot be classified as convictions in which one cannot perceive the inseparable combination of "recognition of responsibility — application of punishment."

In is undisputed in the pronouncement under discussion that the second of the terms of this combination (application of punishment) is present, while the first is absent, that is, the recognition of responsibility, which cannot be obtained without a complete ascertainment on the part of the judge. Here the judge is even denied the possibility of making a preliminary ascertainment and is only obligated to limit himself to examining if, "based on the file," one can exclude the possibility of proof of innocence. It is true that the Constitutional Court recently affirmed that "the application of punishment upon request of the parties (...) serves to indicate an agreement between the public prosecutor and the defendant on the merits of the accusatory pleading. (...). But this "agreement" may certainly not be substituted for the ascertainment of the truth which is the proper and exclusive duty of the judge and may not be delegated to anyone else, and that even a full admission by the accused of his complete responsibility for the commission of the crime and the absence of any cause of justification (which in the request for application of punishment could implicitly be reviewed) could not bind the judge as to an affirmation of the guilt of the person under investigation.

And such conclusions are reinforced in the end by considerations that recourse to this form of anticipated definition of the procedure is only permitted during the phase of the preliminary investigation (§ 447 CPP) and therefore when, at least theoretically, evidence has not yet been gathered sufficient for a request for committal for trial.

In conclusion, one is dealing with a new institution in our laws introduced to deflate the trial through pronouncement of a judgment in which, having separated the formula "recognition of responsibility — application of punishment," there is no ascertainment by the judge of an effective violation by the defendant of the interests protected by the norm which was presumed to be violated and the guilt of the person under investigation. The prosecution is exempted from the burden of proving responsibility and the accused accepts, based on his own evaluation of its convenience, the anticipated definition of the procedure while enjoying a kind of "reward."

If one wanted to categorize the institution one could definitely insert it among those defined as a "hypothetical judgment" and, in this specific case, "a hypothesis of responsibility."

Again one sees that the defendant, in consummating a "deal," does not admit guilt, and the judge of the investigation does not make a guilt-finding, but merely determines the legal sufficiency of the evidence underlying the charge (what Americans would call "probable cause") and the proportionality of the punishment were there to be a guilt-finding.

§ 655 LECr (Spain)

If the punishment requested by the prosecuting parties has a correctional character, the representative of the defendant, upon being notified of the pleadings, may express his absolute conformity with the most serious pleadings, if there be more than one, and with the punishment requested; defense counsel may also indicate, nonetheless, if he deems it necessary to continue to trial.

If it is not deemed necessary, the judge, with previous ratification by the defendant, pronounces judgment without more, according to the pleadings mutually accepted and may not impose a punishment more serious than that requested.

If this was not, as it were, the appropriate pleading and should have been a more serious one, the court shall order the continuation of the trial.

The trial also continues if there were several defendants and not all have expressed their conformity.

If the defendant or defendants disagree only with respect to their civil responsibility, the trial shall be limited to evidence and argument as to the points relative to this responsibility.[229]

---

229. *Conformidad* with the most serious charges and punishments requested by the prosecuting parties is equally possible whether trial would be before professional

On the one hand, the Spanish *conformidad* and the Italian *patteggia-mento* appear to be like a plea of *nolo contendere* in American courts, for no admission of guilt is required. On the other hand, the Italian procedure, unlike the *conformidad* and the *nolo* plea, does not result in a finding of guilt. Note that the victim's position is secured in the Spanish procedure because the defendant must stipulate to the highest punishment and quali-fication of the unlawful act pleaded by all of the prosecuting parties, in-cluding private and popular prosecutors. In 2004 France introduced a pro-cedure, however, which involves a "recognition of guilt" and applies to crimes punishable by no more than five years deprivation of liberty. In issu-ing judgment, however, the judge may not impose a prison sentence of more than one year, and must suspend at least half thereof, and may only impose fines in one-half of the amount which otherwise would have been applicable.[230]

IV. Submitting the Case on the Investigative Dossier: Return of the Written Inquisitorial Trial?

The CCP (Italy) of 1988 also introduced the "abbreviated trial," which is, in essence, a submission of the case to the judge of the investigation to be de-cided on the basis of the contents of the investigative dossier in exchange for a one-third reduction in the sentence. There is some irony in this procedural innovation. The 1988 Italian code was designed, on the one hand, to intro-duce an adversarial trial, with party-driven presentation of the evidence and strict observance of the principles of orality and immediacy epitomized by the elimination of the investigative dossier from the courtroom. But here, for a reduction of one-third in the punishment, the defendant can choose what amounts to a written trial which resembles the ancient inquisitorial review of the investigative dossier.

---

judges, §§ 699, 787 LECr (Spain), a jury court, § 50 LOTJ (Spain), or according to so-called "abbreviated procedure," § 787 LECr (Spain). Under Spain's "expedited pro-cedures," introduced in 2004, a *conformidad* may be concluded in flagrant cases and select other cases where no more than five years punishment may be imposed, but deprivation of liberty is limited to three years and may be suspended. §§ 795, 800, 801(1)(2), 802(2) LECr (Spain).

230. *See* §§ 495-7, 495-8 CPP (France).

Decision of November 21, 1991
(Italian Supreme Court)[231]

In the second point the petitioner complains, as he already did at the hearing on appeal, that the court, confronted with an accusation of possession of a small quantity of narcotics, requalified the charge within the ambit of a more serious type of offense (...). The petitioner maintains that, in relation to the agreement on the procedure made by the public prosecutor and the defense (abbreviated trial), the court had the duty to decide on the basis of the dossier at the moment it gains possession thereof and this, in his opinion, imposes an obligation on the judge to accept the terms of the accusatory pleading formulated at the moment of the agreement as to the procedure and prohibits any modification of it to the detriment of the defendant. (...)

On the contrary, as has been pointed out in a considerable part of the literature and as has emerged from not a few decisions articulated by the Constitutional Court (...), the current Constitution implies (and constitutionalizes) a criminal procedure of the Latin-Continental type and, therefore, per definition, inquisitorial, to the extent that the judge in every cases is involved in the control over the exercise of the criminal action by determining which legal definition of a criminal act corresponds to the facts brought to his attention. Within this comprehensive process of judicial ascertainment is included a power-duty to present new evidence and to attribute to the facts ascertained their exact legal definition, even to the detriment of the person against whom the criminal action is directed. These are power-duties which are completely unknown, and moreover unimaginable, in the accusatory procedure of the Common Law. (...)

In substance, to deny to the judge of the abbreviated trial the power-duty to control the congruence of the legal hypothesis (the abstract offense) charged in the accusatory pleading, to identify the essential elements (in relation to an episode of life lived and past), would be a step towards a clear violation of a constitutional disposition. (...)

It follows, therefore, that the Court of Messina had the duty-power to control the correspondence between the charged fact and the provision hypothesized in the accusatory pleading and, therefore, (...) to specify the corresponding penal offense and apply it even if, by happenchance, as in the instant case, the result would be a more serious punishment.

---

231. Cass. penale, No. 354, 585, 585–87 (1993).

No substantial violation of the right to a defense is apparent in the instant case, given that it is the articulation of the "act" in its essential identifying terms (the censured behavioral episode) which fixes the terms of the pleading and to which the defense must adjust its mission, bearing in mind that, in case of an omission or error in the charge, the judge will make it the object of verification and adjustment. (…)

And the contrary argument cannot be accepted (…) because the agreement between the parties concerns, pointedly, the procedure and not the rules of evaluating the facts and the results of the trial, the one and the other which is the domain of the judge. Not even in the procedure for application of punishment upon request of the parties (§ 444 CCP) (…), where the autonomy of the parties to reach a disposition reaches the maximum scope, is the judge deprived of the power-duty to verify the correspondence between "act" and the "offense charged" (…); nor, as has been previously explained, may it be done without violating the Constitution.

While the above procedure has similarities with the Italian *patteggimento*, the procedure is supposed to be the equivalent of a "trial," that is, the judge of the investigation, acting as judge of the abbreviated trial, may weigh the evidence and even convict of an offense more serious than that preliminarily charged by the public prosecutor.

There has been a substantial reform of the provisions for abbreviated procedure and application for punishment which have eliminated the possibility for the public prosecutor to oppose the defendant's choice of the procedures.[232] The defendant has also been given an opening, not only to agree to be interrogated at the abbreviated trial, but also to present new ev-

---

232. *See* §§ 438 (1–5), 441 (1–3,5), 448 (1,2) CPP (Italy) (Appendix, 255–56). These changes came on the heels of a series of decisions of the Constitutional Court. *See* Judgment No. 81 of January 29, 1991, Sentenze e ordinanze della Corte costituzionale, Vol. XCVIII at 637 (if prosecutor objects to the abbreviated trial without sufficient reasons, the trial judge may give the one-third discount after an ordinary trial); Judgment No. 23 of January 31, 1992, 37 Giur. cost. 109 (if the judge of the investigation rejects a request for an abbreviated trial without sufficient reasons, the trial judge may still impose the one-third reduction after trial; Judgment No. 127 of March 29, 1993, 38 Giur. cost 1027 (if the prosecutor rejects a "deal" without sufficient reasons, the judge may impose the one-third reduction after trial). The one-third discount after an abbreviated trial applies to all crimes. The punishment in cases subject to life imprisonment is reduced to 30 years. § 442(2) CPP (Italy). For a scathing attack on the new Italian consensual procedures, *see* Ferrajoli, *supra* note 14, at 625, 637.

idence which will be heard along with the evidence in the investigative dossier.[233]

V. Significance of Alternative Procedures

Alternative procedures, whether American plea bargain, penal order, German *Absprache*, Italian *patteggiamento*, Italian abbreviated trial or Spanish *conformidad*, must be justified in terms of the governing principles of criminal procedure: the presumption of innocence, principle of material truth, etc. By understanding the theoretical underpinnings of these "deviant" forms, we can better understand the substance of the old principles as they continue to be applied in the "normal" criminal trial. However, the reality of all modern criminal procedure is that the "normal" trial with all of its guarantees is rapidly becoming the "alternative" procedure. The overcrowded dockets of modern courts, have induced the legislator, as in Italy, or the participants themselves, as in Germany, to create new simplified or abbreviated procedures. The principle of "procedural economy" has thus progressively challenged the hallowed principles of due process applied in the trial "with all the guarantees."

Questions

1. Which approach to "procedural economy" do you prefer, the informal German procedure of giving the defendant a break on sentence in exchange for a judicial confession or the Italian or Spanish approaches which are strictly delineated by statute?

2. Should the trial "with all the guarantees" be reserved only for the most serious cases or those where the defendant absolutely denies guilt?

3. Do you think a written inquisitorial trial (with or without the possibility of adding additional evidence) in the form of the Italian "abbreviated procedure" can be a just procedure in ascertaining the truth of the charges?

4. How does American plea bargaining compare in your mind with the German, Italian and Spanish procedures?

---

233. *See* §§ 438, 441 CCP (Italy) (Appendix, 255) and § 441-bis CCP (Italy). These amendments to the code also came on the heels of decisions of the Constitutional Court. *See*, for instance, Decision No. 318 of July 8, 1992, 37 Giur. cost. 2635.

5. If, in the U.S., the prosecutor insists on capital punishment or a very long prison term if the defendant insists on a jury trial and is convicted, but offers a substantially lesser term of imprisonment if one pleads guilty, can one characterize such a guilty plea as "voluntary?" Could an innocent person plead guilty in such a situation?

6. Should plea bargaining be used in the prosecution of international war crimes and genocide?[234]

Suggested Readings

NANCY AMOURY COMBS, GUILTY PLEAS IN INTERNATIONAL CRIMINAL LAW. CONSTRUCTING A RESTORATIVE JUSTICE APPROACH (2007).

Julian A. Cook, III, *Plea Bargaining At The Hague*, 30 YALE J. INT'L L. 473 (2005).

Mirjan Damaska, *Negotiated Justice in International Criminal Courts*, 2 J. INT'L CRIM. JUST. 1018 (2004).

Herbert M. Kritzer, *Disappearing Trials: a Comparative Perspective*, 1 J. EMPIRICAL LEGAL STUDIES 735 (2004).

John H. Langbein, *Torture and Plea Bargaining*, 46 U. CHI. L. REV. 3 (1978).

Joachim Herrmann, *Bargaining Justice—a Bargain for German Criminal Justice?*, 53 U. PITT. L. REV. 755 (1992).

HEDIEH NASHERI, BETRAYAL OF DUE PROCESS. A COMPARATIVE ASSESSMENT OF PLEA BARGAINING IN THE UNITED STATES AND CANADA (1998).

Máximo Langer, *From Legal Transplants to Legal Translations: the Globalization of Plea Bargaining and the Americanization Thesis in Criminal Procedure*, 45 HARV. INT'L L. J. 1 (2004).

Stephen C. Thaman, *Plea-Bargaining, Negotiating Confessions and Consensual Resolution of Criminal Cases* in GENERAL REPORTS OF THE XVIITH CONGRESS OF THE INTERNATIONAL ACADEMY OF COMPARATIVE LAW 951 (2007).

---

234. For discussions of plea bargaining in cases before the International Criminal Tribunal for the Former Yugoslavia and the International Criminal Court, *see* in general, NANCY AMOURY COMBS, GUILTY PLEAS IN INTERNATIONAL CRIMINAL LAW. CONSTRUCTING A RESTORATIVE JUSTICE APPROACH (2007); Mirjan Damaska, *Negotiated Justice in International Criminal Courts*, 2 J. INT'L CRIM. JUST.1018 (2004).

Chapter Seven

The Trial

I. Presumption of Innocence and Burden of Proof

A. Presumption of Innocence and Right to Remain Silent

1. The Use of a Defendant's Silence as Evidence of Guilt

Murray v. United Kingdom (European Court of Human Rights) (February 8, 1996)[235]

The applicant was arrested by police officers at 5:40 p.m. on 7 January 1990 under section 14 of the Prevention of Terrorism (Temporary Provisions) Act 1989. Pursuant to Article 3 of the Criminal Evidence (Northern Ireland) Order 1988 ("the Order"), he was cautioned by the police in the following terms: "You do not have to say anything unless you wish to do so but I must warn you that if you fail to mention any fact which you rely on in your defence in court, your failure to take this opportunity to mention it may be treated in court as supporting any relevant evidence against you. If you do wish to say anything, what you say may be given in evidence." In response to the police caution the applicant stated that he had nothing to say.

[The Applicant at no time during the proceedings made any statements, incriminating or otherwise.]

In May 1991 the applicant was tried by a single judge, the Lord Chief Justice of Ireland, sitting without a jury, for the offences of conspiracy to murder, the unlawful imprisonment with seven other people, of a

---

235. 22 E.H.R.R. 29, 31–34, 57–63 (1996).

certain Mr. L. and of belonging to a proscribed organisation, the Provisional Irish Republican Army (IRA).(...)

At the close of the prosecution case the trial judge, acting in accordance with Article 4 of the Order, called upon each of the eight accused to give evidence in their own defence. The trial judge informed them inter alia: "I am also required by law to tell you that if you refuse to come into the witness box to be sworn or if, after having been sworn, you refuse, without good reason, to answer any question, then the court in deciding whether you are guilty or not guilty may take into account against you to the extent that it considers proper your refusal to give evidence or to answer any questions."

Acting on the advice of his solicitor and counsel, the applicant chose not to give any evidence. No witnesses were called on his behalf. Counsel, with support from the evidence of a co-accused, D.M., submitted, inter alia, that the applicant's presence in the house just before the police arrived was recent and innocent.

On 8 May 1991 the applicant was found guilty of the offence of aiding and abetting the unlawful imprisonment of Mr. L. and sentenced to eight years' imprisonment. He was acquitted on the remaining charges. (...)

The applicant alleged that there had been a violation of the right to silence and the right not to incriminate oneself contrary to Article 6(1) and (2) of the Convention. (...) The relevant provisions provide as follows:

"1. In the determination of (...) any criminal charge against him, everyone is entitled to a fair and public hearing within a reasonable time by an independent and impartial tribunal established by law. (...)

2. Everyone charged with a criminal offence shall be presumed innocent until proved guilty according to law." (...)

In the submission of the applicant, the drawing of incriminating inferences against him under the Criminal Evidence (Northern Ireland) Order 1988 ("the Order") violated Article 6(1) and (2) of the Convention. It amounted to an infringement of the right to silence, the right not to incriminate oneself and the principle that the prosecution bear the burden of proving the case without assistance from the accused. He contended that a first, and most obvious element of the right to silence is the right to remain silent in the face of police questioning and not to have to testify against oneself at trial. In his submission, these have always been essential and fundamental elements of the British criminal justice system. (...) To use against him silence under police questioning and his refusal to testify during trial amounted to subverting the presumption of innocence and the onus of proof resulting from that presumption: it is for the prosecution to prove the accused's guilt without any assistance from the latter being required.

Amnesty International submitted that permitting adverse inferences to be drawn from the silence of the accused was an effective means of compulsion which shifted the burden of proof from the prosecution to the accused and was inconsistent with the right not to be compelled to testify against oneself or to confess guilt because the accused is left with no reasonable choice between silence—which will be taken as testimony against oneself—and testifying. It pointed out that Article 14(3)(g) of the United Nations International Covenant on Civil and Political Rights explicitly provides that an accused shall "not be compelled to testify against himself or to confess guilt". Reference was also made to Rule 42(A) of the Rules of Procedure and Evidence of the International Criminal Tribunal for the Former Yugoslavia which expressly provides that a suspect has the right to remain silent and to the Draft Statute for the International Criminal Court, submitted to the United Nations General Assembly by the International Law Commission, which in Draft Article 26(6)(a)(i) qualifies the right to silence with the words "without such silence being a consideration in the determination of guilt or innocence". (...)

The Court must, confining its attention to the facts of the case, consider whether the drawing of inferences against the applicant under Articles 4 and 6 of the Order rendered the criminal proceedings against him—and especially his conviction—unfair within the meaning of Article 6 of the Convention. (...)

Although not specifically mentioned in Article 6 of the Convention, there can be no doubt that the right to remain silent under police questioning and the privilege against self-incrimination are generally recognised international standards which lie at the heart of the notion of a fair procedure under Article 6. By providing the accused with protection against improper compulsion by the authorities these immunities contribute to avoiding miscarriages of justice and to securing the aims of Article 6.

The Court does not consider that it is called upon to give an abstract analysis of the scope of these immunities and, in particular, of what constitutes in this context "improper compulsion". What is at stake in the present case is whether these immunities are absolute in the sense that the exercise by an accused of the right to silence cannot under any circumstances be used against him at trial or, alternatively, whether informing him in advance that, under certain conditions, his silence may be so used, is always to be regarded as "improper compulsion".

On the one hand, it is self-evident that it is incompatible with the immunities under consideration to base a conviction solely or mainly on the accused's silence or on a refusal to answer questions or to give evidence himself. On the other hand, the Court deems it equally obvious that these immunities cannot and should not prevent that the accused's silence, in situations which clearly call for an explanation from him, be taken into account in assessing the persuasiveness of the evidence adduced by the prosecution. Wherever the line between these two extremes is to be drawn, it follows from this understanding of "the right to silence" that the question whether the right is absolute must be answered in the negative. It cannot be said therefore that an accused's decision to remain silent throughout criminal proceedings should necessarily have no implications when the trial court seeks to evaluate the evidence against him. In particular, as the Government have pointed out, established international standards in this area, while providing for the right to silence and the privilege against self-incrimination, are silent on this point. Whether the drawing of adverse inferences from an accused's silence infringes Article 6 is a matter to be determined in the light of all the circumstances of the case, having particular regard to the situations where inferences may be drawn, the weight attached to them by the national courts in their assessment of the evidence and the degree of compulsion inherent in the situation.

As regards the degree of compulsion involved in the present case, it is recalled that the applicant was in fact able to remain silent. Notwithstanding the repeated warnings as to the possibility that inferences might be drawn from his silence, he did not make any statements to the police and did not give evidence during his trial. (...) Thus his insistence in maintaining silence throughout the proceedings did not amount to a criminal offence or contempt of court. Furthermore, as has been stressed in national court decisions, silence, in itself, cannot be regarded as an indication of guilt (...).

Admittedly a system which warns the accused — who is possibly without legal assistance (as in the applicant's case) — that adverse inferences may be drawn from a refusal to provide an explanation to the police for his presence at the scene of a crime or to testify during his trial, when taken in conjunction with the weight of the case against him, involves a certain level of indirect compulsion. However, since the applicant could not be compelled to speak or to testify, as indicated above, this factor on its own cannot be decisive. The Court must rather concentrate its attention on the role played by the inferences in the proceedings against the applicant and especially in his conviction.

In this context, it is recalled that these were proceedings without a jury, the trier of fact being an experienced judge. Furthermore, the drawing of inferences under the Order is subject to an important series of safeguards designed to respect the rights of the defence and to limit the extent to which reliance can be placed on inferences. In the first place, before inferences can be drawn under Article 4 and 6 of the Order appropriate warnings must have been given to the accused as to the legal effects of maintaining silence. Moreover, (...) the prosecutor must first establish a prima facie case against the accused, i.e. a case consisting of direct evidence which, if believed and combined with legitimate inferences based upon it, could lead a properly directed jury to be satisfied beyond reasonable doubt that each of the essential elements of the offence is proved. The question in each particular case is whether the evidence adduced by the prosecution is sufficiently strong to require an answer. The national court cannot conclude that the accused is guilty merely because he chooses to remain silent. It is only if the evidence against the accused "calls" for an explanation which the accused ought to be in a position to give that a failure to give any explanation "may as a matter of common sense allow the drawing of an inference that there is no explanation and that the accused is guilty". Conversely if the case presented by the prosecution had so little evidential value that it called for no answer, a failure to provide one could not justify an inference of guilt. In sum, it is only common-sense inferences which the judge considers proper, in the light of the evidence against the accused, that can be drawn under the Order. (...)

Furthermore in Northern Ireland, where trial judges sit without a jury, the judge must explain the reasons for the decision to draw inferences and the weight attached to them. The exercise of discretion in this regard is subject to review by the appellate courts.

In the present case, the evidence presented against the applicant by the prosecution was considered by the Court of Appeal to constitute a "formidable" case against him. It is recalled that when the police entered the house some appreciable time after they knocked on the door, they found the applicant coming down the flight of stairs in the house where Mr. L. had been held captive by the IRA. Evidence had been given by Mr. L. — evidence which in the opinion of the trial judge had been corroborated — that he had been forced to make a taped confession and that after the arrival of the police at the house and the removal of his blindfold he saw the applicant at the top of the stairs. He had been told by him to go downstairs and watch television. The applicant was pulling a tape out of a cassette. The tangled tape and cassette recorder were later found on the premises. Evidence by the applicant's co-accused that he had recently arrived at the house was discounted as not being credible.

The trial judge drew strong inferences against the applicant under Article 6 of the Order by reason of his failure to give an account of his presence in the house when arrested and interrogated by the police. He also drew strong inferences under Article 4 of the Order by reason of the applicant's refusal to give evidence in his own defence when asked by the court to do so.

In the Court's view, having regard to the weight of the evidence against the applicant, as outlined above, the drawing of inferences from his refusal, at arrest, during police questioning and at trial, to provide an explanation for his presence in the house was a matter of common sense and cannot be regarded as unfair or unreasonable in the circumstances. (...) [T]he courts in a considerable number of countries where evidence is freely assessed may have regard to all relevant circumstances, including the manner in which the accused has behaved or has conducted his defence, when evaluating the evidence in the case.

As can be seen from the *Murray* case, the presumption of innocence and the right to remain silent are recognized as part of the right to a fair trial guaranteed in Art. 6 ECHR. The presumption of innocence in the U.S. is inextricably intertwined with the substantial burden to prove guilt beyond a reasonable doubt which is placed on the prosecution in all criminal cases. One could argue that *Murray* shifts the burden to the defendant to explain away incriminating evidence, thus undermining the presumption of innocence, in cases where he/she is arrested *in flagrante*.[236]

Before 1994 an accused's failure to give evidence in England could neither be commented on by the prosecution nor given any independent evidentiary weight.[237] However §35 of the Criminal Justice and Public Order Act (CJPOA) of 1994 repealed the earlier test and enacted a law which is virtually

---

236. A French law reversing the burden of proof in cases when a person is arrested entering the country in possession of contraband has been upheld by the Eur. Ct. HR. *See* Salabiaku v. France, 13 E.H.R.R. 379 (1991); Hoang v. France, 16 E.H.R.R. 53 (1993).

237. Criminal Evidence Act 1898, § 1(b), cited in R. v. Martinez-Tobon [1994] 1 W.L.R. 388 (Lord Taylor of Gosforth).

identical to the Northern Irish law discussed in *Murray*.[238] Under the CJPOA of 1994 a suspect's silence before being charged when confronted by a police officer or other person with incriminating evidence or accusations, or his failure to mention any evidence or defense later relied on in court, may be used against him at trial.[239] When arrested *in flagrante*, a statutory burden is placed on the suspect to explain the suspicious circumstances, reminding one of the old *Carolina* provisions which allowed torture in such cases.[240]

Compare *Murray* and the English statutes with the following German case:

Decision of October 26, 1965 (German Supreme Court)[241]

[Defendant was arrested for theft from telephone booths. He remained silent during police interrogation. He then gave an exculpatory story to the judge, saying he intended to turn in the money.]

Whether the right of the accused, not to make a statement about the case, also completely prohibits drawing disadvantageous conclusions from his silence, may be doubtful. This is especially the case when the accused remains silent only partially, or during only one or some of multiple judicial interrogations in a judicial proceedings. In the instant case the Chamber need not, however, answer this question.

Such conclusions are legally inadmissible in any case when the accused, as was the case here, availed himself of this right to the full extent at arrest and in the following police interrogation because he, regardless of for what reason, deemed it to be correct to first make statements about the case at a judicial interrogation.

A contrary view limits the right of the accused not to make a statement about the case in a legally impermissible manner. For it means that the accused, who is aware thereof, would feel himself compelled

---

238. SEABROOKE & SPRACK, *supra* note 179, at 73–74. *See* § 35 CJPOA (England) (Appendix, 242–43).

239. § 34 CJPOA (England) (Appendix, 242–43).

240. *See* §§ 23, 25–27 Constitutio Criminalis Carolina, *supra*, at 5–6. *See* §§ 36, 37 CJPOA (England) (Appendix, 244–45). Interestingly enough, the Eur. Ct. HR held that Art. 6 ECHR was violated in a jury trial in England in which the jury was instructed under § 36 CJPOA (England) that it could use the defendants' silence to prove guilt in a drug case in which their lawyers told them not to talk to police due to their state of intoxication. The Court held that there had not been a *prima facie* showing of guilt sufficient for the silence to be used as an inference of guilt. Condron v. United Kingdom, 31 E.H.R.R. 1 (2001).

241. BGHSt 20, 281, 282–83.

to give a statement immediately at his first police interrogation, if he did not want to run the risk that disadvantageous inferences could be drawn in a later judicial proceeding from his conduct during that interrogation. An interpretation which leads to such results contradicts § 136a StPO, which fundamentally prohibits undermining the accused's freedom to determine his own will through coercion.

The law of criminal procedure must also be just to accuseds who are innocent. Even such accuseds can, for reasons of the most varied sort, consider it proper to make a statement about the case before a judge rather than before a police officer. The fear, that a corresponding attitude could be considered to his disadvantage during the evaluation of the evidence would make such conduct in many cases well-nigh impossible and therefore limit the right to remain silent before the police in a manner which is unacceptable. As to accuseds who are guilty, the same applies. He should be treated like an innocent person up until a judgment of guilt has become final.

Questions

1. Do you agree with the Eur. Ct. HR when it claims that allowing comment on a person's silence in the face of incriminating evidence does not compel that person to testify and does not undermine the presumption of innocence?

2. Why does the Eur. Ct. HR stress the fact that the trier of fact in *Murray* was a professional judge and not a jury? Should that make a difference?

3. Compare the English rule, allowing comment in both jury and non-jury trials, with the German approach. Which approach seems more old-fashion, more akin to the old inquisitorial approach of the German *Carolina*?[242]

4. Can the silence of an accused be commented on in the U.S.? If she refuses to testify at trial? If she refuses to waive her *Miranda* rights? If she re-

---

242. A report on justice reform in England and Wales noted that those in favor of comment on the exercise of the right to remain silent found it to be a "way of seeking the truth by encouraging suspects to provide explanations which can be further investigated and which may exonerate them." THE ROYAL COMMISSION ON CRIMINAL JUSTICE. REPORT 52, § 12 (1993) (hereafter RCCJ Report). A post-inquisitorial country, Portugal, like Germany, does not allow comment on the exercise of the right to remain silent. §§ 343(1), 61(1) CCP (Portugal), cited in Jorge De Figueiredo Dias, *Die Reform des Strafverfahrens in Portugal*, 104 ZEITSCHRIFT FÜR DIE GESAMTE STRAFRECHTSWISSENSCHAFT 448, 462 (1992).

fuses to give a statement before being advised of *Miranda* rights? If she refuses to give a statement before or at the time of arrest?

Relevant U.S. Case Law

Griffin v. California, 380 U.S. 609 (1965)

Doyle v. Ohio, 426 U.S. 610 (1976)

Jenkins v. Anderson, 447 U.S. 231 (1980)

Fletcher v. Weir, 455 U.S. 603 (1982)

B. Role of the Trial Judge: Investigator of the Truth, Impartial Evaluator of the Evidence, or Impartial Guarantor of a Fair Adversarial Trial?

1. The Judge's Power to Question Witnesses and Introduce Evidence

Decision of October 10, 1991 (Italian Supreme Court)[243]

[Defendant was acquitted in the trial court of killing a deer in violation of the hunting laws. The public prosecutor appealed. Documents filed by the trial prosecutor indicated the presence of witnesses who had seen defendant with a dead deer but the prosecutor neglected to deposit the list of his witnesses with the court per § 468 CPP (Italy) and thus was precluded from calling these crucial witnesses. The trial prosecutor then asked the judge to call the witnesses *sua sponte* but the judge refused.]

The municipal judge deemed that the introduction of such material was precluded because of the forfeiture incurred by the public prosecutor per § 468 CPP but also excluded the possibility of taking any initiative per § 507 CPP,[244] maintaining that the discretionary power of the judge cannot be exercised to frustrate the preclusions and forfeitures provided by the law and, therefore, to thus provide a remedy for the inactivity or negligence of the parties. (...)

In this light the absolute necessity for introducing new means of proof can be viewed in relation to the goal of criminal procedure, which is

---

243. CASS. PENALE No. 648, 1258, 1258–59 (1992).
244. *See* § 507(1) CPP (Italy) (Appendix, 257).

that of ascertaining the truth and to draw the consequences there-from, and there cannot be any absolute necessity beyond that goal. This having been postulated, the means of proof at the disposal of the judge for purposes of introduction of evidence can be none other than those which are absolutely necessary to achieve the aforemen-tioned goal. The absolute nature of the necessity surpasses, obviously, and according to logic, any preclusive barrier and any obstacle. Other-wise the necessity would not be absolute, but conditional, limited, circumscribed. (...)

In the contest between the parties it is precisely § 507 CPP which grants the judge in the trial phase a role which is not that of a simple controller or a director of an orchestra without any power of initia-tive, linked to that of each party and conditioned by preclusions, forfeitures, negligence and, more banally, by simple errors or forget-fulness, even if excusable, which the parties will always be suscepti-ble to.

The judgment shall be reversed (...).

Decision of March 26, 1993 (Italian Supreme Court)[245]

[T]he interpretation of § 507 CPP to which the remitting judges ad-here, according to which the power of the judge to introduce *ex offi-cio* means of proof would be precluded by the lack of evidentiary ac-tivity by the parties and the forfeitures they have incurred, takes as its point of departure (...) a conception according to which the new procedural code "does not aspire to the discovery of the truth, but only to a decision correctly made in a dialectical contest between the parties, according to an abstract accusatorial model in which 'one result counts the same as another, as long as they are correctly obtained.'"

Expressed in other terms, a criminal trial responding to such a model would be a technique of resolving conflicts in the ambit of which the judge, essentially, would be reserved a role of guaranteeing the obser-vance of the rules of a contest between opposing parties and the trial would not have the function of ascertaining the real facts in order to reach a decision corresponding as well as possible to the result desired by the substantive law, but to attain — on the presupposition of an ac-centuated goal-oriented autonomy of the procedure — only that pro-cedural "truth" which is possible to obtain by means of the dialectical

---

245. CASS. PENALE, No. 1317 2224, 2231–32, 2234 (1993).

logic of adversary procedure and with respect to the rigid methodological and procedural rules coherent with the model. (...)

In relation, however, to the technique of the trial it is of course true that the necessity of accentuating the tertiary role of the judge—inasmuch as he is programmatically ignorant of the preceding developments in the procedural phases—has led to the introduction of an extreme model of functional separation of the procedural phases in order to give priority to the oral method of collecting evidence, which is conceived as an instrument favoring the dialectic of adversary procedure and the formation in the judge of a conviction free of prior influences. But such methodological options have not overlooked, nor could they have intended to, the fact that the primary and inescapable goal of the criminal trial cannot but remain that of discovering the truth (...) and that a procedure imprinted with the legality principle (Art. 25(2) Const.)—which makes the punishment of criminally sanctioned conduct an obligation—and which, connected with the principle of the obligatory nature of the penal action, (...) is not consonant with norms of procedural methodology which hinder in an irrational manner the process of ascertainment of the historical facts necessary to arrive at a just decision (...).

Similar rules of legal predetermination of the persuasive value of evidence are, on the other hand, in dissonance with the principles at the base of the new code, which has preserved (and in adherence to constitutional principles it could not be otherwise) the principle of free conviction, understood as the freedom of the judge to evaluate the evidence according to his own prudent judgment with the obligation of making an account of the criteria adopted and the results achieved in the judgment reasons (...). More generally—as has been explained in this decision—if the new code has chosen the dialectic of the adversary trial and the oral method as those criteria which to the greatest extent respond to the need to discover the truth, it has at the same time needed to temper in an opportune manner its reach in relation to those elements of proof not completely (or genuinely) acquirable through those means, adopting in this case a principle of non-dispersion of elements of proof. (...)

The power attributed to the judge by § 507 CPP is, therefore, a supplementary power but not, to be sure, exceptional.

The preceding two Italian Supreme Court cases illustrate the tensions between the move to adversary procedure which was the key feature of the CCP (Italy) of 1988 and the inquisitorial principle of the judge's duty to ascertain the truth. On the one hand, if the judge is to effectively exercise evidentiary initiative in an inquisitorial manner, she would need access to the investigative file, the repository of potentially admissible evidence, yet the Italian code has denied the trial judge access to the dossier in order to strengthen the orality and immediacy of the taking of the evidence.

The following cases shows how an active judge in a Common Law jury case can affect the presumption of innocence by excessively participating in the evidentiary portion of the trial or, as the English say, "descending into the arena:"

Regina v. Foxford
(Northern Ireland Court of Appeals) (1974)[246]

[Defendant, a police officer, was convicted of homicide of a boy during a disturbance in Northern Ireland. He claimed he had been fired upon and this was corroborated by other police witnesses. Civilian witnesses, however, testified that only one shot was fired.]

[The appeal claims that] the learned trial judge precluded himself from arriving at the correct verdict, and from a proper and satisfactory assessment of the evidence and witnesses in the case, by: (...) (iii) intervening, during the course of the trial, in the examination and cross-examination of witnesses, in such a way as to indicate that he was biased against the accused, and was seeking to establish in evidence facts which would point to the guilt of the accused. Having heard certain of the crown witnesses at an early stage in the trial, and having expressed himself at this time as impressed by these witnesses (although in the contention of the defence their evidence was unreliable and in conflict with many of the other Crown witnesses and although they were established as prejudiced and unsatisfactory persons) throughout the remainder of the trial, he repeatedly sought to find support for their evidence, ignored the true purport and effect of the remaining Crown evidence, and the weight and substance of the evidence for the defence, and appeared to close his mind to any suggestion or argument that the evidence of these witnesses should or could be open to criticism. (...)

This trial perfectly exemplifies the difficulty attendant on a procedure where the judge of law is also the tribunal of fact. According to one theory, if an irregularity occurs or inadmissible evidence is given and has to be ignored, the trained mind of a judge is less vulnerable to its harmful effects than that of a juror. This may not always be true when one considers that, if there is a jury, the judge assumes the duty of warning them as to what they may take into account, and that the content and significance of an irregularity may fade from the lay mind

---

246. [1974] Northern Ireland L. Rep. 181, 200–01, 212–13.

when it has ceased to be part of the case but stick firmly in the mind of the judge, who is trained to marshal and evaluate evidence. One may also mention the discussions which if there were a jury might be held in their absence and, as specially relevant to this case, the nuances and overtones, which would be lost on the jury, not for want of intelligence but for lack of specialised knowledge, and which at the same time might speak volumes to the judge. Magistrates, of course, and county judges sitting on appeal from them, as well as judges sitting without a jury in civil cases, are tribunals of fact as well as judges of law, but rarely do these jurisdictions throw up problems so numerous and important as are encountered in a long and hard-fought trial on indictment.

We quash the conviction and allow the appeal.

Regina v. Roncoli (English Court of Appeal) (1997)[247]

[Roncoli (R) was convicted of inflicting grievous bodily harm. He claimed self-defense.]

On appeal, objection was taken (1) to the fact that the judge, in the absence of the jury, had on three occasions indicated that she did not think "self-defence was a runner"; and (2) to a series of questions asked by the judge of R.

Held, allowing the appeal, (1) the judge should not have made the comments she did about whether it was possible to run self-defence. Although the jury were not present, she did so in the presence of R, and on one occasion, in the presence of the chief prosecution witness. They were bound to give the appellant the impression that the judge had formed a strongly adverse view of his cases. On its own, this complaint may not have led to the quashing of the conviction, but the effect of the complaints made was cumulative.

After R's examination in chief, the judge effectively cross-examined him, asking hostile questions which when transcribed took up six pages of text. In her questions, the judge set out the law and pressed R as to whether he still maintained that he had acted in self-defence, in terms which would be expected from prosecution counsel ("I am putting to you quite simply that the danger [said to have been presented by the victim] had gone"). The Court set out a number of the questions asked and concluded that the jury would be bound to conclude

---

247. [1998] Crim. L. Rev. 584, 584–85.

that the judge was of the view that R had no defence. The fact that the Crown case was a strong one did not deprive R of his right to be tried fairly. It had been said by the Court in other cases that it was perhaps even more important that the defence was fairly presented where the Crown evidence was strong. The Court considered (...) that intervention by the judge in a criminal trial was generally undesirable because [it] might unsettle the witness, prevent counsel from pursuing proper points, appear to belittle counsel in the eyes of the defendant and indicate a preconceived belief in guilt.

In Italy and Spain the trial judge is not the primary questioner of the defendant and other witnesses.[248] Note how the Spanish judge's role in aiding the ascertainment of the truth is formulated:

§ 683 LECr (Spain)

The presiding judge shall direct the trial, taking care to impede irrelevant discussions that do not lead to ascertainment of the truth, without restricting for this reason defense counsel in the liberty necessary for the defense.[249]

Compare the Spanish and Italian approaches with the more clearly inquisitorial role of the judge in the French criminal trial:

§ 310 CPP (France)

The presiding judge is invested with a discretionary power by virtue of which he is able, according to his honor and conscience, to take all measures which he believes are useful to uncover the truth (...).

During the course of the trial he may call, or if he wishes, subpoena and hear all persons or introduce any new piece of evidence which ap-

---

248. §§ 503(1), 506 CPP (Italy) (Appendix, 257); § 708 LECr (Spain) (Appendix, 261). In the U.S. judges are nearly always allowed to question witnesses. Cf. Fed. Rules of Evidence 614. But, as has been noted in the literature, "the more active the judge is, the greater threat to the independence of the jury." STEPHEN A. SALTZBURG & DANIEL J. CAPRA, AMERICAN CRIMINAL PROCEDURE 1163 (6th ed. 2000).

249. For a similar provision in Russia, see § 15(3) UPK (Russia) (Appendix, 258).

pears to him, according to the developments in court, to be useful for the determination of the truth (...).[250]

The presiding judge in French and German trials has a similar task as that of the prosecutor or the investigating magistrate during the preliminary investigation, that of investigating and ascertaining the truth. Naturally, in both countries the presiding judge has access to and has studied the investigative dossier which is the repository of evidence from which he or she attempts to explore and confirm the truth of the charges.

2. The Judge as Investigator and Evaluator of the Evidence
Decision No. 145 of July 12, 1988 (Spanish Constitutional Court)[251]

[The Court first discusses the prohibition against the investigating magistrate acting as a trial judge.]

It is not a question, of course, of doubting the personal rectitude of the magistrates who conduct the investigation, nor of failing to recognize that this presupposes an objective investigation of the truth in which the investigating magistrate must investigate, record and appreciate the circumstances both adverse to and favorable to the presumed offender (...). But it happens that the investigative activity, to the extent that it places the person who conducts it in direct contact with the accused and with the facts and information which can serve to prove the crime and the persons possibly responsible therefor, can provoke in the mind of the investigator, even despite his best wishes, prejudices and impressions in favor of or against the accused which can exert influence at the hour of passing judgment. Even when this does not happen it is difficult to avoid the impression that the judge is not fulfilling the function of judging with the full impartiality which is required. Thus, the Eur. Ct. HR, in its decision in the case of *DeCubber* of October 26, 1984, and even before in that made in the case of *Piersack* of October 1, 1982, insisted in the importance which appearances have in such matters, such that any magistrate should abstain in cases of those as to whom one could legitimately fear a lack of impar-

---

250. Cf. § 244(2) StPO (Germany) (Appendix, 249).
251. 1988–89 BJC 1168, 1174.

tiality, for with that goes the confidence which the courts of a democratic society must inspire in those before the courts, beginning, in the criminal trial, with the defendants themselves.

Note how strict the Spanish Constitutional Court and the Eur. Ct. HR are in preventing one judge from engaging in investigative acts during the preliminary investigation and then judging the case as a trier of fact and law at the trial. At issue, of course, is the presumption of innocence and the appearance of impartiality of the trial judge.

Decision No. 455 of December 30, 1994 (Italian Constitutional Court)[252]

The municipal judge of Padua maintains that § 342(2) CPP, in the part in which it does not provide for the incompatibility of the judge who issued an order to remand the file to the public prosecutor within the meaning of § 521(2) CPP to participate at the trial (...).

The argument is well-founded.

A principle has developed from the jurisprudence of this Court, which affirms the incompatibility to function as presiding judge at trial, of a judge who has, at an earlier stage of the proceedings, expressed an evaluation on the merits of the same procedural material regarding the same accused; and this, whether the evaluation has been completed at the concluding moment of the preliminary investigation (...) or whether it has been completed in an earlier trial on the merits which could not be concluded with a judgment (...).

There cannot be any doubt, without considering the theoretical construction which one wants to give to the institution under examination, that the judge, when he ascertains at the end of the taking of the evidence, that "the act is different from that described in the committal order," that he has completed a penetrating analysis of the merits of the *res judicanda*, not dissimilar to that which, while lacking an evaluation of the distinctiveness of the act, leads to a conclusion in a judgment on the merits following the trial.

A "new trial" concerning the same historical act and the same defendant cannot, therefore, not be assigned to another judge for decision, it being a case of the same *ratio* of protection of the impartiality and serenity of the trial which informs the rule provided in § 34(1) CPP

---

252. 39 GIUR. COST. 3940, 3944–45.

which declares the incompatibility of the judge who has pronounced judgment at an earlier stage of the trial relating to the same proceedings.

Note how the Italian Constitutional Court insists that the trial judge not in any way be prejudiced by having adjudged the merits of the charges in any prior proceedings. According to this view, the trial judges in German and Russian trials would be *per se* suspected of partiality for they have previously ruled on the sufficiency of the evidence in the investigative dossier to hold the defendant to answer at trial. But if an assessment preliminary to the trial[253] compromises the objectivity (or appearance of objectivity) of the trial judge, what about clearly investigative conduct during the trial itself, i.e., when the trial judge acts as investigator and evaluator of the facts simultaneously?

Decision of April 20, 1999
(Russian Constitutional Court)[254]

[A petition from the Irkutsk Regional Court challenged the power of the presiding judge to issue an order returning a case for supplementary investigation per § 232 UPK RSFSR (which was replaced by the 2001 UPK (Russia)).]

The court realizes judicial power through constitutional, civil, administrative and criminal court proceedings (Art. 118 Const.), which, in accordance with Art. 123(3) Const., is based on the principle of adversary procedure and equality of arms of the parties. This principle in criminal proceedings means above all a strict delimitation of the judicial function of deciding cases and the function of the prosecution which, thus, is realized by different subjects.

In deciding the case, the court, on the basis of evidence adduced at the trial, formulates conclusions as to established facts, as to the legal norms which must be applied in a given case, and as to the conviction or acquittal of persons in relation to whom the criminal prosecution was conducted. In relation thereto, adversary procedure in criminal proceedings presupposes, at any rate, that the initiation of the criminal prosecution, the formulation of the charge and its prosecution in court is undertaken by organs, civil servants and also aggrieved parties as provided by law. Burdening the court with the duty in one

---

253. This could also be in the form of evaluating the evidence to determine if the defendant should be held in pretrial detention. *See* Hauschildt v. Denmark, 12 E.H.R.R. 266 (1990).

254. Konstitutsionnyy sud Rossiyskoy Federatsii. Postanovleniia. Opredeleniia. 1999, 78 (2000).

form or another to substitute for the activity of these organs and persons in realizing accusatory functions does not conform to the provisions of Art. 123(3) Const. and hinders the court from independently and impartially realizing justice as is required by Art. 120(1) Const. and norms of international treaties ratified by the Russian Federation (Art. 6 ECHR and Art. 14 ICCPR).

The provisions of §§ 232, 258 UPK RSFSR under consideration allow the court, even *sua sponte*, to remand a criminal case to investigative organs to conduct supplementary investigation, when the inquest or preliminary investigation has been incomplete, or where there are reasons for filing a new charge or amending to charge a more serious crime than that contained in the accusatory pleading or one which is substantially different in terms of its factual circumstances. Thus the court, by itself initiating the continuation of investigative activities to lay the foundation for the charge, in essence fulfils an accusatory function alien to itself. The remand of a case for supplementary investigation for the aforementioned reasons in the absence of a corresponding motion by the parties, that is, where neither the prosecution nor the defense insists on it, can only reflect the interests of the prosecution, because this guarantees the correction of prosecutorial inadequacies in situations when neither the public prosecutor nor the aggrieved party have eliminated doubts as to the proof of the charges (including during the trial). From the point of view of the interests of the defense, remanding the case to conduct supplementary investigation in such situations is not necessary, for in the case of a complete or partial lack of proof or the doubtfulness of the charges, the defense has the right to expect the court to return a judgment of acquittal or, in the proper case, of finding the defendant guilty of a less serious crime than that charged by the prosecutorial organs. Such a defense posture is a permissible way of defending the interests of the defendant, for the court under such circumstances is required to follow the principle of the presumption of innocence incorporated in Art. 49 Const.

In accordance with the aforementioned constitutional principle, every person accused of having committed a crime is considered innocent until his guilt is proved and established with a final judgment according to the procedure provided in federal law. From this principle, in conjunction with the principle of adversary procedure (...), it follows that the court has the right to establish the guilt of a person only on condition that it is proved by organs and persons realizing the criminal prosecution. Inasmuch as, within the meaning of Arts. 118 and 123(3) Const., the court, in hearing criminal cases, realizes exclusively the function of administering justice and should not substitute for organs and persons who formulate and substantiate the charges, then doubts which are not eliminated by them as to the guilt of the accused are interpreted to the benefit of the former pursuant to Art. 49(3) Const. Thus, if the organs of criminal prosecution could not prove guilt of the accused in its full magnitude (...), then that should lead—in the current system of criminal procedure norms as constitutionally interpreted—to the return of a judgment of acquittal in relation to the accused or a judgment of conviction establishing guilt of a less serious act. (...)

In addition (...), the court in an adversary proceeding, on the other hand, is obligated to provide for a just and impartial resolution of the case, giving the parties equal possibilities to defend their positions, and may not assume in a supplementary fashion the fulfillment of the procedural functions of a party representing the prosecution, for that would violate the constitutional principle of adversary procedure and would result in a worse position for the party realizing the defense. (...)

In addition, by making a decision to remand a case to the public prosecutor for supplementary investigation, the court, in complying with § 232(2) UPK RSFSR, should indicate on what basis the case is being remanded and which circumstances must be clarified in a supplementary fashion. Fulfilling these requirements of the statute, the court thus specifies the tasks of the prosecutorial party by prescribing for the organs of the criminal prosecution (...) in what manner the formation and substantiation of the charge should be realized. (...)

Thus, §§ 232(1)(1,3) and 258(1) UPK RSFSR do not exclude arbitrary application, whether in relation to the refusal to render a judgment of acquittal, i.e., to publicly rehabilitate someone who is illegally charged with criminal responsibility, or to a failure to provide timely defense to aggrieved parties to the extent that a remand to the investigative organs can, without basis, make the aggrieved party's prospect for a judicial resolution of her rights more remote. (...)[255]

---

255. A similar procedure for remanding a case to the investigative organs exists in France in non-jury cases (§ 463 CCP (France)), and is commonly used in the Netherlands when the evidence the judge seeks to admit during the trial is not in the investigative dossier. Sending the case back to the investigating magistrate can cause delays of from three to four months. It is also often the defense which requests the case to bounce back to the investigative stage. Field et al, *supra* note 49, at 229–42. In Russian jury cases judges would occasionally dissolve a jury and send the case back to the investigator for supplementary investigation instead of allowing the jury to acquit based on insufficiency of evidence. Thaman, *Resurrection*, *supra* note 170, at 99–102.

Compare the Russian procedure with the protection guaranteed by the double jeopardy clause of the U.S. Constitution. Once a jury is sworn or the first witness is examined in a non-jury trial, the trial may not be suspended for further investigation or taken from the designated trier of fact unless there is a hung jury.[256] The tendency in some post-inquisitorial systems for the case to bounce back and forth from the trial stage to the investigative stage has clear implications for the presumption of innocence, for is one not presuming that there exists more incriminating information that could be uncovered with a re-opened investigation? The procedure also unduly mixes the investigative and adjudicative stages of the procedure and potentially undermines the impartiality of the triers of fact and guilt.

Questions

1. Does an active judge compromise the presumption of innocence at the trial? If she vigorously questions witnesses? If she calls for the introduction of supplementary evidence?

2. Does the judge's duty to ascertain the truth in many European countries compromise the presumption of innocence at trial? Does mixing the investigative and adjudicative roles of judges undermine their impartiality?

3. If the trial judge has read the investigative dossier containing the prosecutor's or investigating magistrate's evidence of guilt and has determined that it is sufficient to support a judgment of guilt before trial, can that judge be impartial in weighing the evidence and ascertaining guilt at trial?

4. Should there be "procedural acquittals," i.e., when the prosecution does not meet its burden of proof (whether due to incompetent investigators, the exclusion of evidence gathered in violation of the law, the violation of statutory rules) yet the person is likely guilty? Should the duty to ascertain the truth trump these procedural protections?

5. Do you think judges are more likely to intervene to "ascertain the truth" where it will benefit the prosecution or the defense?

---

256. Green v. United States, 355 U.S. 184 (1957); Downum v. United States, 372 U.S. 734 (1963); Arizona v. Washington, 434 U.S. 497 (1978); Oregon v. Kennedy, 456 U.S. 667 (1982).

Relevant U.S. Case Law

Green v. United States, 335 U.S. 184 (1957)

Downum v. United States, 372 U.S. 734 (1963)

Arizona v. Washington, 434 U.S. 497 (1978)

Oregon v. Kennedy, 456 U.S. 667 (1982)

Taylor v. Illinois, 484 U.S. 400 (1988)

II. The Evaluation of the Evidence and Rendering of Judgment

A. Who Evaluates the Evidence?

Regina v. Consett Justices, *Ex Parte* Postal Bingo Ltd. (Queen's Bench, England) (1966)[257]

[The applicant company was convicted on three counts of violating the gambling laws.]

The broad general ground upon which this application is moved is, to adopt that well-known expression, that justice must manifestly be seen to be done and that that was not so in the present case in that the decision appeared to be a decision not of the justices alone but of the justices together with their clerk. (...)

It has for long been recognised that the justices are entitled to have the advice of their clerk on law but not on fact. That is all very well to state as the general principle but we all know that there is hardly a decision which falls to be made which is not mixed law and fact. (...)

As regards the manner in which justices may consult their clerk, (...) the decision of the court must be the decision of the justices and not that of the justices and their clerk, and that if the clerk retires with the justices as a matter of course it is inevitable that the impression will be given that he may influence the justices as to the decision or sentence or both. A clerk should not retire with his justices as a matter of course, nor should they attempt to get round the decisions to which I

---

257. [1967] 2 Q.B. 9, 14–17.

have referred merely by asking him in every case to retire with them or by pretending that they require his advice on a point of law. Subject to this, it is in the discretion of the justices to ask their clerk to retire with them if in any particular case it has become clear that they will need his advice. (...)

It was undoubtedly a difficult matter for the justices. It involved not only finding the primary facts, which really were not in dispute at all, but drawing the right inferences from those facts and applying the law so far as it has been laid down in these cases. In my judgment, law and fact were so intimately interwoven that it was really impossible to say that the justices were wrong in keeping their clerk with them throughout. (...)

The matter does not end there because, contrary to what was stated in the *Practice Note (Justices' Clerks)*,[258] which I read, the clerk remained to the very end or almost the very end. That, as it seems to me, is in conflict with the *Practice Note (Justices' Clerks)*, but for my part I do not think that that is a matter in the circumstances of this case which would call for an order of certiorari. (...)

The matter does not end there because even if, as I hold, the clerk and the assistant clerk were right to be there, it is said that the clerk hearing the case so conducted himself and took such a prominent part and was so domineering that anyone in court must have thought that the decision ultimately arrived at was really a decision influenced by the clerk. The matters complained of under this head are several in number. Quite generally it is said that the picture in court was of a silent bench and a dominant clerk. It is said that the clerk cross-examined a number of witnesses, put questions to prosecuting counsel and generally appeared to be taking charge of the case. It is said also that he on his own motion ordered witnesses out of court, and matters of that sort.

The question: "Who decides the case?" is not always easy to answer. Here we have a court composed of three lay magistrates who are supposed to decide all questions of law and fact. The English lay magistrates may, and do invite their legally-trained clerk into their chambers to aid them in deliberation. The clerk may advise the lay judges on "questions of law or mixed law and fact."[259] Note that the clerk does not advise the magistrates in open court as to which

---

258. *See* Practice Direction (Justices: Clerk to Court) (1981) (Appendix, 245).

259. Critics of Germany's jury court claimed that the impossibility of separating questions of law and fact was a ground for transforming the jury court into the mixed court. Peter Landau, *Schwurgerichte und Schöffengerichte in Deutschland im 19. Jahrhundert bis 1870*, in THE TRIAL JURY IN ENGLAND, FRANCE, GERMANY 1700–1900 299–300 (Antonio Padoa Schioppa ed. 1987).

law should be applied and why. This is also true in the German mixed court. Since deliberations are confidential it is impossible to determine whether errors were made in this respect. Some European jury systems permit the jury to vote on a petition by the profession bench to take part in deliberations,[260] or to ask the clerk of the court[261] to aid them in the jury room.

B. Evaluating the Evidence in a Flagrant Case: Circumstantial Evidence of Mental State

In flagrant cases the suspect is usually caught in the act, with blood on his or her hands, in possession of stolen goods, etc. There is no question as to the identity of the perpetrator. But, especially in homicide cases, there is often a dispute as to why a person committed the crime or even how the crime was committed. The culprit's mental state is often the only issue at trial. In the U.S. the guilty mental state or *mens rea* is an element of the crime which, like identity or other external crime elements must be proved by the jury (or professional judge) beyond a reasonable doubt.

Decision of February 9, 1957 (German Supreme Court)[262]

[Defendant was convicted of mishandling his wife without intent to kill and then, believing she was dead, putting her in a car and setting fire to the car. She actually died in the burning car. He was sentenced to six years prison. The public prosecutor appealed.]

Free evaluation of the evidence means that in answering the guilt question one need only ask whether the trier of fact has arrived at an inner conviction as to a certain state of facts or not; this personal certainty is necessary for convicting the defendant, and also sufficient. The concept of such inner conviction does not exclude the possibility of another, even contradictory state of facts; it is rather part of its essence, that it very often remains open to objectively possible doubts. For in the area of facts to be evaluated by the trier of fact, an absolutely certain knowledge about the circumstances of the act, capable of excluding under all circumstances other possible conclusions, is de-

---

260. *See* §324 StPO (Austria), cite from STRAFPROZESSORDNUNG (MANZsche Taschenausgabe, 17th ed. 2006).

261. *See* §61(2) LOTJ (Spain) (Appendix, 264), which allows the clerk to aid in drafting the reasons Spanish jurors must give for their verdicts.

262. BGHSt 10, 208, 209–10.

nied to human knowledge in its state of imperfection. Therefore the task to which the trier of fact is alone obligated and which is decisive for the guilt question is to examine, without being bound by legal rules of evidence, whether he can overcome the theoretically possible doubts and convince himself of a certain state of facts or not.

The principle of free evaluation of the evidence, however, repeatedly received a doubtful and confusing formulation (...). There it was stated that "exceedingly high demands" should not be placed on the judicial inner conviction necessary for convicting the defendant, and the judge "should satisfy himself with such a high degree of probability" as arises after the most exhausting and conscientious use of the existing means of gaining knowledge. Such a formulation does not correctly reflect the principle of § 261 StPO. Just as little as the trier of fact may be prevented from drawing possible, if not binding consequences from certain facts, just as little may the preconditions be prescribed for him upon which he may come to a certain conclusion and inner conviction. It is especially prohibited for the court of cassation to replace the evidentiary evaluation of the trier of fact with its own. For only through an evaluation of the evidence can it be determined if a probability is so great that it borders on certainty. In the end, an inner conviction, even in the presence of the most possible probability of its correctness, cannot be "required."

If the court of cassation wanted to reject an acquittal based really on "last doubts," because on the basis of the determined evidentiary material it came to the conclusion that there existed a probability of the guilt of the defendant which bordered on certainty, then it would exceed the limits of its task. It would burden itself with a responsibility which it can and may not assume according to the legal design of the proceedings in cassation. The task of forming an inner conviction as to the guilt or lack of guilt of the defendant is that of the trier of fact alone.

In Germany as in most continental European countries, acquittals based on reasonable doubt may be appealed by the prosecution. This is not the case in the U.S. In the above case the German mixed court found the defendant not guilty of murder but guilty of a lesser offense of negligent homicide. Note the great amount of deference given the trier of fact.

In most continental European countries trial courts must give reasons for their judgments, whether of guilt or acquittal.[263] Thus, despite the "free eval-

---

263. Cf. §§ 485, 543 CPP (France) (for correctional and police courts); § 267 (1–3) StPO (Germany) (Appendix, 250) (all courts); Art. 120(3) Const. (Spain), § 142 LECr (Spain); Art. 111 (para. 6) Const. (Italy), § 546(1) CPP (Italy).

uation of evidence" by the trier of fact, appellate courts may reverse convictions (or acquittals) if they find that they are not based on proper reasons.[264]

Case of Otegi (Guipuzcoa Regional Court, Spain) (Verdict of March 6, 1997)[265]

[On December 10, 1995, Mikel Otegi, a young Basque sympathizer with the independence movement in the Basque Country, shot two Basque police officers (*ertzaintza*) dead with his shotgun at his farmhouse in Guipuzcoa Province. He had been drinking heavily throughout the preceding day and evening and had been followed home by the police after he had threatened an off-duty police officer in a bar. He had previously had run-ins with the Basque Police and testified that he felt they were harassing him. On March 6, 1997, the jury acquitted Otegi of both murders in a 5–4 majority vote of the nine jurors. The following are selected sections from the special verdict form submitted to the jury and its response to each proposition therein included.][266]

A. *Principal Facts of the Prosecution*

1. UNFAVORABLE FACT: Mr. Mikel Mirena Otegi Unanue [hereafter "Otegi"], on December 10, 1995, around 10:30 a.m., at the farmhouse Oteizabal, voluntarily and with intent to kill, shot Mr. Ignacio Jesús Mendiluce Echeberría [hereafter "Mendiluce"] with a .12 caliber shotgun, hitting him in the lower right clavicular region and killing him instantly. **Not Proved. Majority**

2. UNFAVORABLE FACT: Otegi, on the same day and at the same time in the same place, and voluntarily, with intent to kill, shot José

---

264. *See* § 261 StPO (Germany) (Appendix, 249); § 192 CPP (Italy); § 741 LECr (Spain) (Appendix, 261). The standard of "free evaluation of evidence" was introduced on the European continent along with jury trial in the late 18th and early 19th Centuries to replace the so-called "formal rules of evidence" which required specifically prescribed forms of proof (i.e., two witnesses) and originally allowed torture. Roxin, *supra* note 32, at 90. The freedom jurors had in England and America to acquit or convict according to their inner conviction was transferred to the European system and applied even where professional judges made the decisions. Landau, *supra* note 259, at 281–82.

265. Verdict on file with author.

266. The case caused an uproar in Spain and led to calls to abolish or severely restrict the new jury system, which had been in effect for less than a year at the time of the trial. For more on the *Otegi* case, *see* Stephen C. Thaman, *Spain Returns to Trial by Jury*, 21 HASTINGS INT'L & COMP. L. REV. 241, 380–81, 405–12, 497–503, 517–24 (1998).

Luis González Villanueva [hereafter "González"] hitting him in the left scapular region and killing him instantly. **Not Proved. Majority**

3. UNFAVORABLE FACT: Otegi shot Mendiluce without there having been any provocation on the part of the latter. **Not Proved. Majority**

4. [same as "3" in relation to González]

5. UNFAVORABLE FACT: Otegi shot Mendiluce from a distance of approximately 1.5 meters. **Proved. Unanimously**

6. UNFAVORABLE FACT: Otegi shot González from a distance of approximately 2.5 meters. **Proved. Unanimously**

7. UNFAVORABLE FACT: Otegi shot Mendiluce in a sudden and unexpected fashion. **Not Proved. Majority**

8. UNFAVORABLE FACT: Otegi shot Mendiluce before he had a chance of defending himself. **Not Proved. Majority**

9. UNFAVORABLE FACT: Otegi shot González in the back. **Not Proved. Majority**

10. [same as "7" in relation to González]

11. [same as "8" in relation to González]

12. UNFAVORABLE FACT: In the moment of receiving the mortal wound, Mendiluce was a Basque Police officer, dressed in his official uniform and exercising his lawful duties. **Proved. Unanimously**

13. [identical to "14" in relation to González]

14. UNFAVORABLE FACT: Otegi was conscious that he was shooting at a Basque police officer when he fired at Mendiluce. **Not Proved. Majority**

15. [identical to "14" in relation to González]

[Questions 16–19 relate to issues only relevant to the civil action.]

B. *Facts Which are Object of the Defense*

[Questions 20–47, all favorable to the defense, deal with Otegi's drinking during the day prior to the shootings, his aggressive conduct with an off-duty police officer in a bar, his being followed home by the two victims due to erratic driving, his being awakened by the victims, his getting his shotgun after an argument had started and one officer had pulled his duty revolver. All were found to be proved by the jury.]

48. FAVORABLE FACT: At this location the argument with the Basque Police officers resumed, Otegi now armed with the loaded shotgun. **Proved. Unanimously**

49. FAVORABLE FACT: In the course of the argument, the Basque Police officer González pointed his weapon at Otegi. **Proved. Majority**

50. FAVORABLE FACT: In the course of the argument, Otegi felt that the weapon of the Basque Police officer González was pointed at him. **Proved. Majority**

51. FAVORABLE FACT: Then Otegi completely lost control of his actions. **Proved. Majority**

52. FAVORABLE FACT: (only if the preceding fact "51" has not been proved): Then Otegi partially lost control of his actions. (No answer)

53. UNFAVORABLE FACT: In this situation, Otegi fired the shotgun. **Proved. Unanimously**

54. FAVORABLE FACT: Otegi fired two shots without intending to kill. **Proved. Majority**

55. FAVORABLE FACT: Oregi fired two shots without consciousness of killing. **Proved. Majority**

[Questions 56–68 refer to mitigating circumstances which happened after the killings, such as calling the police, not escaping, remorse, etc.]

C. *Facts Alleged by the Parties Which Can Go Towards Proving a Lack of Criminal Responsibility*

69. FAVORABLE FACT: Otegi has a personality with a propensity or predisposition to experience feelings of harassment and persecution by the Basque Police. **Proved. Majority**

70. FAVORABLE FACT: In Otegi there exists a pre-existing pathological condition or an ailment or an underlying psychic disturbance in connection with the aforementioned sense of harassment and persecution by the Basque Police which he experienced in extreme ways, intolerable for his personality. **Proved. Majority**

[Questions 71–75, all of which were proved, deal with prior incidents Otegi had with the Basque Police and the fact that they patrolled his house.]

76. FAVORABLE FACT: Otegi consumed an excessive quantity of alcoholic beverages between the afternoon and evening of December 9 and 10, 1995, until he achieved a state of inebriation. **Proved. Unanimously**

77. FAVORABLE FACT: The conjunction of all of the facts laid out in numbers "69" through "76" of Part C, or, in the alternative, of those which have been declared proved, had as a result that in the moment

of firing the weapon Otegi was absolutely not in control of his actions. **Proved. Majority**

D. *Facts Which Determine the Modification of Criminal Responsibility*

[Questions 78–91 deal with various favorable and unfavorable facts which could aggravate or mitigate criminal liability.]

E. *Criminal Acts for Which the Defendant Must Be Declared Guilty or Not Guilty*

92. Otegi intentionally killed the Basque Police officer González, who wore the official uniform and was on active duty, shooting in a sudden and unexpected manner from a shotgun which he held without giving him a chance to defend himself. **Not Guilty. Majority**

93. (Only in case the defendant is declared not guilty of the fact contained in the preceding number 92): Otegi intentionally killed the Basque Police officer González, who wore the official uniform and was on active duty, shooting him with the shotgun he held and using the advantage said shotgun gave him. **Not Guilty. Majority**

94. [same as "92" in relation to Mendiluce]

95. [same as "93" in relation to Mendiluce]

F. *Criteria of the Jury in Relation to Whether or Not to Grant a Petition for Total or Partial Clemency in the Sentence*

96. FAVORABLE FACT: In case of a verdict of guilty and that the legal prerequisites exist for its application, the jury favors a conditional punishment. (no answer)

97. FAVORABLE FACT: In case of a verdict of guilty, the jury is in favor of total pardon of the punishment. (no answer)

98. FAVORABLE FACT: In case of a verdict of guilty and of a vote against the preceding fact, the jury favors a partial pardon of the punishment. (no answer)

Reasoning

Referring to the questions "92," "93," "94," and "95," the jury finds that they were "deficiently proved," but finds not proved the circumstances. Had doubts.

Observe how the Spanish jury verdict differs from the American. When France introduced trial by jury in 1789 following the French Revolution, it adopted a kind of special verdict with a list of questions relating to the factual underpinnings for a finding of guilt, mitigating circumstances, etc. All European countries which introduced trial by jury in the 19th Century followed this model, which was adopted again by Spain and Russia in the 1990s when they returned to trial by jury.[267] Continental European jury verdicts universally required only a majority or qualified majority vote of the jurors.[268]

Note how one can trace the logic of the jury's verdict in the *Otegi* case. Such a verdict form enables appellate courts to test whether the conclusions reached are logical in relation to each other and can allow professional judges to write a reasoned judgment as is required in most European countries. Note also the last lines in the verdict, consisting of some "reasons" given by the jury for their verdict. Spain's jury law provides that the jury, besides returning a special verdict addressing the proof of the elements of the crime and grounds for mitigation and aggravation, must also give reasons for having found the case proved or not proved.[269]

Otegi Case: Decision of March 11, 1998 (Spanish Supreme Court)[270]

One of the novel characteristics of the Organic Law on the Jury Court is the inclusion of a fourth section to the verdict in which it shall be stated that "the jurors have considered the following as pieces of evidence in making the preceding declarations." The legislator, in accordance with the constitutional mandate of Art. 120(3) Const., desired that the judgment with which a trial by jury culminates should be constructed on what one author called "reinforced reasons," derived from the content of § 61(1)(d) LOTJ which requires an expression by the jurors in the verdict of the items of evidence they considered in the evaluations underlying the declarations integrated into their verdict.

The omission of this legal requirement causes a nullity (...), for it constitutes a defect in form which implies the absence of an indispen-

---

267. For a comparison of Spanish and Russian "question lists," *see* Stephen C. Thaman, *The Separation of Questions of Law and Fact in the New Russian and Spanish Jury Verdicts*, in THE JUDICIAL ROLE IN CRIMINAL PROCEEDINGS (Sean Doran & John Jackson eds. 2000). *See also* § 52(1) LOTJ (Spain) (Appendix, 262–63); §§ 349–350 CPP (France) (applicable only in the mixed court).

268. In Spain, seven of a jury of nine must agree to prove any fact disadvantageous to the defendant (including guilt). Five votes are sufficient to prove any fact favorable to the defense. § 59 LOTJ (Spain).

269. § 61(1)(d) LOTJ (Spain) (Appendix, 263-64).

270. LA LEY (5.12.98), No. 4226, 6, 12–13.

sable requirement indicated by the law in developing Art. 120(3) Const., and which, moreover, causes an effective denial of due process and prevents the parties from knowing what reasons led the jury to decide in this way. (...)

A reading of the verdict reveals an absolute absence of an explanation in relation to the reasons which led the jury to declare proved or not proved all of the facts enumerated in the verdict form. There is only an allusion to the existence of doubt, without further concretization, which prevents one from knowing if it is a question of reasonable doubt or not about the criminal acts as to which the defendant had to be declared guilty or not guilty, the rubric under which facts 92 through 95 are included in the verdict form.

The fifth reason in the appeal (...), alleges a violation of Art. 24(2) Const. alone, and in relation with §54(3) LOTJ which protects the right to a trial with all the guarantees and the presumption of innocence which are part of a fair trial and due process (Arts. 6(1) ECHR and 14 ICCPR) and require that, in order to pronounce a judgment of conviction the court must act with certainty as to guilt and must acquit if the evaluation of the evidence does not liberate it from doubt. The judgment being appealed [that of the intermediate court of appeal which reversed the acquittal of *Otegi*] allegedly infringes upon, and consequently violates the principles and rights therein expounded by not taking account of the doubt which the jury expresses in the verdict which is a sufficient basis for a declaration of non-culpability of the defendant. (...)

This reason must also be rejected. Guilt and innocence do not admit of anything in between. If the court has doubts about the actual occurrence of the acts it should acquit — and this is obvious — but not erect the expression of this doubt as a basis for acquittal. By thus acting in this case it violated the norms of the LOTJ as to the form in which it should formulate the verdict. The contested judgment (...) expressed it in a manner which cannot be surpassed: "The indication that the circumstances presented to them were not deemed to have been proved is equivalent to reiterating a conclusion not found proved once again in the succinct explication in which reasons should be given. This specification adds nothing — if anything, only laxity and confusion — to the defect consisting in having failed to succinctly explain the reasons which persuaded them. The invocation of a doubt and the appeals to that which the law requires — with which the jury pretends to support the answers for which it did not take care to give reasons earlier — reveal that, disguising with perplexity a psychological state which has nothing to do with serious vacillation, the jury invents the existence of a doubt to gratuitously prejudge, to grab the handle of § 54(3) of the law. Shielded by the prohibition in this principle, the jury proclaims that it is assaulted with doubt, that it finds itself in a position where it is impossible to dissipate it and, because of this, decides to resolve the case in the sense most favorable to the defendant. It does not describe the way in which the doubt arose, nor its scope. (...)

Read through the question list in the *Otegi* case once more. Can you discern from the answers why the jury determined that Otegi was not guilty of the murders? Note that they found a combination of diminished capacity due to alcoholic intoxication and psychological pressures caused by alleged police harassment. The Court seems to claim that the jury did not sufficiently explain why it rejected the evidence of guilt, that is, on what it based its doubts, and thus upheld the reversal of the acquittal. If Otegi was presumed innocent, and the defense questions relating to excuses for the crime or lack of guilt due to unconsciousness were based on evidence presented at the trial, and the jury found these exonerating circumstances to be true, then why must the jury explain the doubts they had about the prosecution's arguments? Is he not presumed innocent *until* the prosecutor proves the elements of a crime beyond a reasonable doubt.[271]

§ 339 (1–5) UPK (Russia)

(1) For each act the defendant has been charged with committing, (...) three principal questions shall be asked: (1) has it been proved, that the act took place; (2) has it been proved, that the act was committed by the defendant; (3) is the defendant guilty of having committed the act.

---

271. Before the LOTJ (Spain) went into effect, scholars felt that giving reasons for an acquittal might violate the presumption of innocence. *See* José Antonio Díaz Cabiale, *Prueba, Veredicto, Deliberación y Sentencia*, in Agustín Pérez-Cruz Martín et al, Comentarios sistemáticos a la Ley del Jurado y a la reforma de la prisión preventiva 276, 333–36 (1996); Francisco Marés Roger & José-Antonio Mora Alarcón, Comentarios a la Ley del Jurado 398 (1996). The Spanish Constitutional Court has upheld the constitutionality of § 61(1)(d) LOTJ (Spain) as it relates to the sufficiency of the reasons for acquitting with a strong dissenting opinion by President of the Court María Emilie Casas Baamonde and two other judges who claimed the requirement violated the presumption of innocence. Decision No. 169 of October 6, 2004 (Spanish Constitutional Court), 283 BJC 5. The majority of the court upheld the reversal of the *Otegi* acquittal as well, based on the same jurisprudence. Decision No. 246 of December 20, 2004 (Spanish Constitutional Court), 285 BJC 263.

(2) It is also possible in the question list to pose only one basic question as to the guilt of the defendant representing a consolidation of the questions indicated in the first part of this section.

(3) After the principal question of the defendant's guilt, specific questions may be asked as to those circumstances which aggravate or mitigate the level of guilt or modify its character or lead to the exoneration of the defendant from responsibility. When required, questions shall also be asked as to the level of realization of the criminal intent, reasons why the act was not carried out to the end, and the level and character of the participation of each of the defendants in the commission of the crime. Questions are admissible which permit the establishment of the defendant's guilt of the commission of less serious crimes if it does not worsen the position of the defendant and does not violate his right to defense.

(4) In the case of a finding of the defendant's guilt, a question shall be asked as to whether he deserves lenience.

(5) Questions may not be asked, either separately or in combination, which require the jurors to make a legal qualification of the status of the defendant (as to his prior convictions) or also other questions requiring strict legal evaluation in the jury's rendering of its verdict. (...)

The Russian verdict form, like the Spanish, may contain questions relating to mitigation, aggravation, or facts relating to excuses or justifications. It seems that this would allow Russian jurors to determine in a homicide case, like the *Otegi* case, whether the defendant intended to kill, labored under heat of passion or diminished capacity, etc. The Russian Supreme Court, however, has ruled that questions posed to the jurors may not include: "the use of such legal terms as intentional or negligent murder, intentional murder with exceptional cruelty, intentional murder with hooliganistic motivation or for personal gain, intentional murder committed in the heat of passion, murder using excessive force in self-defense, rape, robbery, etc."[272]

Whereas the U.S. jury decides the defendant's guilt, or lack thereof, as to the charged *crime*, the Russian Supreme Court has limited the Russian jury

---

272. Postanovlenie Plenuma Verkhovnogo Suda Rossiyskoy Federatsii: *O nekotorykh voprosakh primeneniia sudami ugolovno-protsessual'nykh norm, reglamentiruiushchikh proizvodstvo v sude prisiazhnykh*, No. 9, ¶ 18 (Dec. 20, 1994) (hereafter SCRF, Decision No. 9), published in SBORNIK POSTANOVLENIY PLENUMOV VERKHOVNYKH SUDOV SSSR I RSFSR (ROSSIYSKOY FEDERATSII) PO UGOLOVNYM DELAM 569–80 (1995).

to merely finding whether certain facts have been proved, leaving it to the professional judge to then determine whether there was "intent to kill," "heat of passion," "rape," etc.[273] Note, however, how the jury in the following case responded when confronted with an abused woman arrested *in flagrante*, literally red-handed, and with no statutory defenses after having killed her abuser:

Case of Kraskina (Ivanovo Regional Court, Russia) (Verdict of March 10, 1995)[274]

The following questions are posed to the jury panel for their decision:

(1) Has it been proved, that on October 17, 1994, around 4:00 p.m. in apartment no. 1 on Ul'ianov Street in the city of Navoloki in Kineshma Precinct, Ivanovo Region, serious bodily injury was inflicted on the victim Yuriy Anatol'evich Smirnov in the form of a stab wound to the brain, complicated by spinal shock, from which his death ensued at the scene in a brief period of time, in a matter of minutes?

ANSWER: Yes, proved. Unanimously.

(2) If an affirmative answer was given to the first question, has it been proved, that the aforementioned injury to the victim, who was at a serious level of alcoholic intoxication, was inflicted by the defendant V.A. Kraskina, who threw him to the floor and intentionally administered him one blow with a home-made knife, which she prepared beforehand for this purpose, for she was dissatisfied with the conduct of her living companion, which had expressed itself in drunkenness, filthy language and extortion of money for the purpose of drinking booze?

ANSWER: Yes, proved. Unanimously

(3) If an affirmative answer was given to the second question, is V.A. Kraskina guilty of the intentional infliction of the aforementioned in-

---

273. The original draft of the Spanish jury law would have had the jury find guilt as to the charged crime, but the jury, in the final version, must find guilt as to the "criminal act" or *hecho delictivo*. Luciano Varela Castro, *El enjuiciamiento de ciudadanos por ciudadanos. Algunas prácticas conformadas por una jurisprudencia abrogante*, in LA LEY DEL JURADO: PROBLEMAS DE APLICACIÓN PRÁCTICA 547, 580–81 (Luis Aguiar de Luque & Luciano Varela Castro eds. 2004).

274. GOSUDARSTVENNO-PRAVOVOE UPRAVLENIE PREZIDENTA ROSSIYSKOY FEDERATSII, LETOPIS' SUDA PRISIAZHNYKH, Vol. 5, 19 (1995).

juries to Yu. A. Smirnos, all the while desiring his death and knowingly allowing it to ensue?

ANSWER: No, not guilty. Unanimously.

Decision of June 7, 1995 (*Kraskina* Case) (Russian Supreme Court)[275]

Kraskina, who had a prior conviction for attempted intentional murder, was found to be not guilty by the verdict of a jury of the intentional murder of her living companion, Yu. A. Smirnov, who was born in 1954.

In the appeal in cassation it is requested that the judgment be reversed and the case remanded for a new trial. It is pointed out in the appeal that the jury found that the factual circumstances of Kraskina's commission of the murder of Smirnov were proved, but that they gave a negative answer to the question of guilt. Discerning therein a contradictory verdict, the public prosecutor asserts that the presiding judge, in violation of §456 UPK did not take measures to eliminate the contradiction in the verdict, which substantially violated the law on criminal procedure.

After examining the case file and discussing the arguments presented in the appeal in cassation, the cassational panel finds that there have been no violations of procedural norms which regulate the trial of the case in the jury court.

The questions subject to the decision of the jury were formulated in the question list in conformance with §449 UPK. The summation of the presiding judge was in complete conformance with the requirements of §451 UPK. The parties made no objections as to the content of the summation of the presiding judge claiming violations of the principle of objectivity.

On the basis of the evidence presented, the jury came to the conclusion that Kraskina was not guilty. The parties discussed the consequences of the jury's verdict, taking into account §458 UPK, which prohibits the parties in their arguments from calling into doubt the correctness of the verdict returned by the jury.

The presiding judge properly did not find the verdict to be contradictory. The jury gave a clear answer to the question of the innocence of Kraskina (§456 UPK).

---

275. *Id.*, at 22. All UPK cites refer to the UPK RSFSR (old code of criminal procedure).

Inasmuch as the verdict of the jury is obligatory for the presiding judge (§459 UPK), Kraskina was acquitted properly by the judgment which was rendered.

Note how the jury answered the three principal questions in the Russian question list. They found that a homicide did occur, that Kraskina was responsible for it, and that she had no legal excuses or justifications. Yet they acquitted her. Read the following French instruction, originally designed for the jury but now used in the French mixed court, and ask yourselves whether that court could acquit in a case like that of Kraskina:

§353 CPP (France)

Before the *cour d'assise* retires, the presiding judge reads the following instruction which is, furthermore, posted in large letters in the most visible place in the jury room:

The law does not demand of judges an accounting of the means by which you were convinced; nor does it prescribe rules according to which the completeness or the sufficiency of evidence can be determined; it requires that you reflect in silence and with careful thought in order to determine, in the sincerity of your consciences, what impression has been made upon your reasoning by the evidence adduced against the defendant and the means of his defense. The law asks only one question which sums up your entire duty: Do you have an 'inner conviction' (*intime conviction*).

An inner, personal, or *intime conviction* was a state of mind derived from the standard used in English jury trials, referred to often as "verdict according to conscience." In this spirit, the verdict of acquittal of the French mixed court (nine lay and three professional judges) is final, as is the acquittal of an American or English jury.[276]

Note how the following provision of the Spanish jury law prevents the judge from accepting a verdict as was returned in the *Kraskina* case:

---

276. An appeal of an acquittal in cassation may only address questions of law in France, but may not reverse or nullify the judgment. §§368, 572 CPP (France). On how the outdated, "romantic" standard of *intime conviction* has ceded to the less expansive and more controlled standard of "free evaluation of the evidence" (*freie Beweiswürdigung*), *see* MIRJAN R. DAMASKA, EVIDENCE LAW ADRIFT 21 (1997). Note: in the translation of German opinions in this book, the term *inner conviction* is used to express the German word *Überzeugung*, related to the process of being "convinced," whereas the word "conviction" alone is used to translate the German word *Verurteilung*, meaning a formal judgment of guilt.

§ 63(1)(d) LOTJ (Spain)

(1) The presiding judge will return the verdict to the jury if, after reading a copy thereof, he finds the following circumstances: (...)

(d) the diverse pronouncements are contradictory, either the statements as to the facts declared proved amongst themselves, or the pronouncement of guilt in relation to the declaration of the facts proved.

The Spanish and Russian jury laws allow the jury to decide aggravating and mitigating circumstances and thus, indirectly, the parameters of punishment. The Russian jury may recommend lenience which reduces the maximum punishment and even allows the trial judge to sentence below the statutory minimum. The jury in both systems is made aware of the parameters of punishment applicable in case of a verdict of guilty. In most states in the U.S., as well as in the federal system, the jury is kept completely in the dark as to what sentence will ensue in the event of a guilty verdict, except in capital cases.[277]

C. Evaluating the Non-Flagrant Case Based on Circumstantial Evidence

When a crime has been committed but no suspect has been apprehended *in flagrante*, the crucial element in a case is often that of proving the identity of the perpetrator. In the Common Law bifurcated jury court, in which the jury deliberates without participation of any professional judges, control of the jury's decision in identification cases (as well as in all others) must be provided through the judge's instructions to the jury before it retires to deliberate:

Regina v. Turnbull (English Court of Appeal) (1976)[278]

[The court heard consolidated appeals in three cases in which the convictions were based on eyewitness identification.]

Each of these appeals raises problems relating to evidence of visual identification in criminal cases. Such evidence can bring about miscarriages of justice and has done so in a few cases in recent years. The number of such cases, although small compared with the number in which evidence of visual identification is known to be satisfactory, ne-

---

277. Shannon v. United States, 512 U.S. 573 (1994).
278. [1977] 1 Q.B. 224, 228–31.

cessitates steps being taken by the courts, including this court, to reduce that number as far as is possible. In our judgment the danger of miscarriages of justice occurring can be much reduced if trial judges sum up to juries in the way indicated in this judgment.

First, whenever the case against an accused depends wholly or substantially on the correctness of one or more identifications of the accused which the defence alleges to be mistaken, the judge should warn the jury of the special need for caution before convicting the accused in reliance on the correctness of the identification or identifications. In addition he should instruct them as to the reason for the need for such a warning and should make some reference to the possibility that a mistaken witness can be a convincing one and that a number of such witnesses can all be mistaken. (...)

Secondly, the judge should direct the jury to examine closely the circumstances in which the identification by each witness came to be made. How long did the witness have the accused under observation? At what distance? In what light? Was the observation impeded in any way, as for example by passing traffic or a press of people? Had the witness ever seen the accused before? How often? If only occasionally, had he any special reason for remembering the accused? How long elapsed between the original observation and the subsequent identification to the police? Was there any material discrepancy between the description of the accused given to the police by the witness when first seen by them and his actual appearance? If in any case, whether it is being dealt with summarily or on indictment, the prosecution have reason to believe that there is such a material discrepancy they should supply the accused or his legal advisers with particulars of the description the police were first given. In all cases if the accused asks to be given particulars of such descriptions, the prosecution should supply them. Finally, he should remind the jury of any specific weaknesses which had appeared in the identification evidence.

Recognition may be more reliable than identification of a stranger; but even when the witness is purporting to recognise someone whom he knows, the jury should be reminded that mistakes in recognition of close relatives and friends are sometimes made.

All these matters go to the quality of the identification evidence. If the quality is good and remains good at the close of the accused's case, the danger of a mistaken identification is lessened; but the poorer the quality, the greater the danger.

In our judgment when the quality is good, as for example when the identification is made after a long period of observations, or in satisfactory conditions by a relative, a neighbour, a close friend, a workmate and the like, the jury can safely be left to assess the value of the identifying evidence even though there is no other evidence to support it: provided always, however, that an adequate warning has been given about the special need for caution. Were the courts to adjudge otherwise, affronts to justice would frequently occur. (...)

The trial judge should identify to the jury the evidence which he adjudges is capable of supporting the evidence of identification. If there is any evidence or circumstances which the jury might think was supporting when it did not have this quality, the judge should say so. A jury, for example, might think that support for identification evidence could be found in the fact that the accused had not given evidence before them. An accused's absence from the witness box cannot provide evidence of anything and the judge should tell the jury so.[279] But he would be entitled to tell them that when assessing the quality of the identification evidence they could take into consideration the fact that it was uncontradicted by any evidence coming from the accused himself.

Care should be taken by the judge when directing the jury about the support for an identification which may be derived from the fact that they have rejected an alibi. False alibis may be put forward for many reasons: an accused, for example, who has only his own truthful evidence to rely on may stupidly fabricate an alibi and get lying witnesses to support it out of fear that his own evidence will not be enough. Further, alibi witnesses can make genuine mistakes about dates and occasions like any other witnesses can. It is only when the jury is satisfied that the sole reason for the fabrication was to deceive them and there is no other explanation for its being put forward can fabrication provide any support for identification evidence. The jury should be reminded that proving the accused has told lies about where he was at the material time does not by itself prove that he was where the identifying witness says he was. (...)

A failure to follow these guidelines is likely to result in a conviction being quashed and will do so if in the judgment of this court on all the evidence the verdict is either unsatisfactory or unsafe.

In the notorious German case which follows, the court of cassation must deal with a court's appraisal of circumstantial evidence and issues of eyewitness identification:

---

279. In light of the right to use silence as evidence of guilt introduced by the Criminal Justice and Public Order Act 1994, Appendix (242–45), do you think the lack of such an instruction will mean more innocent people will be convicted based on eyewitness testimony?

Case of *Monika Weimar*. Decision of November 6, 1998 (German Supreme Court)[280]

[Monika Weimar was sentenced to imprisonment for life for the murder of her children M. and K. by the Superior Court of Fulda on January 8, 1988. A new trial was ordered and the Superior Court of Gießen acquitted the defendant. The public prosecutor and the collateral complainant (the victims' father) appealed. The Supreme Court reversed.]

According to the findings, the marriage of the defendant with the collateral complainant was in a rut. It often came to verbal and violent confrontations between the married couple. The defendant turned to another man, the American citizen P. The relationship was not concealed from the collateral complainant. She herself confronted him quite early with her decision to divorce him and that she wanted to live together with P and the children. But the collateral complainant did not accept a divorce. Thereafter the married couple lived "at a distance and to a great extent silent next to each other."

On Sunday, August 3, 1986, there was a violent confrontation between the married couple W. The defendant thereafter drove with the children and P. to go swimming. After she brought the children back home, where the collateral complainant was, she left home around 8:15 p.m. and spent the evening with P. Around 3:20 a.m. she returned home.

Before noon on August 4, 1986, the defendant ran different errands with the family car in a neighboring town. Around 11:00 a.m. she was seen at the place where the body of M. was found three days later. After her return home she participated in the search for the children who had, in the meantime, been missing. On August 7, 1986, the bodies of the children were found.

The defendant explained in several interrogations that the children were still living when she left the home on Monday morning (August 4, 1986). On August 29, 1986, she announced in her interrogation as an accused, that the children were lying dead in their beds when she came home at 3:20 a.m. on August 4, 1986. Her husband, according to her, had killed the children while she was away from home, so that, as he explained, neither of them would get them in the divorce.

---

280. StV 1999/5, 5–7.

According to the findings in the Superior Court, the children M. and K. were killed either in the night from August 3 to August 4, 1986, by the collateral complainant, or before noon on August 4, 1986, by the defendant. The mixed court (*Schwurgericht*)[281] found itself unable to explain whether the collateral complainant killed the children during the absence of the defendant and she found them dead upon her return, or if the defendant killed them before noon on the next day and placed them at the place they were later found.

If the children were still alive before noon on August 4, 1986, only the defendant can be considered as the perpetrator in the view of the Superior Court. The court sitting in judgment acquitted the defendant because it could not convince itself of this fact. However, the Superior Court found a number of circumstances to be true which incriminate the defendant to a great extent. It did not find itself in a position, however, to clarify the identity of the perpetrator with ultimate security because it could not determine a motive for the defendant to kill the children and—as the experts advised—the conduct of the defendant after the death of the children was judged as being "psychologically understandable and consistent with the personality of the defendant." In this context it was not able to follow the statements of the married couple F., which announced that they had seen the children before noon on August 4, 1986 (...).

If the court acquits a defendant, because it cannot overcome doubts as to his identity as the perpetrator, then this must be accepted as a rule by the court of cassation. The evaluation of the evidence is in principle the job of the trier of fact. The determination in cassation is limited to the examination of whether legal errors occurred when the trier of fact evaluated the evidence. This is the case in a substantive legal sense if the evaluation of the evidence is contradictory, unclear, or fraught with gaps or violates laws of thought or secure axioms of experience. Evidentiary conclusions of the trier of fact are also subject to attack if they reveal that the court placed over-stretched demands on the formation of the inner conviction necessary to convict and thereby fails to recognize that an absolute certainty, which of necessity compels the intellect to exclude the opposite and is doubted by no one, is not required; rather a measure of confidence suffices which is

---

281. In trials of serious felonies, the German mixed court consists of three professional judges and two lay assessors but still retains the old name: "jury court." Four of the five votes are needed for a conviction. §76 GVG (Germany). Thus the professional judges need at least one lay vote for a conviction.

sufficient according to life experience and excludes only reasonable doubt and not based on conceptual theoretical possibilities. (...)

Such legal errors are present here. They concern the evaluation of the statements made by the married couple F. as witnesses.

According to the findings which are not legally erroneous, the children were killed either in the evening from August 3 to August 4, 1986 by R.W. or before noon on August 4, 1986, by the defendant. The married couple F. stated, from their first examination on August 11, 1986, on, and at the trial before the Superior Court of Gießen, "confidently and consistently without contradiction in a constant manner," that they had seen the children on Monday before noon. If this is true, then under the given circumstances found to be true by the expanded mixed court, not the husband of the defendant but only she herself could have killed the children.

However the Superior Court did not follow the statements of the married couple F. The reason given therefor is doubtful in many respects.

The Superior Court examines the statements intensively and finds that a "mistake on the part of the married couple F., despite a rather short perception and insufficient lighting, seems improbable." There exists "no serious reason for the presence of problems in their perception." A mistaken identification of the children by the witnesses "seems to be scarcely imaginable," for a consciously untrue statement by the witnesses there is no "plausible reasonable ground." After these explanations, the Superior Court saw no evidence which could be seriously considered for the fact that the statements of the witnesses F. could be incorrect. Why the Superior Court nevertheless did not follow the pronouncements remains unclear. The judgment reasons are contradictory as to this point. If the Superior Court could find no rationally comprehensible reasons for doubt as to the credibility of the witnesses or as to the correctness of the content of the statements after examination of the pronouncements themselves or from other results of the evidence, then they were relevant. Then the Superior Court must draw the conclusions therefrom. It could not, on the one hand, find the witnesses credible and, on the other, refuse to base the judgment on their statements.

The Superior Court also explains, however, that, as a whole, a mistake on the part of the married couple F. would be "improbable." This could indicate, to be sure, that a mistake on the part of the witnesses was not completely excluded and that their statements would not therefore suffice for the finding that the children still lived on Monday before noon. As has been shown, the Superior Court did not consider a mistake on the part of the witnesses to be a possibility which should be seriously taken into consideration. When the mixed court nonetheless doubted the correctness of the pronouncements, this is only explainable by an overstretching of the demands on the formation of judicial [inner] conviction. (…) Greater certainty as to the correctness of the pronouncements of the witnesses than that which was found would only be thinkable in the sense of an exclusion of abstract, theoretical doubts. This can, however, not be required. (…)

The evaluation of the evidence is also subject to doubt to the extent that the Superior Court believes that a conviction could not be based on the testimony of the witnesses F. alone, due to the lack of supplementary incriminating evidence.

To that extent, the penal chamber already neglected to evaluate the statements of the married couple F. along with the pronouncements of further witnesses, who also had seen the children still alive. The witness N. continuously pronounced and the witness A., at least in the early stages of the proceedings, that they saw the children on that day before noon and, to be sure, independently of one another on different occasions and from different observation points.

To be sure, the conclusions of the mixed court that the witness N. and the witness A.(the grandmother of the defendant), who retracted her earlier statement in this regard, could have been mistaken, is possible in itself and must therefore be accepted by the court of cassation. The court did not consider, however, whether it could speak against a mistake on the part of the witnesses that several persons pronounced independently of one another that they saw the children in different situations alive. It was not taken into consideration that the probability of a simultaneous mistake by several persons — independent of one another confirming in essence the same evidentiary material — can be less than in the case of a single witness statement.

This is not contradicted by the fact that other persons, above all the playmates of M. and K. did not see them before noon on that date. Because their possibilities of observation differed temporally from those of the witnesses who saw the children, their pronouncements were without importance for the formation of the [inner] conviction of the Superior Court.

Doubt as to the correctness of the statements made by the witnesses F. was not so obvious in light of the totality of the evidence, but the lack of importance of their pronouncements in the results was obvious. The opposite, rather, is the case.

As weighty reasons for the identity of the defendant as the perpetrator, the Superior Court made the following error-free findings: "the scarcely plausible, non-comprehensible admission of the defendant, her conduct on the days up to the discovery of the bodies of the children, the results of the autopsy, the clothing of the children, the temporal possibility that the defendant could have committed the act before noon on August 4, 1986, as well as the observations of the witness E., the sister of the defendant, in the night from August 3 to 4, 1986.

Above all, the findings of the autopsy indicate a killing of the children after the taking of breakfast, therefore on Monday before noon. The fact that they wore daytime clothing, were partially combed and wore barrettes, which they habitually took off before going to bed, speak contrary to their having been killed at night.

The case must therefore be tried anew. The chamber deems it appropriate to remand the case (...) to a penal chamber competent as an expanded mixed court in the Superior Court of Frankfurt am Main.[282]

Notice how the German Supreme Court picks holes in the output of the mixed court in the *Weimar* case and reverses the judgment. Compare this with the typical scenario in reversals of jury judgments of conviction in U.S. cases: the appellate courts pick holes in the input given to the jury by the professional judge in the form of jury instructions. In mixed courts there are no formal instructions given by the presiding judge to the lay components of the court. The entire procedure of deliberation and discussion of the law is *in camera* and may not be divulged. The court is required, however, to thoroughly document in its reasons the law which was applied and why the court came to the conclusion that certain facts underlying the judgment were proved and others not.

European law places great weight on the importance of having a reasoned judgment which can be reviewed by higher courts. This is considered to be a guarantee against arbitrary justice. But are the reasons given the real reasons for the court having reached the decision it reached in secret deliberations? Consider the following report from a German magazine after the acquittal of Monika Weimar in the case which was the subject of the above decision: "When the Superior Court of Gießen on April 24, 1997, pronounced the acquittal of Monika Böttchers, formerly Weimar, of the charge of murder of her daughters Karola and Melanie, both female lay assessors, touched to tears, shared in the happiness of the defendant. The professional judges appeared cast in stone—as if they had been outvoted by the lay people. The written

---

282. Monika Böttchers (formerly Weimar) was convicted in her third trial. Gisela Friedrichsen, *Ohne Pathos: schuldig*. DER SPIEGEL, Vol. 52 (1999), at 50.

justification of the acquittal strengthened this impression even more.[283] It was generally accepted that the professional judges, who are responsible for writing the judgment even if they are outvoted by their lay colleagues, intentionally drafted reasons for the judgment of acquittal, with which they wre seemingly in disaccord, that they knew would not stand appellate scrutiny.[284]

The following German case arising out of the holocaust involves the German Supreme Court refusing to overturn an acquittal despite some strong circumstantial evidence that the defendants were indeed involved:

Decision of November 17, 1983 (German Supreme Court)[285]

The defendant W. was regional commissar in W. in the Ukraine from October 1941 through the retreat of German troops in early 1944. The defendant Z. was active as his secretary until October 1943. The substantiated accusatory pleading charges the defendant W. with participating as a co-perpetrator in two mass shootings in which the main part of the Jewish population of the region under his administration was murdered and to have himself murdered Jewish persons in six other cases. The accusatory pleading charges the defendant Z. with participating in the first of the two mass killings also as a co-perpetrator, and to have murdered or attempted to murder Jewish children in two other cases.

The Superior Court acquitted the defendants of these charges "due to lack of evidence on factual grounds." Upon an appeal in cassation by the public prosecutor the German Supreme Court reversed the judgment and remanded the case for a new trial and decision. The defendants were again acquitted because it could not be proved that they committed the acts. The appeal in cassation of the public prosecutor is unsuccessful.

To the extent that the appeal in cassation is directed at the acquittal of the defendants of the charge of being co-perpetrators of the "mass killings," its attacks are directed exclusively against the evaluation of the evidence. This is, however, a matter for the trier of fact alone,

---

283. *Weimar-Prozeß: Warten auf den Gnadenakt*, DER SPIEGEL, Vol. 46 (1998), at 98.

284. For some thoughts on the predicament of the professional judge when threatened with being out-voted by the lay assessors, *see* Mirjan Damaska, *Evidentiary Barriers to Conviction and Two Models of Criminal Procedure*, 121 U. PA. L. REV. 506, 540–43 (1973).

285. BGH NStZ 1984, Vol. 4, 180.

whose task is that of arriving at an inner conviction of the guilt or lack of guilt of the defendant. If he cannot overcome present, albeit slight doubts, he must acquit the defendant (...). The court of cassation must, in principle, accept such a decision. It may only review it with reference to legal errors, especially as to whether the evaluation of the evidence was contradictory in itself, unclear or incomplete, whether it deals comprehensively with the evidence, reveals violations of rules of logic or axioms of experience, or the trier of fact has made exaggerated demands on the certainty required for a conviction (...).

Such legal errors are not apparent in the contested judgment. The evaluation of the evidence is, contrary to the opinion of the appeal in cassation, neither incomplete nor does it contain contradictions or violations of the rules of logic.

The opinion of the appeal in cassation was incorrect in maintaining that the judgment is lacking "a comprehensive total evaluation of the evidence introduced in the trial." The Superior Court undertakes in the judgment reasons, rather, an incisive evaluation of the evidence in which it gets all it can out of the evidence available to it. It proceeds from the statements of the eyewitnesses, which it reports in detail, investigates their evidentiary value, and finally reaches the result, that from the "few trustworthy and usable statements" of these witnesses, also "in relation to statements by hearsay witnesses," the "proof of a criminally relevant participation of the defendants in both mass shootings" could not be deduced.

The position of the appeal in cassation that this evaluation of the evidence "lacks a sufficient analysis of the statements of the hearsay witnesses" finds no support in the judgment reasons. The Superior Court explains, rather, in a manner free of legal errors, that the statements of these "hearsay witnesses" do not allow it to make an "image (...) of the personality, and thus the credibility, of the declarant who remained in the dark, whereby in most of the cases it was not even explained who the declarant was or how many other declarants preceded her," especially, whether the respective declarant or the multiple links in the further chain of reports were also hearsay witnesses or whether they had conveyed observations they themselves made to the witnesses who were here evaluating them. On the basis of the statements of two of these witnesses — S. and Ze. — it shows in exemplary fashion how "untrustworthy" in the instant case "statements of identification from the declarants to the hearsay witnesses can be in connection with the complex and interwined events during the acts of annihilation and the multitude of different uniformed participants in the act." The Superior Court has thus sufficiently included the statements of the hearsay witnesses in its considerations. In the described state of the case it was—contrary to the view of the appeal in cassation—not required that all the witness statements were reported in detail.

The opinion of the appeal in cassation, that the Superior Court did not "sufficiently analyze the points to be extrapolated from the official position of the defendants—especially that of the defendant W., can finally not be seconded. The Superior Court has, rather, made incisive findings in relation to the official position of both defendants, their tasks, their activities in W. and their conduct in relation to the mass killings and included them in its evaluation of the evidence. The result to which it thereby came may, of course, seem alienated from reality. In relation to the official position of the defendant who administered the Ghetto, as well as the circumstance that he gave the Jewish Council the order to dig the "death pits" and supervised the continuation of the work thereon before the first "mass killing" of the impending "action against the Ghetto inhabitants" was announced, and was present—as was the defendant Z.—at the time of the transport of the Jewish victims in the Ghetto area, is very close to an assumption of complicity in the acts or at least to aiding and abetting. If the Superior Court nevertheless came to the conclusion that such conduct on the part of the defendants could not be proved, then the result of the evaluation of the evidence by the trier of fact must be accepted. The Court of Cassation cannot reverse an acquittal based on existing doubts even when, based on the evidence adduced, it is of the opinion that a probability of guilt approaching that of certainty exists (...). The responsibility for this acquittal lies alone with the trier of fact.

Can you understand why the German Supreme Court deferred to the mixed court's acquittal in the holocaust case, but not to the acquittal of Monika Weimar? Is it clear that the certainty of Weimar's guilt eclipsed that of W. who allegedly ordered the digging of the "death pits" before the Jewish population was exterminated?

D. Was There a Crime Committed? The Evaluation of the Credibility of Witnesses

In most of our cases we are presuming that a crime was committed. But credibility of witnesses is often crucial to determining whether certain kinds of crimes committed in secret actually occurred. Many sexual assault cases fall into this category. In the U.S., when a jury acquits or convicts in a rape case, it is often because they believed, or did not believe, the testimony of the complaining witness. Can higher courts fashion rules for weighing the credibility of conflicting testimony in such cases that can aid them in appraising the sufficiency of evidence in cassation?

Decision of January 1, 1988 (German Supreme Court)[286]

The Superior Court sentenced the defendant to imprisonment of one year and eight months for rape and suspended the execution of the punishment and imposed probation.

His appeal in cassation against this decision is successful in its factual assertions.

The conviction of the defendant is based on the statement of the witness B. who stated that the defendant forcefully carried out an act of sexual intercourse with her.

The defendant maintains that the witness had consensual sex with him. The statement of the witness B. is counterposed, thus, to the statement of the defendant. The decision as to acquittal or conviction is therefore dependent on whether the assertions of the witness are credible. The defendant may not be convicted if circumstances exist (because they are not susceptible of being disproved) or must be assumed in his favor, which for rational (intersubjectively communicable and understandable) reasons do not allow of the conclusion that a concurrence of the witness' statement and the actual events is probable to a great degree (...). According to settled case law (...), merely "abstract," "theoretical," "unreasonable" doubts, for which there is no real basis and "exaggerated" ("over-stretched") demands on the certainty required from the trier of fact, cannot call into question the "measure of [inner] conviction sufficient from life-experience" for a conviction. It follows, that reasons, on the other hand, which provide the basis for "reasonable doubts" as to a question relevant to a finding of guilt, will speak against a conviction (...). The "reasonable doubt" has its basis in rational argumentation which grasps the circumstances which speak in favor of the defendant completely and in the aspects which are material to the subject matter. If it gains a foothold, then the measure of proof of a high probability required for a conviction may not be achieved.

---

286. BGH NStZ 1988, Vol. 5, 236, 236–37.

Moreover, it is settled in the case law, that the subjective conviction of the trier of fact can only constitute a basis for a conviction of the defendant free of legal errors, if the trier of fact has analyzed all relevant circumstances speaking for and against the defendant.

The penal chamber shortchanges at the outset the foundations of its evaluation and thereby the basis for reasonable doubts which arise. It only inquires as to feelings of revenge of the victim B. and whether there are reasons for believing that the witness has accused the defendant unjustly, "in order to have an excuse in relation to third parties for a voluntary act of sex." But it is not, decisively, alone a question of feelings of revenge and motives for excuse in relation to the origin of the witness's decision to accuse the defendant of rape.

The error which makes the assessment of credibility of the penal chamber appear faulty lies above all in the failure to consider, or the insufficiently rational evaluation of, the peculiarities of the witness B. before and after the "act" and her severe drunkenness.

The witness remained alone with the defendant until around 3:30 a.m. in the kitchen of his tavern. Both had ingested considerable amounts of alcoholic beverages. The witness had a blood alcohol content of .29 and the defendant one of .264. The witness spoke of her Lesbian predilections. After the sexual intercourse she got dressed in order to leave the tavern, but walked — clothed only in shoes, stockings, slip and an undershirt — to the wife of the defendant whom she did not know in the second story of the building, awakened the sleeping woman, and told her that the defendant had raped her.

In connection with this course of events, the penal chamber should, above all, have analyzed the response of the defendant and his explanations for the accusations of the witness. The defendant maintained that the severely drunk witness was not content with the consensual sexual intercourse; his member was — and the Superior Court also proceeds from this premise — not fully erect. She asked whether it perhaps doesn't "work" with him because his wife is home and encouraged him to drive away with her (the witness) so that "it could be done once in peace." When he refused, she said: "Just imagine if I went to your wife and said that you had raped me." Upon his response: "go ahead!" she reported the rape to his wife.

Compare the previous case with the following, in which the defendant remained silent, yet was convicted on the basis of a prior statement by the complaining witness, which had been retracted at trial.

Decision of December 17, 1997
(German Supreme Court)[287]

The Superior Court sentenced the defendant to three years, six months aggregate imprisonment for sexual abuse of a child in three cases. The appeal in cassation of the defendant has success on the factual issue (...).

The evidentiary evaluation of the contested judgment is, however, not free of legal errors.

The defendant, who had no record, did not testify in the case. His conviction is based exclusively on the statements that the victim made at the time of his police examination to the witness PHK S. on February 12, 1996. The victim, who was six to ten years old at the time of the acts and 14 years old at the time of the trial, characterized his police statements as "lies" in the trial court.

In a case in which statement is confronted by statement—or as here where the defendant does not testify and only the statement of the only prosecution witness is available—and the decision alone depends on whether one should believe this one witness, then the judgment reasons must reveal that the trier of fact took notice of all of the circumstances that could influence the decision and included them in his considerations. This applies even more when the only prosecution witness no longer substantiates his charge in the trial and his police statements are only introduced through the interrogator.

The judgment of the trier of fact does not comply with these heightened requirements.

In the judgment reasons, the genesis of the police statement of the victim is not discussed, although special importance is given to this in the evaluation of child witnesses in cases of abuse (...). The trier of fact also did not give close analysis of the personality of the victim and his environment. This was, however, important for judging his credibility and the believability of his statements.

Compare the above case with the cases in the previous chapter relating to conviction on the basis of written statements. Note here, however, that the reversal is not based on an inability to confront and cross-examine the child witness but on a deficient justification given for relying on the prior statement of the child.

---

287. BGH StV 5/98, 250.

E. Concluding Remarks

One can say that the criminal trial in common law and civil law countries is not only a contest between prosecution and defense, which in various, more-or-less adversary fashions wrestle with each other to present persuasive evidence, undermine the evidence produced by the adversary, and to convince the judges of the facts and the law to adopt its positions. But it is also a contest—in a subtle, more institutional sense—between professional and lay judges over which part of the court will control the crucial guilt determination, which fixes the parameters for the state's administration of punishment. In this sense, it is a struggle between a positivistic, more or less inflexible application of laws which finds its justification in the principles of legality and material truth, and a more flexible approach, derived from customary law, of coming to an equitable resolution of the case, bending or even ignoring the law if justice and the social peace will be better served.

Questions

1. Does the German conception of "proof beyond a reasonable doubt" differ in any way from the American conception?

2. Should the trier of fact, whether jury, mixed court or professional judge or judges, have to give reasons explaining why their doubts justify an acquittal? Does this violate the presumption of innocence?

3. Do you believe the appellate courts should be able to set aside "scandalous" acquittals, as was done in the *Otegi* case? Would the Spanish appellate courts have reversed the *O.J. Simpson* acquittal? On what grounds?

4. Which method of control over the deliberations of juries and mixed courts is preferable, that provided by detailed on-the-record instructions on the law before deliberations, as in the U.S. and England, or that provided by reasoned judgments after deliberations in Germany?

5. Do you think professional judges in mixed courts give as detailed instructions to the lay assessors on the dangers of eyewitness identification as are required by the *Turnbull* decision? Does it trouble you that lay assessors in Germany may not reveal what the professional judges tell them in deliberation?

6. Should courts be able to express their own moral judgment as to the punishability of a particular act in a particular case, even it is contradicts settled legal doctrine, i.e., grant a type of clemency? Is this what the French

"inner conviction" or the German and Spanish "free evaluation of the evidence" should mean?

7. Should a jury or mixed court have discretion to acquit regardless of the evidence? Is this any different than the discretion given prosecutors not to charge clear violations of the law in systems where the "opportunity principle" reigns?

8. Do the appellate opinions in the *Otegi* and *Monika Weimar* cases seem any less arbitrary than the verdicts of the jury and mixed courts which preceded them? Do you think appellate courts sometimes also ignore the law to reach results they believe are desirable?

9. Should juries have to give reasons when they convict the defendant? Would this help to reduce the number of innocent persons who have been sentenced to death or long prison terms in the U.S.?[288]

Relevant U.S. Case Law

Allen v. United States, 164 U.S. 492 (1896)

Dunn v. United States, 284 U.S. 390 (1932)

Shannon v. United States, 512 U.S. 573 (1994)

United States v. Gaudin, 515 U.S. 506 (1995)

Apprendi v. New Jersey, 530 U.S. 466 (2000)

Ring v. Arizona, 536 U.S. 584 (2002)

United States v. Booker, 543 U.S. 220 (2005)

United States v. Spock, 416 F.2d 165 (1st Cir. 1969)

United States v. Dougherty, 473 F.2d 1113 (D.C.Cir. 1972)

United States v. Thomas, 116 F.3d 606 (2nd Cir. 1997)

---

288. DNA tests alone led to the exoneration of over 163 convicted persons since 1989. Monica Davey, *A Man Hailed As Exonerated Is Back in Jail*, NEW YORK TIMES, Nov. 23, 2005, at A1, A23. The Spanish Supreme Court recently reversed the conviction of an innocent woman for the murder of a teenage girl, basing it on the fact that the jury only superficially mentioned the evidence it relied on and did not analyze the circumstantial evidence which led it to believe the defendant guilty of the crime in a case where there were no eyewitnesses. In doing so, the court stated, that in circumstantial evidence cases the jury must not only mention the evidence it relies on, but also explain why it thinks one can infer guilt from it. Decision of March 12, 2003 (Spanish Supreme Court), STS 279/2003 of March 12.

Selected Readings

Markus Dirk Dubber, *American Plea Bargains, German Lay Judges and the Crisis of Criminal Procedure*, 59 STAN. L. REV. 547 (1997).

John D. Jackson, *Making Juries Accountable*, 50 AM. J. COMP. L. 477 (2002).

JOHN JACKSON & SEAN DORAN, JUDGE WITHOUT JURY: DIPLOCK TRIALS IN THE ADVERSARY SYSTEM (1995).

John D. Jackon & Nikolay Kovalev, *Lay Adjudication and Human Rights in Europe*, 13 COLUM. J. EUR. L. 83 (2006).

THE JUDICIAL ROLE IN CRIMINAL PROCEEDINGS (Sean Doran & John Jackson eds. 2000).

Nikolay P. Kovalev, *Lay Adjudication of Crimes in the Commonwealth of Independent States: An Independent and Impartial Jury or a Court of "Nodders?,"* 11 J. E. EUR. L. 123 (2004).

John H. Langbein, *Mixed Court and Jury Court: Could the Continental Alternative Fill the American Need?* 1981 AM. BAR FOUNDATION RESEARCH J. 195 (1981).

WILLIAM T. PIZZI, TRIALS WITHOUT TRUTH (1999).

Stephen C. Thaman, *The Resurrection of Trial by Jury in Russia*, 31 STAN. J. INT'L L. 61 (1995).

Stephen C. Thaman, *Spain Returns to Trial by Jury*, 21 HASTINGS INT'L & COMP. L. REV. 241 (1998).

WORLD JURY SYSTEMS (Neil Vidmar ed. 2000).

Case Register

European Court of Human Rights

Kostovski v. The Netherlands (November 20, 1989),
12 E.H.R.R. 434 (1990)   126, 137

Delta v. France (December 19, 1990),
16 E.H.R.R. 574 (1993)   129

Murray v. United Kingdom (February 8, 1996),
22 E.H.R.R. 29 (1996)   171

Doorson v. The Netherlands (March 26, 1996),
22 E.H.R.R. 330 (1996)   140

Teixeira de Castro v. Portugal (June 9, 1998),
28 E.H.R.R. 101 (1998)   78

England and United Kingdom

Court of Common Pleas

Entick v. Carrington, 19 Howell's State Trials 1029 (1765)   14, 81

Divisional Court

Regina v. Canterbury et al [1982] 1 W.B. 398   148

Queen's Bench Division

Regina v. Consett Justices, *Ex parte* Postal Bingo Ltd.
[1967] 2 Q.B. 9   191

Court of Appeal

Regina v. Turnbull [1977] 1 Q.B. 224   206

Regina v. Fulling [1987] 1 Q.B. 426   101

Regina v. Samuel [1988] 2 All ER 135   114

Regina v. Cole [1990] 1 W.L.R. 866   132

Regina v. McGovern [1991] Crim. L. Rev. 124   121

Regina v. Bryce [1992] 4 All ER 569   94

Regina v. Roncoli [1998] Crim. L. Rev. 584   183

Northern Ireland Court of Appeal

Regina v. Foxford [1974] Northern Ireland L. Reports 181   182

France

Supreme Court

Decision of July 18, 1884, Crim. No. 242, 404 (1884)   125

Decision of December 8, 1906 (*Placet*), in LES GRANDS
    ARRÊTS DU DROIT CRIMINEL Vol. 2, 38–40
    (Jean Pradel & André Varinaud eds. 1995)   123

Germany

Supreme Court

Decision of February 16, 1954, BGHSt 5, 332   97

Decision of February 9, 1957, BGHSt 10, 208   193

Decision of June 14, 1960, BGHSt 14, 358   72

Decision of February 21, 1964, BGHSt 19, 325   82, 112

Decision of October 26, 1965, BGHSt 20, 281   177

Decision of February 22, 1978, BGHSt 27, 355   119

Decision of November 3, 1982, BGHSt 31, 140   136

Decision of November 17, 1983, BGH NStZ 1984, Vol. 4, 180   214

Decision of April 28, 1987, BGHSt 34, 362   98

Decision of January 1, 1988, BGH NStZ 1988, Vol. 5, 236   217

Decision of March 31, 1989, BGHSt 36, 159   143

Decision of May 31, 1990, BGH StV 8/1990, 337   92

Decision of February 27, 1992, BGHSt 38, 214   91, 110

Decision of October 29, 1992, BGHSt 38, 372   85

Decision of October 8, 1993, BGHSt 39, 335   76

Decision of May 21, 1996, BGHSt 42, 170   87

Decision of August 28, 1997, BGHSt 43, 195   151

Decision of December 17, 1997, BGH StV 5/1998, 250   219

Decision of June 10, 1998, BGH NStZ 1999, 92   156

Decision of November 6, 1998, BGH StV 5/1999, 5   209

Court of Appeal

Decision of November 25, 1997 (Frankfurt/Main), StV 3/1998, 119   99

Italy

Constitutional Court

Decision No. 313, July 3, 1990, 35 GIUR. COST 1981   159

Decision No. 81, March 11, 1993, 38 GIUR. COST. 731   69

Decision No. 455, December 30, 1994, 39 GIUR. COST. 3940   186

Supreme Court

Decision of July 5, 1988, CASS. PENALE, No. 953, 1043 (1989)   73

Decision of February 19, 1990, CASS. PENALE, No. 15, 44 (1990)   162

Decision of October 10, 1991, CASS. PENALE, No. 648, 1258 (1992)   179

Decision of November 21, 1991, CASS. PENALE, No. 354, 585 (1993)   166

Decision of March 26, 1993, CASS. PENALE, No. 1317, 2224 (1993)   180

Decision of March 27, 1996, GIUST. PENALE 138 (1997)   122

Russia

Constitutional Court

Decision of April 20, 1999, KONSTITUTIONNYY SUD ROSSIYSKOY
    FEDERATSII, POSTANOVLENIIA. OPREDELENIIA. 1999 78 (2000)   187

Supreme Court

Decision of June 7, 1995, GOSUDARSTVENNO-PRAVOVOE
    UPRAVLENIE PREZIDENTA ROSSIYSKOY FEDERATSII,
    LETOPIS' SUDA PRISIAZHNYKH, Vol. 5, 22 (1995)   204

Regional Courts

Case of Kraskina (Ivanovo Regional Court)
    (Verdict of March 10, 1995), GOSUDARSTVENNO-PRAVOVOE
    UPRAVLENIE PREZIDENTA ROSSIYSKOY FEDERATSII,
    LETOPIS' SUDA PRISIAZHNYKH, Vol. 5, 22 (1995)   203

Spain

Constitutional Court

Decision No. 145, July 12, 1988, 1988–89 BJC 1168   185

Decision No. 241, December 21, 1996, 141 BJC 134   28

Decision No. 303, October 25, 1993, 151 BJC 108   52

Decision No. 52, February 23, 1995, 167 BJC 145   135

Decision No. 49, March 26, 1996, 180 BJC 133   61, 115

Supreme Court

Decision of March 29, 1990, RJ 1990, No. 2647, 3534   49

Decision of October 30, 1992, RJ 1992, No. 8553, 11247   59

Decision of November 14, 1992, RJ 1992, No. 9661, 12662   60

Decision of March 5, 1993, RJ 1993, No. 1840, 2400   131

Decision of June 25, 1993, RJ 1993, No. 5244, 6702   66

Decision of July 9, 1993, RJ 1993, No. 6060, 7682   106

Decision of June 28, 1994, RJ 1994, No. 5157, 6797   57

Decision of July 8, 1994, RJ 1994, No. 6261, 7983   55

Decision of June 5, 1995, RJ 1995, No. 4538, 6058   118

Decision of July 12, 1995, RJ 1995, No. 5775, 7737   45

Decision of March 11, 1998, La Ley (5.12.96), No. 4226, 6   199

Provincial Courts

Case of Otegi (Guipuzcoa Provincial Court)
    (Verdict of March 6, 1997), On file with author.   195

Statutes and Other Texts

England

Law II of Edmund (10th Century)   9

Regulations Regarding Exculpation of William I (Late 11th Century)   7

Police and Criminal Evidence Act 1984
PACE-Code of Practice A

§ 1.4   46

§ 2.2   46

§ 2.3   46

PACE-Code of Practice B

§ 5   54

PACE-Code of Practice C

§ 10.1   90

§ 10.5   90

France

Assises de la cour des Bourgeois (Ch. CCLIX)   4

Livre de Jostice et des Plets I, 3 § 7 (12th Century)   12

Code de Procédure Pénale

§80	32
§81 (1,2,4)	32
§82-1 (paras. 1,2)	37
§170	105
§171	105
§174 (para. 3)	106
§310	184
§353	205

Germany

Constitutio Criminalis Carolina (German Empire, 1532)

§16	5
§§23, 25–27	10

Constitution

Art. 13 (1,2)	56

Strafprozessordnung

§98	56
§136a	96

Italy

§63	93
§64(3)(a,b), (3-bis)	88
§65	103
§191	109
§266	64
§267 (1–3)	64

§ 268 (4,6)   65
§ 350   88
§ 352 (1)   51
§ 380 (1)   48
§ 381 (1–4)   48
§ 392 (1)   38
§ 394   39
§ 401 (1,3,5)   39
§ 403 (1)   39
§ 449 (1–5)   43

Russia

Ugolovno-protsessual'nyy kodeks

§ 339 (1–5)   201

Spain

Constitution

Art. 125   28

Ley de Enjuiciamiento Criminal

§ 100   25
§ 101   28
§ 105   25
§ 118   36
§ 270   28
§ 282 (para. 1)   30
§ 286   31
§ 655   164
§ 683   184

Ley Orgánica del Tribunal del Jurado

§ 25   41

§ 27 (1)   41

§ 63(1)(d)   206

Other

Art. 24(2) Canadian Charter of Rights and Freedoms   117

Appendix

England

Police and Criminal Evidence Act 1984

Excerpts from MICHAEL ZANDER, THE POLICE AND CRIMINAL EVIDENCE ACT 1984 (5th ed. 2005).

§ 8

(1) If on an application made by a constable a justice of the peace is satisfied that there are reasonable grounds for believing—

(a) that an indictable offence has been committed; and

(b) that there is material on premises mentioned in subsection 1A below which is likely to be of substantial value (whether by itself or together with other material) to the investigation of the offence; and

(c) that the material is likely to be relevant evidence; and

(d) that it does not consist of or include items subject to legal privilege, excluded material or special procedure material; and

(e) that any of the conditions specified in subsection (3) below applies in relation to each set of premises specified in the application, he may issue a warrant authorising a constable to enter and search the premises

(2) A constable may seize and retain anything for which a search has been authorised under subsection (1) above.

(3) The conditions mentioned in subsection (1)(e) above are—

(a) that it is not practicable to communicate with any person entitled to grant entry to the premises;

(b) that it is practicable to communicate with a person entitled to grant entry to the premises but it is not practicable to communicate with any person entitled to grant access to the evidence;

(c) that entry to the premises will not be granted unless a warrant is produced;

(d) that the purpose of a search may be frustrated or seriously prejudiced unless a constable arriving at the premises can secure immediate entry to them.

§ 10

(1) Subject to subsection (2) below in this Act "items subject to legal privilege" means—

[Subsections a–c list aspects of the attorney-client privilege]

(2) Items held with the intention of furthering a criminal purpose are not items subject to legal privilege.

§ 11(1)(a)

(1) Subject to the following provisions of this section, in this Act "excluded material" means—

(a) personal records which a person has acquired or created in the course of any trade, business, profession or other occupation or for the purposes of any paid or unpaid office and which he holds in confidence (...).

§ 12

In this Part of this Act "personal records" means documentary and other records concerning an individual (whether living or dead) who can be identified from them, and relating—

(a) to his physical or mental health;

(b) to spiritual counselling or assistance given or to be given to him;

(c) to counselling or assistance given or to be given to him, for the purposes of his personal welfare, by any voluntary organisation or by any individual who—

(i) by reason of his office or occupation has responsibilities for his personal welfare; or

(ii) by reason of an order of a court, has responsibilities for his supervision.

§ 25(3)

The general arrest conditions are—

(a) that the name of the relevant person is unknown to, and cannot be readily ascertained by the constable;

(b) that the constable has reasonable grounds for doubting whether a name furnished by the relevant person as his name is his real name;

(c) that—

(i) the relevant person has failed to furnish a satisfactory address for service; or

(ii) the constable has reasonable grounds for doubting whether an address furnished by the relevant person is a satisfactory address for service;

(d) that the constable has reasonable grounds for believing that arrest is necessary to prevent the relevant person—

(i) causing physical harm to himself or any other person;

(ii) suffering physical injury;

(iii) causing loss of or damage to property;

(iv) committing an offence against public decency; or

(v) causing an unlawful obstruction of the highway;

(e) that the constable has reasonable grounds for believing that arrest is necessary to protect a child or other vulnerable person from the relevant person (…).

32(1–5)

(1) A constable may search an arrested person, in any case where the person to be searched has been arrested at a place other than a police station, if the constable has reasonable grounds for believing that the arrested person may present a danger to himself or others.

(2) Subject to subsections (3) to (5) below, a constable shall also have power in any such case—

(a) to search the arrested person for anything—

(i) which he might use to assist him to escape from lawful custody; or

(ii) which might be evidence relating to an offence; and

(b) to enter and search any premises in which he was when arrested or immediately before he was arrested for an indictable offense for evidence relating to the offence for which he has been arrested.

(3) The power to search conferred by subsection (2) above is only a power to search to the extent that is reasonably required for the purpose of discovering any such thing or any such evidence.

(4) The powers conferred by this section to search a person are not to be construed as authorising a constable to require a person to remove any of his clothing in public other than an outer coat, jacket or gloves.

(5) A constable may not search a person in the exercise of the power conferred by subsection 2(a) above unless he has reasonable grounds for believing that the person to be searched may have concealed on him anything for which a search is permitted under that paragraph.

§ 58(1)

A person arrested and held in custody in a police station or other premises shall be entitled, if he so requests, to consult a solicitor privately at any time.

Code of Practice C (PACE)
§ 6.6 (a–c)

A detainee who wants legal advice may not be interviewed or continue to be interviewed until they have received such advice unless:

(a) Annex B applies, when the restriction on drawing adverse inferences from silence in Annex C will apply because the detainee is not allowed an opportunity to consult a solicitor; or

(b) an officer of superintendent rank or above has reasonable grounds for believing that:

(i) the consequent delay might:

- lead to interference with, or harm to, evidence connected with an offence;
- lead to interference with, or physical harm to, other people;
- lead to serious loss of, or damage to, property;

- lead to alerting other people suspected of having committed an offence but not yet arrested for it;
- hinder the recovery of property obtained in consequence of the commission of an offence.

(ii) when a solicitor, including a duty solicitor, has been contacted and has agreed to attend, awaiting their arrival would cause unreasonable delay to the process of investigation.

(c) the solicitor the detainee has nominated or selected from a list:

(i) cannot be contacted;

(ii) has previously indicated they do not wish to be contacted; or

(iii) having been contacted, has declined to attend; and the detainee has been advised of the Duty Solicitor Scheme but has declined to ask for the duty solicitor. In these circumstances the interview may be started or continued without further delay provided an officer of inspector rank or above has agreed to the interview proceeding.

§ 12.2 (a,b)

Except as below, in any period of 24 hours a detainee must be allowed a continuous period of at least 8 hours for rest, free from questioning, travel or any interruption in connection with the investigation concerned. This period should normally be at night or other appropriate time which takes account of when the detainee last slept or rested. If a detainee is arrested at a police station after going there voluntarily, the period of 24 hours runs from the time of their arrest and not the time of arrival at the police station. The period may not be interrupted or delayed, except:

(a) when there are reasonable grounds for believing not delaying or interrupting the period would

(i) involve a risk of harm to people or serious loss of, or damage to, property;

(ii) delay unnecessarily the person's release from custody;

(iii) otherwise prejudice the outcome of the investigation; (...)

§ 12.4

As far as practicable interviews shall take place in interview rooms which are adequately heated, lit and ventilated.

§ 12.6

People being questioned or making statements shall not be required to stand.

§ 12.8

Breaks from interviewing should be made at recognised meal times or at other times that take account of when an interviewee last had a meal. Short refreshment breaks shall be provided at approximately two hour intervals, subject to the interviewer's discretion to delay a break if there are reasonable grounds for believing it would:

(i) involve a:

- risk of harm to people;
- serious loss of, or damage to, property;

(ii) unnecessarily delay the detainee's release

(iii) otherwise prejudice the outcome of the investigation.

Code of Practice D (PACE)
§ 3.5

A "video identification" is when the witness is shown moving images of a known suspect, together with similar images of others who resemble the suspect (...).

§ 3.7

An "identification parade" is when the witness sees the suspect in a line of others who resemble the suspect. (...)

§ 3.9

A "group identification" is when the witness sees the suspect in an informal group of people. (...)

§ 3.11

Except for provisions in paragraph 3.19, the arrangements for, and conduct of, the identification procedures in paragraphs 3.5 to 3.10 [involving video identifications, identification parades (line-ups) and group identifications] and circumstances in which an identification procedure must be held shall be the responsibility of an officer not below inspector rank who is not involved with the investigation, "the identification officer". (...)

§3.12

Whenever:

(i) a witness has identified a suspect or purported to have identified them prior to any identification procedure set out in paragraphs 3.5 to 3.10 having been held; or

(ii) there is a witness available, who expresses an ability to identify the suspect, or where there is a reasonable chance of the witness being able to do so, and they have not been given an opportunity to identify the suspect in any of the procedures set out in paragraphs 3.5 to 3.10, and the suspect disputes being the person the witness claims to have seen, identification procedure shall be held unless it is not practicable or it would serve no useful purpose in proving or disproving whether the suspect was involved in committing the offence. For example, when it is not disputed that the suspect is already well known to the witness who claims to have seen them commit the crime.

§3.17

(...)before a video identification, an identification parade or group identification is arranged, the following shall be explained to the suspect:

(i) the purposes of the video identification, identification parade or group identification;

(ii) their entitlement to free legal advice

(iii) the procedures for holding it, including their right to have a solicitor or friend present;

(iv) that they do not have to consent to or co-operate in a video identification, identification parade or group identification;

(v) that if they do not consent to, and co-operate in, a video identification, identification parade or group identification, their refusal may be given in evidence in any subsequent trial and police may proceed covertly without their consent or make arrangements to test whether a witness can identify them (...)

Annex B. Code of Practice D (PACE)

§ 1

1. A suspect must be given a reasonable opportunity to have a solicitor or friend present, and the suspect shall be asked to indicate on a second copy of the notice whether or not they wish to do so.

§ 2

2. An identification parade may take place either in a normal room or one equipped with a screen permitting witnesses to see members of the identification parade without being seen. The procedures for the composition and conduct of the identification parade are the same in both cases, subject to paragraph 8 (except that an identification parade involving a screen may take place only when the suspect's solicitor, friend or appropriate adult is present or the identification parade is recorded on video).

§ 3

3. Before the identification parade takes place, the suspect or their solicitor shall be provided with details of the first description of the suspect by any witnesses who are attending the identification parade. When a broadcast or publication is made (...) the suspect or their solicitor should also be allowed to view any material released to the media by the police for the purpose of recognising or tracing the suspect, provided it is practicable to do so and would not unreasonably delay the investigation.

§ 8

8. Once the identification parade has been formed, everything afterwards, in respect of it, shall take place in the presence and hearing of the suspect and any interpreter, solicitor, friend or appropriate adult who is present (unless the identification parade involves a screen, in which case everything said to, or by, any witness at the place where the identification parade is held, must be said in the hearing and presence of the suspect's solicitor, friend or appropriate adult or be recorded on video).

§9

9. The identification parade shall consist of at least eight people (in addition to the suspect) who, so far as possible, resemble the suspect in age, height, general appearance and position in life. Only one suspect shall be included in an identification parade unless there are two suspects of roughly similar appearance, in which case they may be paraded together with at least twelve other people. In no circumstance shall more than two suspects be included in one identification parade and where there are separate identification parades, they shall be made up of different people.

§12

12. When the suspect is brought to the place where the identification parade is to be held, they shall be asked if they have any objection to the arrangements for the identification parade or to any of the other participants in it and to state the reasons for the objection. The suspect may obtain advice from their solicitor or friend, if present, before the identification parade proceeds. If the suspect has a reasonable objection to the arrangements or any of the participants, steps shall, if practicable, be taken to remove the grounds for objection. When it is not practicable to do so, the suspect shall be told why their objections cannot be met and the objection, the reason given for it and why it cannot be met, shall be recorded on forms provided for this purpose.

§13

13. The suspect may select their own position in the line, but may not otherwise interfere with the order of the people forming the line. When there is more than one witness, the suspect must be told, after each witness has left the room, that they can, if they wish, change position in the line. Each position in the line must be clearly numbered, whether by means of a number laid on the floor in front of each identification parade member or by other means.

§16

16. Witnesses shall be brought in one at a time. Immediately before the witness inspects the identification parade, they shall be told the person they saw on a specified earlier occasion may, or may not, be present and if they

cannot make a positive identification, they should say so. The witness must also be told they should not make any decision about whether the person they saw is on the identification parade until they have looked at each member at least twice.

Criminal Justice and Public Order Act of 1994

Excerpts from BLACKSTONE'S STATUTES ON CRIMINAL JUSTICE & SENTENCING 212–14 (3rd ed. Barry Mitchell & Salim Farrar eds. 2007)

§ 34

(1) Where, in any proceedings against a person for an offence, evidence is given that the accused—

(a) at any time before he was charged with the offence, on being questioned under caution by a constable trying to discover whether or by whom the offence had been committed, failed to mention any fact relied on in his defence in those proceedings; or

(b) on being charged with the offence or officially informed that he might be prosecuted for it, failed to mention any fact, being a fact which in the circumstances existing at the time the accused could reasonably have been expected to mention when so questioned, charged or informed, as the case may be, subsection (2) below applies.

(2) Where this subsection applies—

(c) the court in determining whether there is a case to answer; and

(d) the court or jury, in determining whether the accused is guilty of the offence charged, may draw such inferences from the failure as appear proper.

(3) Subject to any directions by the court, evidence tending to establish the failure may be given before or after evidence tending to establish the fact which the accused is alleged to have failed to mention.

(4) This section applies in relation to questioning by persons (other than constables) charged with the duty of investigating offences or charging offenders as it applies in relation to questioning by constables; and in subsection (1) above "officially informed" means informed by a constable or any such person.

(5) This section does not—

(a) prejudice the admissibility in evidence of the silence or other reaction of the accused in the fact of anything said in his presence relating to the conduct in respect of which he is charged, in so far as evidence thereof would be admissible apart from this section; or

(b) preclude the drawing of any inference from any such silence or other reaction of the accused which could properly be drawn apart from this section.

(6) This section does not apply in relation to a failure to mention a fact if the failure occurred before the commencement of this section.

§ 35

(1) At the trial of any person for an offence, subsections (2) and (3) below apply unless —

(a) the accused's guilt is not in issue;

(b) it appears to the court that the physical or mental condition of the accused makes it undesirable for him to give evidence; but subsection (2) below does not apply if, at the conclusion of the evidence for the prosecution, his legal representative informs the court that the accused will give evidence or, where he is unrepresented, the court ascertains from him that he will give evidence.

(2) Where this subsection applies, the court shall, at the conclusion of the evidence for the prosecution, satisfy itself (in the case of proceedings on indictment, in the presence of the jury) that the accused is aware that the stage has been reached at which evidence can be given for the defence and that he can, if he wishes, give evidence and that, if he chooses not to give evidence, or having been sworn, without good cause refuses to answer any questions, it will be permissible for the court or jury to draw such inferences as appear proper from his failure to give evidence or his refusal, without good cause, to answer any question.

(3) Where this subsection applies, the court or jury, in determining whether the accused is guilty of the offence charged, may draw such inferences as appear proper from the failure of the accused to give evidence or his refusal, without good cause, to answer any question.

§ 36

(1) Where —

(a) a person is arrested by a constable, and there is —

(i) on his person; or

(ii) in or on his clothing or footwear; or

(iii) otherwise in his possession; or

(iv) in any place in which he is at the time of his arrest, any object, substance or mark, or there is any mark on any such object; and

(b) that or another constable investigating the case reasonably believes that the presence of the object, substance or mark may be attributable to the participation of the person arrested in the commission of an offence specified by the constable; and

(c) the constable informs the person arrested that he so believes, and requests him to account for the presence of the object, substance or mark; and

(d) the person fails or refuses to do so, then if, in any proceedings against the person for the offence so specified, evidence of those matters is given, subsection (2) below applies.

(2) When this subsection applies—

(...)

(c) the court, in determining whether there is a case to answer; and

(d) the court or jury, in determining whether the accused is guilty of the offence charged, may draw such inferences from the failure or refusal as appear proper.

§ 37

(1) Where—

(a) a person arrested by a constable was found by him at a place at or about the time the offence for which he was arrested is alleged to have been committed; and

(b) that or another constable investigating the offence reasonably believes that the presence of the person at that place and at that time may be attributable to his participation in the commission of the offence; and

(c) the constable informs the person that he so believes, and requests him to account for that presence; and

(d) the person fails or refuses to do so, then if, in any proceedings against the person for the offence, evidence of those matters is given, subsection (2) below applies.

(2) Where this subsection applies—

(...)

(c) the court, in determining whether there is a case to answer and

(d) the court or jury, in determining whether the accused is guilty of the offence charged, may draw such inferences from the failure or refusal as appear proper.

Practice Direction (Justices: Clerk to Court (1981))

Reported at 1 WLR 1163 and cited in STEPHEN SEABROOKE & JOHN SPRACK, CRIMINAL EVIDENCE AND PROCEDURE: THE ESSENTIAL FRAMEWORK 219 (1996).

(2) It shall be the responsibility of the justices' clerk to advise as follows:

(a) on questions of law or of mixed law and fact;

(b) as to matters of practice and procedure.

(3) If it appears to him necessary to do so, or he is requested by the justices, the justices' clerk has the responsibility to

(a) refresh the justices' memory as to any matter of evidence and to draw attention to any issues involved in the matters before the court,

(b) advise the justices generally on the range of penalties which the law allows them to impose and on any guidance relevant to the choice of penalty provided by the law, the decisions of the superior courts or other authorities. If no request for advice has been made by the justices, the justices' clerk shall discharge his responsibility in court in the presence of the parties.

France

Code de Procédure Pénale

Excerpts from CODE DE PROCÉDURE PÉNALE (Dalloz, 48th ed. 2007).

§ 1

Public prosecution for the imposition of punishment is initiated and exercised by magistrates or by the officials to whom it is entrusted by law.

Such a prosecution may also be initiated by the aggrieved party under the circumstances provided in this code.

§ 2(1)

(1) A civil action for reparation of the harm caused by a felony, misdemeanor or infraction is reserved to those who have personally suffered harm directly caused by the offense.

§ 53

A felony or misdemeanor is considered to be flagrant if it is in the process of being committed or has just been committed. It also constitutes a flagrant felony or misdemeanor when, at the time close to the criminal act, the suspect is pursued by public hue and cry or is found in possession of objects, or yields clues or circumstantial evidence, leading to the belief that he has participated in the felony or misdemeanor.

The inquest conducted by the public prosecutor following the confirmation of a flagrant crime which is provided for in the present chapter may not be pursued in excess of eight days.

§ 78-1 (para. 2)

Any person present within the national territory shall agree to submit to an identity control carried out under the conditions and by the police authorities provided in the following articles.

§ 78-2 (para. 1)

The officers of the judicial police (...) may request a confirmation by any means of the identity of anyone, as to whom evidence exists giving rise to a presumption:

- that she has committed or attempted to commit a criminal offense;
- that she is preparing to commit a felony or misdemeanor;
- that she may be capable of furnishing information useful in investigating a felony or misdemeanor;
- that she is the object of an investigation ordered by a judicial authority.

§ 78-3(paras. 1,3)

If the interested party refuses or is incapable of confirming his identity, he can, in cases of necessity, be detained at the scene or at the police station where he has been taken for the purpose of verifying his identification (...).

The person who is the object of a verification may not be detained any longer than the time strictly required to establish her identity. The detention may not exceed four hours.

Germany

Strafprozessordnung

Excerpts from STRAFPROZESSORDNUNG 1–185 (dtv 42nd ed. 2007)

§ 94(1,2)

(1) Objects, which as evidence can be of significance to the preliminary investigation, shall be seized or otherwise secured.

(2) If the objects are in the possession of a person and will not be voluntarily relinquished, they may be seized.

§ 100a (para. 1)

The surveillance and copying of telecommunications can be ordered, if certain facts give rise to a suspicion, that someone has committed, as a perpetrator or accomplice [here follows a long list of crimes including treason, crimes against public order, counseling desertion from the army, crimes against federal troops, counterfeiting, slavery, murder, manslaughter, genocide, crimes against personal liberty, theft by a gang, extortion, and many others].

§ 100b

(1) The surveillance and recording of communications can only be ordered by a judge. In exigent circumstances the public prosecutor can issue the warrant. The warrant of the public prosecutor is invalid if it is not confirmed by the judge within three days.

(2) The warrant must be in writing. It must contain the name and address of the affected person against whom it is directed and the telephone number or other identification of the telecommunications connection. The type, magnitude and length of the measures must be specified. The warrant is valid no longer than three months. A prolongation of no longer than three more months is permissible, as long as the prerequisites laid out in § 100a still exist.

(3) Based on the warrant, every person who is in the business of providing telecommunications services or is employed doing so must facilitate the surveillance and recording of telecommunications by the judge, the public prosecutor and their auxiliary police (...).

(4) If the prerequisites of § 100a no longer obtain, then the measures authorized by the warrant must immediately cease. The cessation must be communicated to the judge and the persons under the paragraph 3 obligation.

(5) The personal data acquired by the measures can only be used as evidence in other criminal proceedings, as long as, upon its evaluation, information exists which could be necessary in solving crimes listed in § 100a.

(6) If the information gathered through the measures is not necessary in a criminal prosecution, it should be immediately destroyed under the supervision of the public prosecutor. A record should be made of the destruction.

§ 102

As to anyone who is suspected of being a perpetrator or accomplice in a crime, or of promoting, being an accessory after the fact, or concealing a crime, a search of the dwelling and other rooms as well as the person and things belonging to him may be undertaken to effect an arrest or also, if it is suspected that the search will lead to the discovery of evidence.

§ 105(1,2)

(1) Searches may only be ordered by the judge, or in exigent circumstances by the public prosecutor or his auxiliary officers. Searches pursuant to § 103(1)(2) [of non-suspects] are ordered by the judge; the public prosecutor may make such an order in exigent circumstances.

(2) When the search of a dwelling, business spaces or enclosed property is conducted without the presence of the judge or the public prosecutor, then, when possible, a community official or two members of the community, in whose district the search takes place, should be present. The persons in-

cluded as members of the community may not be police officers or auxiliary officers of the public prosecutor.

§ 106 (1)

(1) The occupant of the places or objects to be searched may be present during the search. If he is absent, his representative or an adult family member, roommate or neighbor should, if possible, be present.

§ 127(1,2)

(1) If one is confronted or pursued *in flagrante*, everyone has the power to arrest him without a judicial warrant, if he is suspected of trying to escape or his identity cannot immediately be confirmed (...).

(2) The public prosecutor and police officers are also authorized to temporarily arrest upon exigent circumstances, if the prerequisites for an arrest warrant or civil commitment order exist.

§ 163a (1,2,4)

(1) The accused shall be examined at the latest before the conclusion of the investigation, unless the proceedings are going to be dismissed. In simple matters, it suffices that he be given an opportunity to express himself in writing.

(2) If the accused moves for the taking of evidence in his defense, it must be secured if it is of significance.

(4) At the first interrogation of the accused by police officers, the suspect must be advised as to which act he is accused of committing. In addition, the provisions of §§ 136(1) (subparagraphs 2–4), (2)(3) StPO and § 136a StPO shall be applied during the interrogation of the suspect by police officials.

§ 244(2)

In order to ascertain the truth, the court must, *ex officio*, extend the taking of evidence to all facts and evidence which are of importance for the decision.

§ 261

As to the results of the evidence-taking, the court decides according to its free conviction derived from the material in the trial.

§ 267 (1,3)

(1) If the defendant is convicted, the judgment reasons shall set forth the facts considered proved in which the legal elements of the crime are found. To the extent that proof is inferred from other facts, such other facts are also to be set forth. (...)

(2) If, during the trial, circumstances specifically provided in the criminal law were alleged, which exclude, decrease or increase liability for punishment, the judgment reasons shall indicate whether such facts are or are not considered established.

(3) The reasons for the criminal judgment shall further indicate the criminal law applied and shall set forth the circumstances which were determinative for the punishment imposed. If according to the criminal law the imposition of a lesser punishment is in general dependent upon the existence of mitigating circumstances, the grounds for the judgment shall reflect the decision made in this respect, if such circumstances were found to exist or if, contrary to a motion made during the trial, they were found not to exist; this applies correspondingly for the imposition of a prison sentence in cases under § 47 of the Criminal Code. The judgment reasons shall further indicate why punishment was suspended during probation or why it was not so suspended contrary to a motion made during the trial; the same applies if the court withholds punishment.

§ 374(1)

(1) The aggrieved party may, without prior referral to the public prosecutor, pursue the following by way of private prosecution: (1) disturbing the peace (...); (2) insults (...), if not directed against a political association named in § 194(4) of the Penal Code; (3) violation of the confidentiality of the mail; (4) battery; (5) threats; (5a) taking or offering a bribe in a business transaction; (6) destruction of property; (6a) a crime under § 323a of the Criminal Code if the crime was committed in a state of intoxication and it is a misdemeanor under sections 1 through 6; (7) a criminal act in violation of (...) the law against unfair competition; (8) [various crimes against laws protecting intellectual property].

§ 377

(1) The public prosecutor is not obliged to participate in a proceeding brought by private prosecution. The court submits the files to him if it deems it necessary that he assume control of the prosecution.

(2) At any stage of the proceeding, before the judgment has become final, the public prosecutor can, by express declaration, also assume control of the prosecution. (...)

§ 407

(1) In proceedings before a penal judge and in proceedings within the jurisdiction of the mixed court, upon written motion by the public prosecutor, the legal consequences of the act in misdemeanor cases can be pronounced in the form of a written penal order without setting a trial. The public prosecutor makes such a motion if she does not think a trial is necessary in view of the results of the investigation. The motion must indicate certain legal consequences. Through it the public charges are brought.

(2) Only the following legal consequences for the offense, either alone or in combination with others, may be imposed by a penal order:

> (1) fine, warning without imposition of punishment, prohibition on driving, confiscation, destruction, rendering unusable, publication of the conviction and civil penalty against a legal entity or collective;

> (2) suspension of driver's license for up to two years;

> (3) suspension of sentence.

If the accused has defense counsel, he may be sentenced up to one year deprivation of liberty if the execution is suspended as a condition of probation.

(3) the accused need not be provided a previous hearing before a court (...).

408 (2,3)

(2) If the judge deems that the accused is not sufficiently suspicious, he refuses to issue the penal order. The decision is equivalent to a resolution refusing to commit the accused for trial.

(3) The judge must agree with the motion of the public prosecutor if he has no doubts regarding the issuance of the penal order. He sets a trial if he has doubts about deciding without a trial, or if he differs with the legal conclu-

sions in the motion for the penal order or wants to impose a legal consequence other than the one in the motion and the public prosecutor insists on the motion. Upon being summoned, the accused is given a copy of the motion for the penal order which does not include the suggested legal consequence.

409(1)

(1) The penal order contains:

(1) the identification of the accused and possible other accomplices;

(2) the name of defense counsel;

(3) the description of the act the defendant has been accused of committing, the time and place of its commission and the description of the statutory legal elements of the crime;

(4) the provisions applied, quoting section, paragraph, number, letter and with the description of the law;

(5) the evidence;

(6) the fixing of the legal consequences;

(7) instructions about the possibility of objection within the precribed time and form therefor and the notification that the penal order will be final and executed if no objection is made per § 410 StPO.

Italy

Codice di Procedura Penale

Excerpts from MARIO CHIAVARIO ET AL, CODICI E LEGGI PER L'UDIENZA PENALE 167–449 (2005–2006)

§ 91

Non-profit entities and associations which, previous to the commission of the act which is the subject of the proceedings, have been recognized by force of law to represent the interests damaged by the offense, can exercise at any stage and level of the proceedings the rights and powers attributed to the person aggrieved by the offense.

§ 92(1)

The exercise of the rights and powers possessed by the entities and associations representing interests injured by the offense is subject to the consent of the aggrieved party.

§ 247

(1) When there is reasonable cause to believe that someone has secreted on his person the *corpus delicti* or things pertinent to the crime, the person may be searched. If there are reasonable grounds to believe that such things are to be found in a certain place, or in such a place the arrest of the accused or a fugitive can be realized, a search of the place is in order.

(2) The search must be based on a reasoned order.

(3) The judicial authority may proceed personally or order that the act shall be completed by officials of the judicial police delegated to do so in the same order.

§ 326

The public prosecutor and the judicial police investigate, within the parameters of their own competence, the evidence necessary for the inherent determination of the exercise of the penal action.

§ 327

The public prosecutor directs the investigation and directly supervises the judicial police which, even after having communicated the notice of the crime, continue to pursue acts on their own initiative in the manner suggested by the following articles.

§ 329(1)

The investigative acts completed by the public prosecutor and the judicial police are protected by secrecy as long as the accused has no right to discover them and, of course, until the closure of the preliminary investigation.

§ 364 (1–4,7)

(1) The public prosecutor, if he is to conduct an interrogation, and inspection or confrontation at which the accused must be present, invites him to be present pursuant to § 375.

(2) The accused who is without defense counsel is again advised that he will be assisted by a publicly appointed defense counsel, but may name a private one.

(3) The publicly appointed or named private defense counsel is advised, at least twenty-four hours before the completion of the acts indicated in paragraph 1 and the searches at which the accused is not allowed to participate.

(4) Defense counsel has the right to be present, in any case, at the acts indicated in paragraph 1 and 3, except when the provisions of § 245 apply.

(7) Those who intervene during the acts are prohibited from giving any signs of approval or disapproval. When they are present during the performance of the acts, defense counsel can make requests, observations and reservations to the public prosecutor which are noted in the record.

§ 365 (1,2)

(1) The public prosecutor, when he proceeds to carry out an act of search or seizure, asks the accused who is present whether she is represented by counsel of her choice, and if not, officially appoints defense counsel according to the provisions of § 97(3).

(2) Defense counsel has the right to be present at the completion of the act to the extent provided in § 249 [which allows for participation of a trusted person in all personal seizures].

(3) The provisions of § 364(7) are applicable.

§ 373 (1,5)

(1) Except where provided in relation to specific acts, a record is prepared of:

(a) the crime report, the private complaint and parts of the procedure presented orally;

(b) the interrogations and confrontations with the accused;

(c) the inspections, searches and seizures;

(d) the summary information gathered pursuant to the provisions of § 362;

(d-bis) the interrogation pursuant to the provisions of § 363;

(e) the technical verifications made pursuant to the provisions of § 360.

(5) The act containing the report of the crime and the documentation relative to the investigation are conserved in a suitable file in the office of the public prosecutor along with the acts transmitted by the judicial police pursuant to the norms of § 357.

§ 438 (1–5)

(1) The accused can request that the trial be carried out at the preliminary hearing on the basis of the file, excepting the provisions of section 5 of this article and § 441(5).

(2) The request may be made orally or in writing (…).

(3) The will of the accused is expressed personally or through a special solicitor (…).

(4) Upon the request, the judge issues an order calling for an abbreviated trial.

(5) The accused, when the evidence in the acts indicated in § 442(1-bis) remains usable, may subordinate the request to a taking of evidence necessary to reach a decision. The judge calls for an abbreviated trial if the taking of evidence requested is deemed necessary to reach a decision and is compatible with the goal of procedural economy inherent in the procedure, taking account of the parts of the file already acquired and usable. In such a case the public prosecutor may request the admission of contrary evidence (…).

§ 441 (1–3,5)

(1) To the extent applicable, the provisions indicated for the preliminary hearing are observed in the abbreviated trial with exception of those in §§ 422 and 423.

(2) The constitution of the civil party who intervenes after the recognition of the order setting the abbreviated trial is equivalent to an acceptance of the abbreviated procedure.

(3) The abbreviated trial takes place in the judge's chambers; the judge orders that the trial shall take place in public session when all the accuseds so request.

(5) When the judge finds he is unable to decide on the basis of the file he takes evidence, *sua sponte* if necessary, essential to making the decision. (…)

§ 444 (1,2)

(1) The accused and the public prosecutor may request the judge to apply, in the form and measure indicated, a substitute sanction or a monetary punishment diminished by a third, or a punishment of deprivation of liberty which, taking into account the circumstances, is diminished by a third and does not exceed five years of imprisonment or detention, either alone or in conjunction with a monetary punishment.

(2) If consent of the party which did not formulate the request is also present and a judgment of dismissal should not be pronounced according to § 129, the judge, on the basis of the file, if he deems correct the legal qualification of the facts, the application and the comparison of the circumstances proposed by the parties and the proportionality of the punishment, imposes in the judgment the application enunciated in the petition which was requested by the parties. If a civil party has been constituted, the judge does not decide the related complaint; the accused is nevertheless sentenced to the payment of the costs sustained by the civil party unless there are just reasons for total or partial compensation. (...)

§ 448 (1,2)

(1) At the hearing provided in § 447, at the preliminary hearing, in the expedited trial and the immediate trial, the judge immediately pronounces judgment if the conditions for accepting the request provided in § 444(1) exist. In the case of the lack of assent of the public prosecutor or accused or rejection of the request on the part of the judge of the investigation, the accused, before the declaration of the opening of the trial in the first instance, can renew the request and the judge, if he deems it well-founded, immediately pronounces sentence. The request is not renewable later before another judge. In the same way, the judge may proceed after the close of the trial in the first instance or in the trial on appeal if he deems the lack of assent of the public prosecutor or the rejection of the request to be unjustified.

(2) In the case of lack of consent, the public prosecutor can file an appeal; in all other cases the judgment may not be appealed.

§ 453(1)

(1) When the evidence appears to be clear, the public prosecutor may request an immediate trial if the accused has been interrogated as to the facts from

which emerge the bases for the charges or, subsequent to an invitation to appear issued in observance of the forms indicated in § 375(3)(2), he has failed to appear, providing that there has not been a legitimate impediment and it is not a case of a person with unknown whereabouts.

§ 503(1)

(1) The presiding judge provides for the examination of the parties who have made a request or have consented in the following order: civil party, civil defendant, person civilly liable for a fine, and accused.

§ 506

(1) The presiding judge, also upon request of another member of the court, as a result of the evidence adduced in the trial upon the initiative of the parties, or as a result of the reading provided under the provisions of §§ 511, 512 and 513 CPP, can indicate to the parties new or broader areas of evidence useful for completing the examination.

(2) The presiding judge, also upon the request of another member of the court, can question witnesses, experts, technical consultants, all persons indicated in § 210 and the parties who have already been examined. The parties then have the right to conclude the examination according to the order indicated in §§ 498(1,2), 503(2).

§ 507(1)

(1) Once the taking of evidence has been concluded, the judge, if it proves to be absolutely necessary, can provide *ex officio*, for the introduction of new means of proof (...).

Russia

Ugolovno-protsessual'nyy kodeks Rossiyskoy Federatsii

Excerpts from UGOLOVNO-PROTSESSUAL'NYY KODEKS ROSSIYSKOY FEDERATSII (Os' 89 2006) (with amendments through January 9, 2006)

§ 15(3)

(3) The court is not an organ of the criminal investigation and speaks neither for the prosecution nor the defense. The court creates the necessary conditions for the parties' fulfillment of their procedural duties and the realization of the rights accorded them. (...)

§ 75 (1), (2)(1–3)

(1) Evidence gathered in violation of the requirements of this Code is inadmissible. Inadmissible evidence has no legal weight and may neither serve as the basis for a prosecution nor be used to prove any of the circumstances listed in § 73 of this Code [that is, to prove the fact a crime was committed, the guilt of the accused, the level of guilt of the accused, and the character and amount of damages sustained by the victim.]

(2) The following are to be considered as inadmissible evidence:

(1) statements of the suspect or accused given during the course of pretrial proceedings in a criminal case in the absence of defense counsel, including cases involving a waiver of the right to defense counsel, and not confirmed by the suspect or accused in court;

(3) other evidence acquired in violation of the requirements of this Code.

Spain

Ley de Enjuiciamiento Criminal

Excerpts from LEY DE ENJUICIAMIENTO CRIMINAL Y OTRAS NORMAS PROCESALES 29–207 (10th ed. Julio Muerza Esparza ed. 2005)

§ 297 (para. 1)

The police reports compiled by officials of the judicial police and the assertions they make as a result of the verifications they have realized shall be considered as crime reports with respect to their legal effect.

§ 302

The appearing parties may take notice of the acts and intervene in all the acts during the proceedings.

Notwithstanding that provided in the previous paragraph, in cases of a public offense, the investigating magistrate, upon motion of the public prosecutor or any of the parties appearing, or *ex officio*, may issue an order declaring it to be totally or partially secret for all the parties appearing for no longer than a month, and must necessarily terminate the secrecy ten days prior to the conclusion of the preliminary investigation.

§ 311 (para. 1)

The magistrate who conducts the preliminary investigation performs the investigative acts proposed by the public prosecutor or any of the parties present if he does not consider them useless or prejudicial.

§ 384 (paras. 1,2)

As soon as the results of the preliminary investigation provide any rational evidence of criminality as to a determinate person, an order is issued declaring her to be an accused and ordering that investigative acts be conducted as to her according to the form and procedure provided in this Title and the other parts of this law.

From the moment of being thus named, the accused may consult with a barrister, if he is not *incommunicado*, and through him solicit the conduct of investigative acts in his behalf, and to make motions which affect his situation (...).

§ 396 (para. 1)

The defendant is permitted to make declarations to the extent he wishes to exculpate himself or to explain the facts, and the meetings he desires or the investigative acts he proposes shall be carried out with urgency if the magistrate deems them appropriate for the proof of his assertions.

§ 400

The defendant may make declarations as many times as he wishes and the magistrate will immediately take the declaration if it is related to the case.

§ 520(2)(a–c)

(2) Every arrested or imprisoned person shall be informed immediately, and in a way she can understand, of the acts she is accused of having committed

and the reasons for the deprivation of her liberty, as well as the rights she possesses and especially the following:

(a) The right to remain silent and not to speak if she does not want to, and not to respond to any of the questions which are formulated, or to state that she only wants to declare in front of a magistrate.

(b) The right not to give a statement against oneself and not to confess guilt.

(c) The right to designate a lawyer and to request his presence to help during the police and judicial acts of interrogations and to intervene in any identification procedure no matter what its object. If the arrested or imprisoned person or prisoner does not designate a lawyer, one will be officially designated.

§ 558

The warrant for the entry and search of a private dwelling shall always contain reasons and the magistrate shall concretely include therein the building or locked place to be examined and whether it will take place only in the daytime, and the authority or functionary who will conduct it.

§ 569 (paras. 1–4)

The search is conducted in the presence of the interested party, or the person who legitimately represents him.

If he is not present or does not want to consent or name a representative, it is conducted in the presence of an adult member of his family.

If there is none, it is conducted in the presence of two witnesses, residents of the same town.

The search shall always be conducted in the presence of the clerk of the court which authorized it or the secretary of the security service which has substituted for him, who shall make a record of the results of the investigative act and its circumstances, which shall be signed by all those present (...).

§ 573

Searches of books and papers of account of the defendant shall not be ordered unless there is grave evidence that the results of this investigative act will be discovery and proof of an important fact or circumstance in the case.

§ 579 (1–3)

(1) The judge may order the detention of private postal or telegraphic correspondence which the defendant sends or receives and its opening and examination, if there is evidence that the discovery or the proof of an important fact or circumstance in the case can be obtained by these means.

(2) The judge also may order, with a reasoned decision, intervention in the telephonic communications of the defendant, if there is evidence that the discovery or the proof of an important fact or circumstance in the case can be obtained by these means.

(3) The judge may in a similar manner order, with a reasoned decision, for a period of up to three months, extendable for equal periods, the observation of postal, telegraphic or telephonic communications of persons as to whom there exists evidence of criminal responsibility, as well as the communications used by them for the realization of their criminal aims.

§ 708

The presiding judge shall question the witness in relation to aspects in the first paragraph of § 436 [name, address, if related to accused, etc.], after which the party who is offering the witness can ask questions it deems appropriate. The other parties can also ask questions they feel are opportune and pertinent in view of their answers.

The presiding judge, on his own motion, or at the urging of other members of the tribunal, may direct questions to the witnesses he deems appropriate for clearing up the facts about which they are declaring.

§ 714 (para. 1)

If the declaration of a witness in the trial does not substantially conform to that made in the preliminary investigation, the reading of the statement at the preliminary investigation can be demanded by any of the parties.

§ 741

The court, appreciating according to its conscience the evidence presented at the trial, the reasons provided for the prosecution and the defense, and that manifested by the defendants themselves, dictates the sentence in the time fixed by law.

The court always makes use of its free discretion in qualifying the crime and in imposing the sentence provided by the Criminal Code, and should place on the record, whether it took into consideration the pieces of evidence at trial which the applicable provisions thereof oblige them to take into account.

Ley Orgánica del Tribunal del Jurado

Excerpts from Ley de Enjuiciamiento Criminal y otras normas procesales 209–41 (10th ed. Julio Muerza Esparza ed. 2005)

§ 52(1) Verdict Form

(1) After the trial has concluded, the arguments have been made, and the defendants heard, the presiding judge shall proceed to submit to the jury in writing a verdict form according to the following rules:

(a) In separate, numbered paragraphs, it shall narrate the acts alleged by the parties which the jury shall declare to be proved or not, differentiating between those which are contrary to the accused and those which would yield favorable results. It shall not include in one paragraph acts, some of which could be susceptible to being proved and others not.

It shall commence by describing the principal act of the prosecution, and then shall narrate those alleged by the defense. But if the simultaneous consideration of the former and latter as proved is not possible without contradiction, only one proposition shall be included.

If the declaration of proof of one fact necessarily infers a similar declaration as to another, the former must be proposed with the necessary priority and separation.

(b) It shall then explain, following the same criteria of separation and numeration of paragraphs, the facts alleged which can determine a basis for exemption from responsibility.

(c) There shall be included, in continuation, in successive separated and numbered paragraphs, the narration of the act which determines the degree of execution, participation and modification of responsibility.

(d) It shall finally specify the criminal act for which the accused must be found guilty or not guilty.

(e) If different crimes were prosecuted, there shall be effectuated a separate formulation successively for each crime.

(f) The same shall apply if there are multiple defendants.

(g) The presiding judge, taking into account the results of the evidence, can add facts or legal qualifications favorable to the accused, only if they do not implicate a substantial variation of the charged facts or violate defense rights.

If the presiding judge believes that from the evidence a fact has been derived which implicates a substantial variation, he shall require an assessment of the corresponding amount of guilt.

§61

(1) Once the voting is completed, a document is prepared with the following paragraphs:

(a) A first paragraph, beginning as follows: The jurors have deliberated concerning the acts submitted for their resolution and have deemed proved, by a vote of (unanimous or majority), the following (...).

If the approved facts were those proposed by the presiding judge, it will suffice to name them by their number.

If the approved text includes some modification, the text will be written as it was voted.

(b) A second paragraph, beginning as follows: They have also found not proved by a vote of (unanimity or majority) the facts described in the following numbers of the text submitted to us for decision. Thereafter, the numbers of the paragraphs of that text are indicated, and it is possible to reproduce the text.

(c) A third paragraph, beginning as follows: Because of the aforementioned, the jurors by (unanimity or majority) find the defendant guilty/not guilty of the crime of (...).

In this paragraph they will make a separate pronouncement for each crime and defendant. In the same form they will pronounce, when appropriate, the jury's recommendation concerning the application of the benefits of conditional suspension of sentence for the guilty person in case the legal preconditions exist, as well as concerning a petition, or lack thereof, for clemency.

(d) A fourth paragraph, beginning as follows: The jurors have relied on the following pieces of evidence in making the preceding declarations (...). This paragraph will contain a succinct explication of the reasons why they have declared, or refused to declare, certain facts as having been proved.

(e) A fifth paragraph in which they will relate any incidents that occurred during the deliberations, avoiding any identification which would destroy the secrecy thereof, except that relating to a refusal to vote.

(2) The document will be edited by the foreperson, unless he dissents from the apparent majority, in which case the jurors will designate the editor.

If requested by the foreperson, the presiding judge can authorize that the clerk or another official help the jury, only in the composition or writing of the document. In the same terms, the person designated as editor in substitution for the foreperson, can request the same.

(3) The document will be signed by all the jurors, the foreperson signing for those who are unable to do so. If any of the jurors refuse to sign, this will be noted in the document.

Ley Orgánica del Poder Judicial

Excerpt from Ley de Enjuiciamiento Criminal y otras normas procesales 252 (10th ed. Julio Muerza Esparza ed. 2005)

§ 11.1

Evidence obtained, directly or indirectly in violation of fundamental rights and liberties, is without effect.

Constitution (Spain)

Art. 18(2)

The dwelling is inviolable. No entry or search may be made therein without the consent of the owner or a judicial resolution except in the case of a flagrant crime.

Glossary

LEGEND: (E) English; (F) French; (G) German; (I) Italian; (R) Russian; (S) Spanish.

A

abbreviated trial (E), F-G (nothing), giudizio abbreviato (I), sokrashchennaia protsedura (R), procedimiento abreviado (S)

accusation (E), prévention (F), Beschuldigung (G), imputazione (I), imputación, obvinenie (R), acusación (S)

accusatory pleading (E), décision de renvoi (F), Anklagesatz (G), accusa (I), obvinitel'noe zakliuchenie (R), calificación (S)

accused (E), prévenu, accusé (F), Angeschuldigter, Beschuldigter (G), persona sottoposta alle indagine (I), obviniaemyy (R), inculpado (S)

acquit (E), acquitter (F), freisprechen (G), proscioliere (I), opravdat' (R), absolver (S)

acquittal (E), acquittement (F), Freispruch (G), proscioglimento (I), opravdanie (R), absolución (S)

act (criminal) (E), action (F), Akt (G), fatto (I), deianie (R), hecho (S)

act (procedural) (E), acte (F), Akt (G), atto (I), deystvie (R), diligencia (S)

adversarial (E), contradictoire (F), kontradiktorisch (G), contraddittorio (I), costiazatel'nyy (R), contradictorio (S)

aggrieved party (E), partie lésée (F), Verletzte(r) (G), persona offesa (I), poterpevshiy (R), ofendido (S)

appeal in cassation (E), pourvoi en cassation (F), Revision (G), ricorso per cassazione (I), kassatsionnaia zhaloba (R), recurso de casación (S)

appeal (E), appelation (F), Berufung (G), appello (I), apelliatsiia (R), apelación (S)

appearance (E), comparution (F), Erscheinung (G), comparizione (I), yavka (R), comparecencia (S) appellant (E), appellant (F), Beschwerdeführer(in) (G), ricorrente (I), zhalobshchik (R), recurrente (S)

appellate remedy (E), pourvoi (F), Rechtsmittel (G), impugnazione (I), obzhalovanie (R), recurso (S)

arrest (noun) (E), détention (F), Festnahme (G), arresto, fermo (I), zaderzhanie (R), detención (S)

B

Bar (E), bâtonnier (F), Rechtsanwaltschaft (G), avvocatura (I), advokatura (R), abogacía (S)

C

case law (E), jurisprudence (F), Rechtsprechung (G), giurisprudenza (I), yurisprudentsiia (R), jurisprudencia (S)

chamber of investigation (E), chambre de l'instruction, G-I-R-S (nothing)

circumstantial evidence (E), indice (F), Indiz (G), prove indiziarie (I), kosvennye dokazatel'stva (R), prueba indiciaria (S)

civil action (E), action civile (F), Privatklage (G), azione civile (I), grazhdanskiy isk (R), acción civil (S)

civil party (E), partie civile (F), Privatkläger(in) (G), parte civile (I), grazhdanskiy istets (R), parte civil (S)

clerk of court (E), greffier, greffe (F), Sekretär(in) (G), segreteria (I), sekretar' (R), secretario (S)

code of criminal procedure (E), Code de Procédure Pénale (F), Strafprozessordnung (G), Codice di procedura penale (I), Ugolovno-protsessual'nyy kodeks (R), Ley de Enjuiciamiento Criminal (S)

collateral complainant (E) Nebenkläger(in) (G) no F-I-R-S

committal order (E), décision de renvoi (F), Eröffnungsbeschluß (G), rinvio al giudizio, decreto che dispone il giudizio (I), naznachenie sudebnoe zasedanie (R), apertura del juicio oral (S)

compel prosecution (motion) (E) Klageerzwingungsverfahren (G) no F-I-R-S

complaint (private) (E), plainte (F), Privatklage (G), querela (I), zaiavlenie (R), querella (S)

complainant (E), plaignant (F), Privatkläger(in) (G), querelante (I), chastnyy obvinitel' (R), querellante (S)

confession (E), aveu, confession (F), Geständnis (G), confessione (I), priznaniia viny (R), confesión (S) confrontation (E), confrontation (F), Gegenüberstellung (G), confronto (I), ochnaia stavka (R), careo (S)

consent (E), consentement (F), Einwilligung, Zustimmung (G), consenso (I), soglashenie (R), consentimiento (S)

constitution (E), constitution (F), Grundgesetz, Verfassung (G), costituzione (I), konstitutsiia (R), constitución (S)

constitutional appeal (E), Verfassungsbeschwerde (G), ricorso costituzionale (I), konstitutsionnaia zhaloba (R), recurso de amparo (S), no F

constitutional court (E), conseil constitutionnel (F), Verfassungsgericht (G), corte costituzionale (I), konstitutsionnyy sud (R), tribunal constitucional (S)

constitutional right (E), droit constitutionnel (F), Grundrecht (G), diritto costituzionale (I), konstitutsionnoe pravo (R), derecho constitucional (S)

contest (E), attaquer (F), angreifen, anfechten (G), impugnare (I), obzhalovat' (R), recurrir (S)

convicted person (E), condamné (F), Veurteilte(r) (G), condannato (I), osuzhdennyy (R), condenado (S)

conviction (E), condamnation (F), Verurteilung (G), condanna (I), osuzhdenie (R), condena (S)

conviction (inner) (E), intime conviction (F), Überzeugung (G), vnutrennoe ubezhdenie (R), convicción moral (S), no I

corpus delicti (E), corps du délit (F), Tatbestand (G), corpo del reato (I), soderzhanie ugolovnogo deianiia (R), cuerpo del delito (S)

court (E), tribunal (F), Gericht (G), tribunale (I), sud (R), tribunal (S)

court of appeal (E), cour d'appel (F), Oberlandesgericht, Berufungsgericht (G), corte d'appello (I), apelliatsionnaia instantsiia (R), tribunal superior de justicia (S)

court of cassation (E), cour de cassation (F), Revisionsgericht (G), corte di cassazione (I), cassatsionnaia instantsiia (R), tribunal de casación (S)

crime (E), crime (F), Straftat (G), delitto (I), prestuplenie (R), delito (S)

crime report (E), dénonciation (F), Anzeige (G), denuncia (I), zaiavlenie (R), denuncia (S)

criminal act (E), fait punible (F), Straftat (G), fatto punibile (I), ugolovnoe deianie (R), hecho punible (S)

criminal action (E), action pénale (F), öffentliche Klage (G), azione penale (I), publichnoe obvinenie (R), acción penal (S) criminal procedure (E), procédure pénale (F), Strafverfahren, Strafprozeß (G), procedura penale (I), ugolovnyy protsess (R), procedimiento penal (S)

D

deal (plea agreement) (E), reconnaissance préalable de culpabilité (F), Absprache (G), patteggiamento (I), soglasie s pred"iavlennym obvineniem (R), conformidad (S)

decision (E), arrêt (F), Entscheidung (G), decisione (I), reshenie (R), decisión, resolución (S)

declaration (E), déclaration (F), Aussage (G), dichiarazione (I), pokazanie (R), declaración (S)

defendant (E), accusé (F), Angeklagte(r) (G), imputato (I), podsudimyy (R), procesado (S)

defense counsel (E), avocat (F), Verteidiger(in) (G), difensore (I), zashchitnik (R), defensor (S)

deliberation (E), délibération (F), Beratung (G), deliberazione (I), soveshchanie (R), deliberación (S)

detention (E), rétention (F), Haft (G), fermo (I), soderzhanie (R), detención (S)

dismissal (E), renvoi (F), Einstellung (G), archiviazione (I), prekrashchenie (R), sobreseimiento (S)

due process (E), rechtstaatliches Verfahren (G), procès equitable (F), giusto processo (I), spravedliviy protsess (R), debido proceso (S)

due process (denial) indefensión (S), no F-G-I-R

E

evidence (E), pièce, preuve (F), Beweis, Beweismittel (G), prova (I), dokazatel'stvo (R), prueba (S)

evidentiary prohibition (E), Beweisverbot (G), prova illicita (I), prueba prohibida (S), no F-R

examination (E), audition (F), Vernehmung (G), esame (I), dopros (R), interrogatorio (S)

exigent circumstances (E), urgence (F), Gefahr im Verzug (G), emergenzia (I), ne terpit otlagatel'stva (R), urgencia (S)

expedited trial (E), comparution immédiate (F), beschleunigtes Verfahren (G), giudizio direttissimo (I), juicio rápido (S), no R

F

facts (E), faits (F), Tatsachen (G), elementi, fatti (I), dannye (R), hechos (S)

fair trial (E), procès equitable (F), faires Verfahren (G), giusto processo (I), spravedliviy protsess (R), proceso con todas las garantias (S)

felony (E), crime (F), Verbrechen (G), delitto (I), prestuplenie (R), delito (S)

fine (E), amende (F), Geldstrafe (G), multa (I), shtraf (R), multa (S)

flagrante (*in*), flagrant (E), flagrant (F), auf frischer Tat (G), in flagranza (I), so polichnom (R), in flagrante (S)

free evaluation of evidence (E), freie Beweiswürdigung (G), libero convincimento (I), svobodnaia otsenka (R), libre valoración (S), no F

fruit of poisonous tree (E), fruit de l'arbre empoisonné (F), Frucht des verbotenen Baumes, Fernwirkung (G), plod otravlenogo dereva (R), fruto del árbol envenenado (S), no I

G

guilt (E), culpabilité (F), Schuld (G), colpavolezza (I), vina (R), culpabilidad (S)

guilty (E), culpable (F), schuldig (G), colpevole (I), vinovat (R), culpable (S)

H

hearing (E), audience (F), Verhandlung, Anhörung (G), udienza, sede (I), slushanie (R), audiencia (S)

hearsay (E), ouï-dire (F), Hörensagen (G), diceria (I), slukh, pokazanie s chuzhikh slov (R), testimonio de oídas, de referencia (S)

hue and cry (E), clameur (F), no G-I-R-S

I

idenfication (E), identification (F), Identifikation (G), identificazione (I), opoznanie (R), identificación (S)

illegality (E), illegalité (F), Rechtswidrigkeit (G), illegittimità (I), pravonarushenie (R), ilicitur (S)

infraction (E), contravention (F), Ordnungswidrigkeit (G), contravvenzione (I), pravonarushenie (R), falta (S)

immediacy (E), immédiateté (F), Unmittelbarkeit (G), immediatezza (I), neposredstvennost' (R), inmediatez, inmediación (S)

inquest (E), enquête (F), Vorerhebungen (G), attività a iniziativa della polizia giudiziaria (I), doznanie (R), diligencias de prevención (S) inquisitorial (E), inquisitorial (F), inquisitorisch (G), inquisitorio (I), inkvizitsionnyy (R), inquisitorio (S)

inspection (E), inspection (F), Augenschein (G), ispezione (I), osvidetel'stvovanie (R), inspección ocular (S)

instant (case) (E), espèce (F), vorliegender Fall (G), fattispecie (I), v dannom dele (R), presente caso (S)

interception (E), interception (F), Abfang (G), intercettazione, captazione (I), nalozhenie aresta (R), interceptación (S)

interrogation (E), interrogatoire (F), Vernehmung (G), interrogatorio (I), dopros (R), interrogación (S)

investigate (E), instruire, informer (F), ermitteln (G), indagare (I), issledovat' (R), indagar, investigar, instruir (S)

investigation (E), information (F), Ermittlungsverfahren (G), investigazione, indagini (I), issledovanie (R), investigación (S)

investigating magistrate (E), juge d'instruction (F), Untersuchungsrichter (G), giudice istruttore (I), issledovatel'skiy sud'ia (R), juez instructor (S)

investigative dossier (E), dossier d'information (F), Akten (G), atti (I), expediente, delo (R), autos (S)

J

jail (E), prison (F), Gefängnis (G), carcere (I), sledstvenniy isolator' (R), cárcel (S)

judge (E), magistrat (F), Richter (G), giudice (I), sud'ia (R), magistrado (S)

judge of the investigation (E), Ermittlungsrichter (G), giudice delle indagine preliminari (I) no F-R-S

judgment (E), jugement (F), Urteil (G), sentenza (I), prigovor (R), sentencia (S)

judgment reasons (E), motivation (F), Urteilsbegründung (G), motivazione (I), motivirovanie (R), motivación (S).

judicial police (E), police judiciaire (F), Kriminalpolizei (G), polizia giudiziaria (I), policía judicial (S), no R

jurisdiction (E), juridiction (F), Gerichtsbarkeit (G), giurisdizione (I), yurisdiktsiia (R), jurisdicción (S)

juror (E), juré (F), Geschworene(r) (G), prisiazhnyy zasedatel' (R), jurado (S), no I jury court (E), cour d'assise (F), Schwurgericht (G), corte d'assise (I), sud prisiazhnykh (R), tribunal del jurado (S).

justice (E), justice (F), Gerechtigkeit (G), giustizia (I), spravedlivost' (R), justicia (S)

L

law (legislative) (E), loi (F), Gesetz (G), legge (I), zakon (R), ley (S)

law (discipline) (E), droit (F), Recht (G), diritto (I), pravo (R), derecho (S)

lawyer (E), avocat (F), Rechtsanwalt (G), avvocato (I), advokat (R), abogado (S)

lay assessor (E), echévin (F), Schöffe, Schöffin (G), giudice popolare (I), narodnyy zasedatel' (R), escabinado (S)

M

magistrate (E), juge (F), Richter (G), magistrato (I), juez (S), no R

misdemeanor (E), délit (F), Vergehen (G), delitto (I), prostupok, menee tiazhkoe prestuplenie (R), delito (S)

mixed court (E), cour d'assises (F), Schöffengericht (G), corte d'assise (I), sud sheffenov (R), tribunal de escabinado (S)

municipal court (E), tribunal correctionnel (F), Amtsgericht (G), pretore, giudice di pace (I), rayonnyy sud, mirovoy sud (R), juzgado (S)

N

natural person (E), personne naturelle (F), natürliche Person (G), fizicheskiy litso (R), persona física (S)

non-usable (E), inadmissible (F), unverwertbar (G), inutilizzabile (I), nedopustimyy (R), inadmisible (S)

non-usability (E), inadmissibilité (F), Unverwertbarkeit (G), inutilizzabilità (I), nedopustimost' (R), inadmisibilidad (S)

nullity (E), nullité (F), Nichtigkeit (G), nullità (I), nedeystvitel'nost' (R), nullidad (S)

O

orality (principle of oral trial) (E), oralité (F), Mündlichkeit (G), oralità (I), ustnost' (R), oralidad (S)

P

paragraph (E), alinéa (F), Absatz (G), comma (I), abzats (R), párrafo (S) party (E), partie (F), Verfahrensbeteiligte(r) (G), parte (I), storona (R), parte (S)

penal order (E), ordonnance pénale (F), Strafbefehl (G), decreto penale (I), ugolovnyy prikaz (R), no-S

petitioner (E), demandeur (F), Beschwerdeführer(in) (G), deducente (I), prositel' (R), demandante, recurrente (S)

police report (E), atestado (S), no F-G-I-R

popular prosecution (E), acción popular (S), no F-G-I-R

preserve evidence (procedure to) (E), Beweisversicherung (G), incidente probatorio (I), prueba anticipada (S), no F-R

preliminary investigation (E), information (F), Vorverfahren (G), indagini preliminari (I), predvaritel'noe sledstvie, rassledovanie (R), sumario (S)

pretrial detention (E), détention provisioire (F), Untersuchungshaft (G), custodia cautelare (I), soderzhanie pod strashey (R), prisión provisional (S)

privacy (E), vie privée (F), Privatsphäre (G), vita privata (I), lichnoe tayno, chastnaia zhizn' (R), vida privada (S)

private prosecution (E), Nebenklage, Privatklage (G), chastnoe obvinenie (R), acusación particular (S), no F-I

probable (reasonable) cause (E), cause fondée (F), dringender (hinreichen-der) Tatverdacht (G), fondato motivo (I), dostatochnye osnovaniia (R), no S

prohibition of evidence gathering (E), Beweiserhebungsverbot (G), no F-I-R-S

prohibition on using evidence (E), Beweisverwertungsverbot (G), prohibi-ción de valoración (S), no F-I-R

proportionality (E), proportionalité (F), Verhältnismäßigkeit (G), propor-tionalità (I), proportsional'nost' (R), proporcionalidad (S)

prosecution (E), poursuit (F), Verfolgung (G), persecuzione (I), enjuici-amiento, presledovanie (R), procesamiento (S).

provision (E), disposition (F), Vorschrift (G), disposizione (I), polozhenie (R), disposición (S)

public prosecutor (E), procureur de la République, procureur géneral, min-istère publique (F), Staatsanwaltschaft, Staatsanwalt (G), pubblico ministero (I), prokuror (R), ministerio fiscal (S)

public prosecution (E), action publique (F), öffentliche Klage (G), azione pubblica (I), publichnoe obvinenie (R), acción pública (S) publicity (E), publicité (F), Publizität (G), pubblicità (I), glasnost' (R), publicidad (S)

punishment (E), peine (F), Strafe (G), pena (I), nakazanie (R), pena (S)

R

record (noun) (E), procès verbal (F), Protokoll, Niederschrift (G), verbale (I), protokol' (R), acto (S)

recording (E), enregistrement (F), Aufnahme (G), registrazione (I), zapis' (R), grabación (S)

right (E), droit (F), Recht (G), diritto (I), pravo (R), derecho (S)

S

secrecy (E), secret (F), Geheimnis (G), segretezza (I), tayno (R), secreto (S)

seizure (E), saisie (F), Beschlagnahme (G), sequestro (I), vyemka (R), secuestro (S)

state under the rule of law (E), état de droit (F), Rechtsstaat (G), stato di diritto (I), pravovoe gosudarstvo (R), estado de derecho (S)

statement (E), déclaration (F), Aussage (G), dichiarizione (I), pokazanie (R), declaración (S)

stop-and-frisk (E), fouille (F), Leibesvisitation (G), perquisire (I), obyskivat' (R), cacheo (S)

superior court (E), tribunal de grande instance (F), Landgericht (G), tribunale ordinario (I), oblastnoi (kraevoy) sud (R), audiencia provincial (S)

supreme court (E), cour de cassation (F), Bundesgerichtshof (G), corte di cassazione (I), verkhovnyy sud (R), tribunal supremo (S)

suspect (E), suspect (F), Verdächtige(r) (G), indiziato (I), podozrevaemyy (R), sospechoso (S)

T

testimony (E), témoignage (F), Zeugenaussage (G), testimonianza (I), pokazanie (R), testimonio (S)

trial (E), débat (F), Hauptverhandlung (G), dibattimento, giudizio (I), sudebnoe sledstvie, razbiratel'stvo (R), juicio oral, debate (S)

trial court (E), tribunal d'instance (F), Tatgericht (G), corte di merito (I), sud pervoy instantsii (R), tribunal de instancia (S)

trial judge (E), Tatrichter (G), guidice del dibattimento (I), predsedatel'stvuiushchiy sud'ia (R), magistrado (S)

V

verdict (E), verdict (F), Wahrspruch (G), verdetto (I), verdikt (R), veredicto (S).

victim (E), victime (F), Opfer (G), vittima (I), poterpevshiy (R), victima (S)

violation (E), violation (F), Verletzung, Verstoß (G), violazione (I), narushenie (R), vulneración, quiebra, infracción (S)

W

warrant (E), mandat (F), Anordnung (G), decreto (I), order (R), mandamiento, auto (S)

watched custody (E), garde-à-vue (F), no G-I-R-S

wiretap (E), écoute téléphonique (F), Abhören (G), intercettazione telefonica (I), kontrol' (R), escucha telefónica (S)

witness (E), témoin (F), Zeuge (G), testimone (I), svidetel' (R), testigo (S)

Index

abbreviated procedures, 6, 18–19,
  50, 165, 168
abbreviated trial, 165–168, 255,
  265
Absprachen, 168, 268,
accusatory pleading, 32, 156–158,
  163, 166, 188, 214, 265
accusatory procedure, 7, 166
adversarial (adversary) procedure,
  4, 8, 18–20, 181–182, 187–89,
  265
aggrieved party, victim (procedural
  rights of), 7–10, 12–13, 16, 18,
  20, 23–24, 26–27, 30, 37–40,
  42, 69, 140–141, 150, 165,
  188–189, 246, 250, 253, 265
anonymous witnesses (informants),
  126, 128, 137–144
anticipated evidence, 34, 38–39, 42,
  132, 136
application of punishment on request of the parties, 159,
  161–164, 167
arrest, 4, 6, 11, 31, 37, 43, 46–53,
  55,59, 78–79, 89, 93, 101, 121,
  129–130, 136–137, 171
  176–177, 203, 235–237,
  243–244, 248–249, 253, 266
arrest warrant, 100
automobile search, 52–53
blood revenge, 5, 8–9

bugging, 63
burden of proof, 7, 164, 171–173,
  176–177, 190
burden of proof (reversal of), 162
circumstantial evidence, 100, 145,
  157, 193, 206, 208, 214, 221,
  246, 266
circumstantial evidence crime, 3, 7,
  9, 11, 221
civil action, 24–26, 29–30 196, 246,
  266
civil party, 23–24, 26, 30, 255–257,
  266
civilian witness (to investigative
  acts), 60–61
clerk (of court), 32, 55, 60, 65,
  106–109, 191–193, 245, 260,
  264, 266
combat (trial by), 7–8
committal order (procedure), 32,
  38, 41, 130, 133, 163, 186, 266
communications (confidentiality,
  secrecy, privacy of), 61–62, 66,
  68, 70, 75–6, 116, 120, 124
communications (interception of),
  63–66, 70–72, 74, 247–248,
  261
communications, stored (seizure
  of), 65, 71
communist, 18, 20

complaint, 23–28, 32–33, 37, 41, 161, 254, 256, 266

compurgators (see oath-helpers)

confession, 6, 11–12, 43, 75, 86, 89, 96, 99–103, 115, 120–122, 144, 151–158, 168, 175, 266

conformidad, 164–165, 168, 268

confrontation (investigative measure), 37–38, 254, 267

confrontation (right to question, examine), 8, 19, 36, 39, 42, 52, 60, 125, 128, 130, 132, 134–138, 140, 142, 145, 219

consensual resolution (of criminal case), 9, 18–19, 160, 168

consent (to search, listen to conversations), 14, 20, 54–56, 59–60, 73, 76, 107, 260, 264

correctionnalisation, 147

counsel (right to), 20, 36–37, 39–41, 52, 55–56, 59–60, 66, 85–93, 100, 103, 110–111, 122, 124, 127–128, 130, 133, 138–139, 254, 258

crime report (police report), 37, 41, 131, 254–255, 258, 267

deal (consensual resolution of case), 151–156, 159, 162, 164, 167, 268

death penalty (capital punishment), 6, 18, 44, 169, 206, 221

deliberations (jury, judgment), 16–17, 153–155, 192–193, 213, 220, 264, 268

deposition, 34, 39, 126, 128, 133, 142, 148

detention (pretrial, investigative), 18, 31, 33–34, 43–44, 48, 60, 85, 89, 95, 99–100, 114, 155, 187, 272

detention (preventive), 136

detention (temporary), 11, 45–47, 50, 247

discovery, 38

dossier, file (investigative), 13, 16, 18, 20, 32–33, 36, 100, 103, 106, 128, 150, 160–163, 165–166, 168, 182, 185, 187, 189–190, 270

due process, 4, 60, 63, 73, 80, 86, 97, 99, 152, 168, 200, 255–256, 268

duel, 8, 149

dwelling, home (constitutional protection, warrant requirement before entry of),14–15, 50, 52–53, 55–61, 78, 106–107, 122–124, 248, 260, 264

ecclesiastical courts, 13

"either-way" offenses, 147–148

entrapment, 80

equality of arms, 28, 30, 115, 117, 187

evidentiary motions, 37–38

exclusionary rule (see prohibition on the use of evidence)

exigent circumstances (emergency circumstances): 6, 39, 48, 51–53, 56–57, 59, 89, 118, 123, 247–249, 268

expedited (trial) procedures, 6, 43–44, 165, 256, 268

eyewitness identification, 7, 11–13, 40, 206, 208, 220–221

Fascism, 17

felony, 23–26, 49, 147, 156, 246, 269

file (defense), 36

flagrant crime, flagrancy, in flagrante, 3–7, 11, 43–44, 46,
48–52, 89, 107, 134, 149, 165,
176–177, 193, 203, 206, 246,
249, 264, 296

free evaluation of the evidence, 112,
128, 145, 156–158, 181,
193–195, 205, 221, 269

free will (determinination of, right
to freely determine will), 87,
96–99, 102, 153, 178

French Revolution, 16, 18–19, 126,
198

fruit of the poisonous tree,
118–119, 122, 269

grand jury, 13, 42

guilty plea, 11, 148, 151, 158, 162,
169

hearsay, hearsay rule, 16, 128,
130–135, 143–145, 215–216,
269

human dignity (protection of, inviolability of), 12, 34, 70, 72, 75,
86, 97–98, 102, 111

identification procedures (line-ups,
show-ups, etc.), 34, 39–40,
238–242, 260

immediacy (principle of), 20, 126,
132, 136, 150, 165, 182, 269

immediate trial, 43, 256

independent source, 119, 121

informant (secret, jailplant, undercover, wired), 20, 72, 74–78,
80, 99, 142

inner conviction (see intime conviction)

inquisitorial procedure, inquisitorial system, 3–5, 9, 11–20, 24,
32–33, 40, 42, 86, 93, 98, 110,
125, 128, 149–150, 165, 168,
178

inquisitorial role of judge, 17, 19,
166, 181, 184

instructions (jury), 20, 206, 213,
220

interrogation (of the suspect, accused), 13, 18, 34, 37, 43,
85–88, 90, 92–100, 103–104,
110–112, 120–121, 177–178,
209, 249, 254, 260, 270

intime conviction (inner conviction, free conviction): 181
193–195, 205, 210, 212, 215,
217–218, 221, 249, 267

judicial authorization (warrant), 6,
48, 50–53, 56–63, 66–68,
77–78, 80, 83, 107–109, 118,
122, 249, 264

judicial police, 30, 32–33, 35, 48,
51, 67, 80, 88–89, 93, 108,
119, 123, 135, 246, 253, 255,
258, 270

judge of the investigation, 34, 40,
60, 64–65, 103, 137, 162,
164–165, 167, 256, 270

jury, jury court, 16–17, 19, 40–41,
125–126, 135, 147–148, 150,
165, 184, 190, 192, 199,
201–202, 204–206, 210,
220–222, 242–245, 271

jury trial, trial by jury, 16–17, 20,
28, 40, 128, 134, 148–150, 169,
175, 177–178, 182–183, 189,
193, 195, 198–208, 213, 216,
242–245

lay assessors (court with …) (see
mixed court)

lay courts, 16–17

lay judges, 5, 16–17, 20, 147, 192, 205, 220, 222

lay participation, 147

legality principle, 13, 17–19, 26, 181, 220

line-ups (see identification procedures)

magistrate, investigating, examining (juge d'instruction), 13, 16, 18–20, 23–24, 31–35, 37–38, 40–42, 57, 60, 62–63 67, 93, 103–105, 107, 116, 126–128, 131–132, 135–136, 138–139, 185, 189–190, 245, 259–260, 270

Magistrate's Court, lay magistrate, 192

Miranda rights, warnings (Miranda v. Arizona), 85–86, 88, 90–92, 94, 99, 103, 110, 112, 122, 124, 178–179

misdemeanor, 24–26, 33, 49, 82, 150–151, 156, 158, 246, 250–251, 271

mixed court, court with lay assessors, 11, 17–18, 150 154, 192–194, 199, 205, 210–214, 216, 220–221, 251, 271

Nazism, 17

nolo contendere, plea of, 165

non-usability (see prohibition on use)

nullity, 55, 105, 107–108, 119, 124, 142, 199, 271

oath, 7–8, 10, 133

oath-helpers (compurgators), 7–8, 12, 149

opportunity principle, 25–26, 221

oral trial (principle of), orality, 16, 19, 125–126, 131, 165, 181–182, 271,

ordeal, 7–8, 12–13, 149

peace (keeping, restoring the), 8–9, 12–13, 220

personality (free development of, right of), 38,68, 70, 72–73, 76–77, 82–83, 97–98, 110–113

plea bargaining, 19, 150, 158, 168–169

police inquest, 30–31, 45, 130, 142, 188, 269

political crimes, 12–13

popular prosecution, popular prosecutor, 28–30, 33, 165, 272

post-inquisitorial, 24, 93, 105, 112, 178, 190

preconstituted evidence, 34, 60, 108, 136

preliminary hearing, 42, 255–256

preliminary investigation, 16, 18–20, 28, 31–38, 40–43, 58, 69, 78–79, 103, 105, 126–128, 130–131, 142, 150, 162–163, 185–186, 188, 247, 253, 259, 261, 272

presumption of guilt, 5, 11, 117, 190

presumption of innocence, 19–20, 33, 43, 115–119, 162, 168, 171–173, 176, 178, 182, 186, 188, 190, 200–201, 220

pretext (arrests), 49

preventive detention, 136

privacy, private life (right to, protection against invasions of), 15, 18, 20, 32, 34, 45, 48, 56,

59–63, 68–75, 77, 113, 120, 124, 272

private complaint, 25–27, 254, 266

private interests, 12, 25–26

private prosecution, private prosecutor, 23–27, 30, 33, 165, 250–251, 272

privilege against self-incrimination (right to silence, right to remain silent), 15, 19, 32, 55, 73, 83, 85–86, 88, 90, 93, 99–100, 103, 111–112, 120, 122, 124, 171–176, 178, 260

probable cause, 11, 47, 49, 52, 56–59, 65, 67, 100, 113, 124, 164, 272

prohibition on the gathering of evidence, 110

prohibition on the use of evidence (non-usability) (exclusionary rule) 18, 74–75, 88 106, 109, 110, 120–121, 271

proportionality (principle of), 46, 48, 54, 58, 62–63, 110, 155, 164, 256, 272

public prosecutor (public prosecution), 20, 23–35, 38–39, 41–43, 51, 56, 59–60, 64–65, 69, 74, 77–78, 89, 100, 103, 105, 116, 127, 131, 143–144, 151–152, 161, 163, 166–167, 179, 186, 188–189, 193, 204, 209, 214, 245–256, 259, 272

public trial (principle of publicity), 8, 16, 19, 150, 153–154, 156, 273

question list (see verdict, special)

reasonable doubt, 175–176, 193–194, 200–201, 211, 217–218, 220

reasonable expectation of privacy, 71

reasonable suspicion (grounds, cause), sufficient reasons, 11, 46–47, 49, 51, 53, 58, 62, 65, 92, 99, 118, 233, 235–236, 244, 253

reasons (judgment) 17–18, 85, 109, 117, 119, 144, 151, 157–158, 160, 167, 175, 181, 194–195, 199, 211, 213–215, 219–220, 250, 270

reasons (jury verdict), 193, 198–201, 221, 263–264

rogatory commission, 32–33

rules of evidence, 13, 16, 134, 194–195

science (law as), 13

secrecy, crimes committed, secret crimes, 3, 11–12, 14–15, 46, 81, 216

secrecy, secret investigative procedure, 12–13, 15–16, 33, 35, 40, 66, 68, 75–77, 82, 259

search incident to arrest, 51–53

show-ups (see identification procedures)

silence, comment on, use as evidence of guilt, 90, 171–174, 177–178, 208, 236, 242–243

silence, right to (see privilege against self-incrimination)

simplified procedures, 18–19, 43, 168

social peace, 8, 68, 76, 220

spoken word (right to), 72

submitting the case on the investigative dossier, 165–168

temporary detention (see detention, temporary)

torture, 6, 10–11, 13, 18, 43, 47, 86, 96, 115, 125, 151, 177, 195

truth, principle of material, search for, ascertainment of, 4, 11, 13, 15, 19, 32, 35–37, 41–42, 45, 66–68, 73, 86, 90, 97–98, 106, 110–111, 120, 143, 150, 152, 156–158, 163, 168, 178–181, 184–185, 190, 220, 249

unavailability (of witnesses), 39, 128, 131, 134, 143,

undercover (police) agents, 15, 78–80, 94–96

undercover interrogation, 94–96, 99

vendetta, 9

verdict (of jury) 16–17, 198–200, 202–206, 208, 226–227, 262–263, 274

verdict, special (question list), 17, 21, 195, 198–199, 201–202, 204–205

Vichy France, 17

victim (procedural rights of)(see aggrieved party)

victimless crime, 3, 12, 15, 46

victim-offender conciliation, 9

voluntariness (of confessions), 96, 99, 102–103, 115, 120, 151

wergeld (composition), 9, 12

wiretapping, 15, 20, 33, 62–63, 65–68, 70, 73–74, 77, 83, 115, 118–119, 121, 274

writings (private, confidentiality of), 20, 81

written trial, 125, 128, 165,